REAL WORLD ECONOMICS

CHRISTOPHER HUHNE

REAL WORLD ECONOMICS

ESSAYS ON IMPERFECT MARKETS AND FALLIBLE GOVERNMENTS

M
MACMILLAN
REFERENCE
BOOKS

First published 1990 by
THE MACMILLAN PRESS LTD.
London and Basingstoke

Associated companies in Auckland, Delhi, Dublin, Gaborone, Hamburg, Harare, Hong Kong, Johannesburg, Kuala Lumpur, Lagos, Manzini, Melbourne, Mexico City, Nairobi, New York, Singapore, Tokyo.

British Library Cataloguing in Publication Data

Huhne, Christopher
real world economics.
1. Great Britain. Economic policies
I. Title
330.941

ISBN 0-333-52683-X

Printed in Great Britain by
Antony Rowe Ltd, Chippenham, Wiltshire

For Lydia, Nicholas, Alexandra and Georgia

Contents

List of Figures

List of Tables

Preface

This book is intended for those who find economics mysterious yet pervasive, whether they are interested citizens who recognize that economic ideas are now the essential language of public affairs, or students who want to have a taste of the excitement of their subject in its applications to the real world.

The essays span a wide range of subject matter from the economics of the National Health Service and the tax system to the economics of a single European currency and the dollar. There are, though, unifying themes which run through the essays. The most persistent is the question of the right balance between the role of the market and the role of government. Despite the fiery and often ideological debates of the last two decades, all economists, even those on the extremes of the profession, recognize that there is a balance to be struck. Even more important, it is quite frequently impossible for markets to work properly without government support and regulation. There have to be markets *and* governments. The real questions concern the appropriate roles for each.

Another theme is the essential need for modesty about what economic research and economic ideas can tell us. Economic thinking is immensely valuable, but it has important limits of which people should be aware. Economics cannot be a science like the physical sciences because of the impossibility of laboratory experiments. There are a large number of different influences which can at any one time be held to have an effect on a particular event. Even the progress of statistical and econometric techniques is often agonizingly slow in rejecting particular theories, so that several competing explanations of a phenomenon can co-exist. Yet particular theories can wreak untold havoc with the lives of many innocent people if applied with excessive zeal. Circumspection is required, along with policies that are robust under a series of different circumstances.

Nevertheless, I would not have written this book if I did not passionately believe in the importance and usefulness of economics. Ultimately, economists are empiricists. If the evidence does not square with a theory, it must eventually wane. Some fashionable theories of the seventies and eighties have not stood the test of time, and that too is a theme of the book. Some have called this a crisis of economics; but in reality competing theories are the stuff of scientific method. The only difference between economics and the physical sciences in this respect (with the possible exception of medicine) is that the impact of mistaken theory can be so much more intrusive into ordinary people's lives. There are new theories and explanations to be tested in the nineties.

The essays in this book owe a great deal to what I have learned while writing a column for *The Guardian* since 1983, but they are not journalism. All the essays have been written specifically to address longer-term questions than the ones that typically concern the journalist and columnist, and stand in relationship to those pieces rather as a template of opinion against which events can be sized up. I have used the opportunity offered by a book to write at greater length than a newspaper would suffer, and at times to go deeper than it would allow. Nevertheless, any essay must of course be highly selective. I make no pretence at comprehensiveness. This book is merely an attempt to separate some wood from the trees,

My debts are substantial. First and foremost, I have a debt to colleagues first on *The Economist* and then on *The Guardian*, especially perhaps to the non-economists who regularly bring one back to earth by asking the simple but difficult questions. Why, for example, is there still unemployment when the London Underground cannot get staff? Secondly, I owe an enormous debt to the small and select band of economic journalists on other papers. We have as much or more in common with each other than we do with the rest of the staffs of our newspapers, and though there is always rivalry, there is also a certain deft comradeship. Journalists of a particular speciality sometimes seem like gold prospectors, sifting and assessing the slurry of official information, and sharing the nuggets that can be gleaned. Over the years, I have learned a lot from our joint efforts.

I should also like to thank the many officials at the Treasury, the Bank of England and the international institutions who have helped me with useful conversations and working papers over the years, but whose careers would not necessarily benefit from explicit acknowledgement. For reading parts or the whole of the manuscript and for making helpful suggestions which have improved the exposition and saved me from many an error, I should like to thank Nicholas Barr, Robert Cassen, Graham Hacche, Gerald Holtham, John Kay, Mervyn King, Richard Layard, Colin Mayer, Keith Pavitt, Sig Prais, Dermot Roaf, Tony Thirlwall and Tony Travers. Whatever errors of fact or judgement this book may contain are indisputably mine.

My thanks also go to David Turner for his help in producing the many figures in this book.

My special thanks too to Vicky Pryce, who has been unsparing in her economic expertise, and who has also had to put up with a lot during the writing of this book as she is my wife. For the second time, I have managed to give birth to a book as she was giving birth to a child, which may be psychologically significant but does not help promote the household division of labour.

Christopher Huhne
London
October 1989

1 The Power and Limits of Economic Ideas

The new economic consensus

The omnipresence of economic ideas

- economics and the Thatcherite agenda
- the rise of the free-market movement
- the taming of the radicals by experience
- a deeper consensus on micro-economics
- market failure and government failure: the false dichotomy
- the new synthesis

'The ideas of economists and political philosophers, both when they are right and when they are wrong, are more powerful than is commonly understood,' John Maynard Keynes wrote. 'Indeed, the world is ruled by little else. Practical men, who believe themselves to be quite exempt from any intellectual influences, are usually the slaves of some defunct economist.'[1] Things have, from the layman's point of view, become worse since Keynes's day. One of the most remarkable features of the eighties has been the way in which economics in some shape or form has forced itself on to the political agenda in most of the western democracies, in part because of dissatisfaction with their economic performance during the seventies. The trend has been even more pronounced in Britain, where Mrs Thatcher's radical Government elected in 1979 was informed largely by liberal and market ideas. It is a common complaint that there is now hardly any area of national life that has not been touched by the Government's essentially economic perspective.

The Government has attempted to reduce subsidies and other items of public spending because it believes in the virtues of private decisions: money spent by individuals will be more wisely spent than money by Governments. For the same reason, tax cuts are a preferable way of spending any excess Government revenue than increases in public expenditure. The education reforms attempt to set up schools which can elect to opt out of local government control and which will expand or contract their state funding according to the enrolment of their pupils: this is an idea modelled on the economic theory of the competitive firm. The National Health Service proposals will set up independent hospitals which will compete to provide services to general practitioners, whose finite budgets will ensure that they shop around for the best bargains. The limitations on trade union action – on the ability to picket another firm which may have no legal connection with the firm in dispute, on strike action before ballots have been called and so forth – hail from the belief of economic liberals that welfare is best maximized when individuals are able to bargain over their situation in the market. If they decide to accept a pay offer rather than move to a new job it is because it is to the mutual benefit of employer and employee. Collective action impedes the free working of the market. Most encompassing of all, the Government pursued an experiment with the monetary control of inflation which led to the worst British recession since the fateful attempt to put Britain back on to the gold standard at the pre-First World War exchange rate in 1920–21.

All of these ideas are economic, but it is equally true that they are not the ideas of most economists. Mrs Thatcher pushed through a programme whose intellectual underpinnings were the essentially free-market schools of thought represented by the monetarist strain of neo-classical economics, the Chicago school of Milton Friedman and the Austrian school of Friedrich von Hayek. Those ideas had been developed in Britain by a small group of active economic liberals at the London School of Economics – Harry Johnson, Sir Alan Walters and others – and were popularized by the skilful and imaginative Mr Ralph Harris (now Lord Harris) and Mr Arthur Seldon at the Institute of Economic Affairs. They did not and do not necessarily accord with the mainstream thinking of the economics profession, and this has been particularly the case in the more macro-economic areas of decision. The persistence in the pursuit of targets for the money supply, despite immense difficulties and the lack of any clear relationship with anything in the real economy, shocked the economic consensus. That episode was followed by the stern Budget of 1981, which raised taxes in the teeth of a recession, contrary to orthodox advice. Neither before nor since has a British Government managed to provoke a protest from 364 members of the economics profession. Several of the essays in this book deal with this seminal period.

Nevertheless, the heat generated by particular controversies should not disguise a broader economic consensus over many issues than has existed for a decade or more. Certainly, the shadows of the old debates are still there. The Liverpool University group still holds to its monetarist faith. The post-Keynesians, rejecting the neo-classical synthesis of Keynesian and market ideas, develop an alternative outside the mainstream of economic thinking although they no longer have a major British research and computer model-building group to give some focus to their activities. But amongst the policy-makers and those with most influence over them there is a new humility about the uncertainties of managing the economy, and a recognition that it is better to design policies which will withstand the test of a variety of circumstances than to persist with measures which depend on one fragile view. The old Keynesians who used to believe that you could fine-tune demand to ensure that growth remained on a sensible non-inflationary track no longer have such faith in their ability to forecast the economy accurately, and therefore have little faith in their ability to offset any likely disturbance. The old monetarists who used to believe that all you needed to do was to set a rule for the money supply have discovered that money is not easy to control, and that active management is required just to maintain the outward appearance of stability. Like ducks stationary on the surging river, there is a lot of paddling going on underneath. Amongst the teams that build the major computer models of the economy – the summation of the research which goes on elsewhere in the profession – the new tentativeness has been enforced by the creation of the Warwick University macro-economic modelling bureau, a sort of economists' policeman or Consumers' Association which attempts to find out why different modelling groups come up with different answers.

Within micro-economics – the study of particular areas of the economy rather than the economy as a whole – there has always been much less disagreement. It is a rare economist who does not broadly believe in the usefulness of markets. Even the New Cambridge group, for so long regarded as the left-wing pariahs of the profession by its neo-classical and free-trading establishment, advocated import controls operated not through bureaucratic fiat but through either tariffs or sales of foreign currency to the highest bidder in the market. In that way, those with most need of the imports would win out without Whitehall having to make a corruptible political judgement.[2] There has been a broad measure of sympathy amongst professional economists for the introduction of market ideas into more areas of national life; for the attempt to promote competition; for the stress on earning money rather than merely redistributing it. In the age-old debate about whether a decision should be left to markets or taken by Governments, economists have increasingly been on the side of markets, a trend that has been part of the *Zeitgeist* of the eighties worldwide.

This trend was a belated recognition of something that the economic liberals had been pointing out for some time. It was not enough merely to say that the market was in some respect failing, and therefore the Government should intervene, because the Government can fail too. Take three examples which at the time were regarded as market failures. The electricity companies underinvested in power supplies in the thirties. There were severe cases of hardship caused by the operation of Rachmanite landlords in the housing market. Private businesses did not make adequate provision for research and development for the future, and lost market share to more long-sighted overseas rivals.

These examples of market failure were replaced by equivalent examples of Government failure. The Morrisonian nationalized corporation, a monopoly in its field, was both exploitative and subject to the will-o'-the-wisp of its political masters, which did not make for rational decision-making. The undeniable faults of the housing market were remedied by the provision of high-rise blocks which no one now wants to live in, and a system of rent control which eliminated all incentive to maintenance of property, and effectively strangled the private rented sector altogether. The Government's policies for high technology and research and development landed us with two wasteful defence cancellations in the form of Blue Streak and the TSR2, and two examples of economic idiocy in the shape of Concorde and the advanced gas-cooled nuclear reactor.

This list of Government failure could be extended to Whitehall's involvement in incomes policy, to capital-intensive plants in the regions which promptly shut down when the industrialists pocketed the cash, to bail-outs of lame-duck car plants which happened to be in marginal constituencies, and even to the building of the Humber Bridge in order to secure for a Labour Government a by-election which it believed it was about to lose. These examples of the political system's ability to act either incompetently or in its own interest rather than that of the commonality provided fertile ground for the attempt to get Government out of economic decision-making, and to ensure that politicians were held at one remove from the honey pot. Government is not always good. Indeed, it is likely to be just as self-serving as any other economic actor – a perception which gained ground in the seventies and which sounded the death knell for the simple nostrums of Fabian interventionism and faith in the beneficence of the state.

The pendulum between markets and Governments is now swinging back the other way as an increasing number of problems require regulation. The most prominent issue is the environment, a long-standing concern of economists which is the subject of the third essay in this chapter. Whether because of the greenhouse gases or the effects of traffic congestion in the inner cities, there is an increasing recognition of the need for law to curb those private activities that economists call negative externalities – they are 'external' to the private bargains between individuals which create them. Congestion, for example, could potentially be tackled by subsidising car drivers to use public transport (assuming that a means could be devised of ensuring that those subsidies actually reduced the fares, rather than boosting the pay packets of those in the transport industry). Alternatively, car drivers could be taxed, thereby raising the cost of driving, and encouraging people to take public transport while raising revenue.

There is also a traditional economic case for intervention in other markets where the full social consequences – either costs or benefits – are not taken into account when individuals make their decisions. Education, training, and research and development, which determine an economy's long-term growth path, all entail wider social consequences than those taken into account by the people involved. Spending on these areas may, indeed, be complementary to private sector activity rather than corrosive of it. The same may well apply to spending on economic infrastructure such as motorways and other transport facilities. As Professor Mancur Olson has shown with the results reproduced in figure 1, there is no relationship between levels of public spending and the growth rates of countries in the post-war period.[3] Big-government countries have done badly and well; small government countries have also done badly and well. The implication is that it is the type of government spending, and the type of government intervention, that is crucial to economic performance.

Most people would also argue that poverty is another case which merits intervention in the market. The bag people sleeping rough in the Charing Cross area of London are a further cost, though not a necessary one, of the excessive pursuit of market remedies. Nor is public spending on welfare inimical to individuals' decisions. After all, transfers of income from rich to poor enlarge the choices of those in poverty by at least as much as they restrict the choices of those who pay the extra taxes. Indeed, it is arguable that a pound spent by a poor man is better appreciated than one spent by a rich man for the best of economic reasons: the utility of anything diminishes the more you have of it. The market is the most powerful means of achieving prosperity, but it must be aided, supported and tempered if it is to be allowed to do its work.

'The intelligent radical keeps his head;' wrote James Meade, the Nobel laureate, in a passage to which most of the economics profession would say amen, 'he argues the virtues of the free market when the tendency is to think only of the need for particular interventions and he stresses the need for social

Figure 1

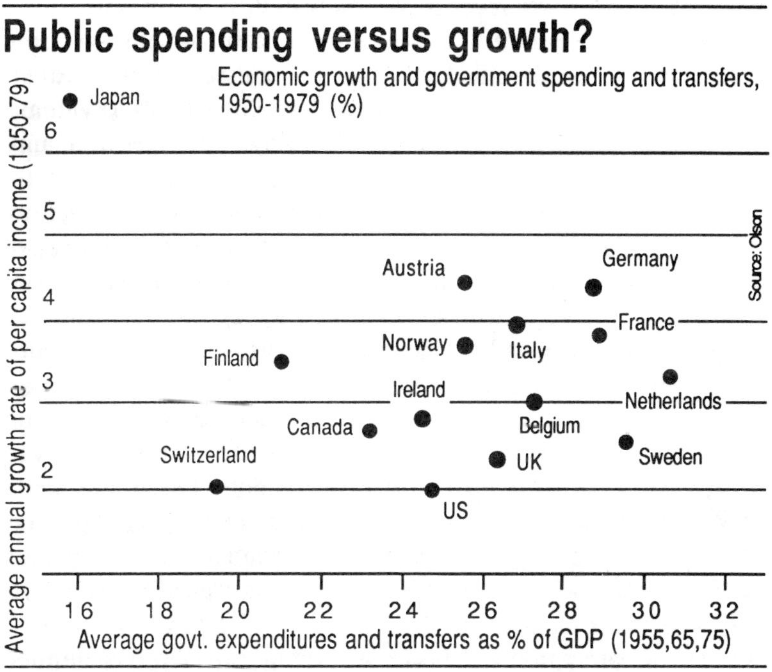

interventions whenever *laissez faire* becomes an object of religious devotion.'[4] This sounds like fence-sitting, the plea of centrists through the ages for balance and harmony, but it can be more. In reality, the dichotomy between markets on the one hand and government activity on the other is a false one. No economy can survive without a measured dollop of both, and the only real question is the correct field of action for each. The Government has traditionally laid down weights and measures, a crucial condition of the proper operation of even the most humble street market. It has provided a framework of law and property rights, and upholds contracts. In other words, there has to be a Government-imposed framework of law for markets to work. Nor is this a trivial area of agreement. Although some neo-Austrians have gone as far as to argue for the privatization of the currency, most economists would recognize that this is a state responsibility, albeit one which may beneficially be administered by an independent central bank.[5] Almost all economists would argue for a tough competition policy to curtail and break down monopoly power wherever it is exercised. Almost all economists would criticize restraints to trade such as a manufacturers' right to dictate the final selling price to the consumer. Almost all economists would agree that there is an irreducible collection of public goods – law and order and defence – which the state must provide.

Most of the essays in this book are an attempt to sketch out the correct balance between the use of markets and the influence of Government, which is the great agenda for economics in the nineties. Real world economics must take account not only of the failure of markets but also the fallibility of bureaucrats and the venality of politicians. As the lines of the new economic consensus take some sort of shape, they will tend to stress the importance of general rules rather than specific actions, so as to limit the discretionary power of Government. Thus an extension service to provide advice on computerization to any business that requests it is a policy which works with the grain of the market (and is broadly what the Department of Trade and Industry now does), whereas a policy to target specific subsidies to firms with particular claims to merit is almost certainly doomed to failure. Bureaucrats are a good deal worse than the market at picking winners. A change in the patent law, or the provision of tax breaks, are ways of encouraging research and development that are preferable to a subsidy paid at the discretion of ministers or civil servants. In short, practical economics is coming of age as it moves away from the single combat of market versus state, and attempts to grapple with the problems that arise from the inevitable intertwining of the two.

Notes

1 John Maynard Keynes, *The General Theory of Employment, Interest and Money*, (London, 1935), book 6, chapter 24.

2 Conversation between author and Professor Wynne Godley. See also *Cambridge Economic Policy Review*, no. 4 (March 1978), no. 5 (April 1979).

3 Mancur Olson, lecture at the London School of Economics, 25 October 1988 (mimeo). See also Olson, *The Rise and Decline of Nations* (New Haven: University of Yale Press, 1982).

4 James E. Meade, *The Intelligent Radical's Guide to Economic Policy: the Mixed Economy*. (London: George Allen and Unwin, 1975)

5 See Kevin Dowd, *Private Money* (London: Institute of Economic Affairs, 1988).

The limits of economic ideas

Economic thinking

- the imprecision of economic data
- embarrassing predictions
- why forecasting is nevertheless crucial
- the Treasury record
- data revisions
- the impossibility of fine tuning
- impractical academic economics
- economics as ideology
- psychopathic economic man
- the burden of empiricism

The development of economic thinking is arguably one of the greatest steps forward in the human understanding of the world. The classical economists led by Adam Smith and David Ricardo explained the advantages of a market where the 'invisible hand' guided producers to specialize in skills at which they excelled and to maximize their benefit and the social benefit by free exchange. The marginalist revolution under the auspices of W.S. Jevons, Leon Walras and Carl Menger gave the world an explanation of why some things were valued more than others. Instead of thinking that things were more valuable according to the amount of labour used to make them, prices were determined by the utility placed upon a good by the last buyer and the last seller in the market. Marginal cost and marginal utility were held to determine price, and an entire theory of how the economy worked was built on the notion that prices would adjust to allocate resources to their fullest and most efficient use. When the depression of the thirties exposed the limitations of such ideas, the Keynesian revolution explained that prices would not always change to ensure that a market cleared. Unemployment could result from lack of spending power in the economy, caused in part by falls in wages: the idea of a circular flow of income from earner to spender and back to earner sired the sophisticated computer models which today attempt to represent the reality of our economic system.

For all the insights which economics, the queen of the social sciences, has been able to bring to bear on the world, its most successful practitioners are generally acutely aware of its limitations. The first limitation is the nature of the real world. Inevitably, economic theories must be abstract because a level of abstraction is crucial if the mass of events and interactions that make up an economy is to be understood. In any modern economy in any hour of any day there is a multiplicity of transactions, many of which cannot be recorded, and others of which will only be recorded imperfectly. Economic data for retail sales, consumer spending, investment, exports, imports and even Government spending are quite frequently far more fragile than the practitioner would like. Data may be collected for purposes which are not those of the economist and by people who have very little interest in either accuracy or timeliness. One of the more curious outgrowths of the boom in the financial services industry has been the equally pronounced boom in private sector economic analysts hired to tell market practitioners what particular numbers mean, even though many of those monthly statistics may not pass even the primary condition of meaningfulness. They may be revised, as further information becomes available, by more than the original estimate of the change in the series.[1]

Successful prediction is the ultimate test of whether a theory is true, but the economists' record of splendidly incorrect predictions is a humbling one. One of the most distinguished economists of his day, Professor Irving Fisher of Yale, declared only months before the great crash in 1929 that 'stock prices have reached what looks like a permanently high plateau'.[2] In 1972 the United States National Petroleum Council estimated that world petroleum demand in 1981 would be 76 million barrels a day; it was less than 47 million barrels a day.[3] Nor is this inaccuracy confined to relatively complex phenomena (though certainly it is most prevalent in such areas: distrust an economist who claims to be able to predict exchange rates). Simple demography can represent an appalling hazard for medium-term economic projections. The British Central Policy Review Staff, reviewing population projections made between 1955 and 1974, found that the size of the population forecast for the year 2000 had varied between 50 million and 70 million, while the projected number of live births annually varied between 650,000 and 1,500,000.[4]

Perhaps the most crucial mistake in recent British economic history was the assessment of 1976, the year in which Britain became the first developed economy ever to subject itself to International Monetary Fund policy conditions in exchange for a loan. The growth rate projected from official statistics in the first half of 1976 was 1.5 per cent, while the early figures suggested a balance of payments deficit of £1,500 million, a total which would have represented little improvement on the year before and which was putting extreme pressure on sterling. By 1980 the growth rate had been revised up to an encouraging 3.7 per cent and the deficit revised down to £842 million.[5] Ironically, the Treasury's internal forecast of the deficit on this occasion proved to be more accurate than the projections based on the balance of payments figures which so alarmed the Bank of England and the markets.

None of this is to argue that the whole exercise of economic forecasting is futile, because it is quite inevitable that it will be done so long as policy-makers and others have to make decisions and assess options. 'A chief purpose of every study of human action,' wrote Alfred Marshall, 'should be to suggest the probable outcome of present tendencies and thus to indicate, tacitly if not expressly, such modifications of those tendencies as might further the well-being of mankind.'[6] At the very least, the process of forecasting imposes a consistency of view upon policy-makers which ensures that their arguments hang together logically. At best, it can improve policies substantially. In an assessment of the Treasury's own forecasts, Sir Terence Burns, the Chief Economic Adviser, has argued that forecasts have been consistently better than straightforward projections of past trends. Moreover, they have improved compared with the turbulent years of the seventies, as one would expect.

Nevertheless, the difficulties with data revisions are formidable. For example, the average absolute error for a Treasury forecast of growth in the year ahead has been about 1.6 percentage points since the 1970s. (In other words, a forecast of a 2 per cent growth rate would on average reflect an outcome of 0.4 per cent to 3.6 per cent.) However, the official estimate of growth in the four quarters *before* each forecast was made was revised by an average 1.3 per cent. The statisticians were moving the baseline by almost as much as the economists proved to be wrong. 'It is almost inevitable that errors in the data will have materially affected the accuracy of the GDP forecasts,' Sir Terence concluded.[7] In the 1989 Financial Statement and Budget report, the annual average error in the Treasury's GDP forecasts for the year in progress is given as 1 per cent: in other words a 3 per cent forecast could be consistent with an outcome from 2 to 4 per cent, and the range could easily be wider.

Clearly, it beggars belief to suppose that policy-makers can fine-tune the economy when the technical means of forecasting are still so imprecise. A forecast of 1.5 per cent growth might imply that policy-makers should take measures to boost growth to 2.5 per cent, the possible long-run trend of the economy needed to stop unemployment rising. But if they do, and the forecast is wrong, they may end up with 3.5 per cent growth and an inflationary problem. Policy can be used to deal with persistent problems, like unemployment during the eighties, but not to make small adjustments to growth. Equally, any hope of applying techniques of optimal control of the sort used to guide spacecraft in flight is still remote. A study of forecasts of all the main computer modelling teams showed that the models are still far from a state in which they could be left unimpeded to produce sensible forecasts. In assessing forecast error, the researcher found that the judgements of the forecasters, in over-riding the results of their unalloyed computer models alone clearly improved the forecasts.[8]

There need be nothing dishonourable or dishonest about such adjustments to the untainted model. The forecasters may be dissatisfied with the way in which a part of the model – say, the equations explaining consumption – captures past reality. Or they may believe, as was the case with both the two main forecasting teams at the National Institute and the London Business School in 1989, that the improvement in manufacturing performance justified some judgemental improvement in their models' predictions of the current account deficit.[9] It is a muddy world in which policy-makers and their forecasters are often trying to navigate in a pea-souper. Nevertheless, decisions about interest rates, tax rates, public spending and foreign exchange intervention will not wait.

Practical economics has often been likened more to an art than a science, and this is sadly true in more ways than one. Economics is not only limited by the difficulties of data and by its inability to conduct laboratory experiments, unlike the physical sciences; it is also hamstrung by constraints of its own imposition. It has increasingly fallen prey to the 'Ricardian vice' – the habit of deducing elegant logical constructions on the basis of premises which may be wholly removed from reality. This tendency is less marked in Britain than in the United States, but it is still noticeable. Wassily Leontief, the Nobel laureate, calculated that 54 per cent of all the articles which appeared in the *American Economic Review*, the flagship of academic journals, over the period from March 1977 to December 1981 were mathematical models without any data whatsoever. This was an increase on the 50.1 per cent of such articles in the *AER* between March 1972 and December 1976.[10] Moreover, a further 12 per cent of articles concerned themselves with analysis without any data, or with statistical methodology.

In its extreme form, this escape from empiricism merely turns economics into an ideology. Some members of the Austrian free market school come closest to giving economics the hallmark of an ideology by denying the usefulness of evidence at all. Ludwig von Mises said: 'There are, in the field of economics, no constant relations, and consequently no measurement is possible.'[11] This is the voice of the Christian theologian, part of whose armoury, when the empirical going gets tough, is the appeal to faith. It has the same self-sealing quality as an ideology like Marxism, which, when confronted with the evidence that the working classes prefer capitalism, ascribes their perverse lack of appreciation of their own interests to 'false consciousness'. Here too went Hitler. The reason why he was unable to adduce sound evidence for the international conspiracy of Jewish bankers and revolutionaries was, of course, that the conspiracy was far too cunning to leave any trail behind it. The lack of evidence merely showed how effective the conspiracy was.

Mainstream economics is not an ideology, because it is still open to empirical testing by means of statistical analysis, even though such testing is still fragile and able to sustain a wide variety of theories. However, economics does tend to worship at the old altars of marginalism even when the real world passes it by. Economic man, according to neo-classical economics, is motivated by self-interest, and maximizes his profits. He is, as Professor Peter Wiles has argued, someone who acts without regard to other people except possibly the family (and then only if he has to rely on it in the absence of sickness insurance) and ignores moral principles unless they are embodied in well-enforced laws (for other ethical behaviour is a money-loser). 'There are a few such people,' says Professor Wiles, 'and we have a word for them: psychopaths.'[12] His plea is for an economics which abandons this presumption, even though it may be 80 per cent true, because human beings diverge from it in a way which can be studied and even predicted. People do not always behave rationally; they are altruistic; they do waste things and indulge their own idleness; they can be irrational. After all, trade unions do not maximize their short-term gains, since it is a matter of record that most strikes do not repay the strikers. Moreover, firms even in apparently competitive industries do not maximize profits, since they raise prices when they concede a wage claim. In other words, they were previously charging a lower price than they needed.

The most interesting economics today is often the result of research in forecasting institutions and policy-making bodies, and a handful of universities with a long tradition of being plugged into a policy-making world which is inevitably oriented towards solving problems. Good economics is a balance of theory and abstraction on the one hand against hard reality on the other. It is a growing body of work, which is the best hope both for good policy-making and for pushing back the limits of economics as a discipline. It is doubtful, though, whether economics will ever be able to aspire to the exactitudes of a physical science, even though its methods of inquiry may be similar. The theory of rational expectations tells us that people will not make the same mistakes over and over again in forecasting the future. On this basis, economics is doomed to chase perpetually after an ever-changing world. For the closer it comes to predicting behaviour on the basis of past events, the quicker it is likely to change that behaviour itself. Uncertainty may be the historical burden of the social scientist.

Notes

1 The neglected classic on this subject is Oscar Morganstern, *On the Accuracy of Economic Observations* (Princeton: Princeton University Press, 1950; 2nd edn 1963).

2 Quoted in John Kenneth Galbraith, *The Great Crash* (Harmondsworth: Penguin, 1961), p. 95.

3 Andrew M. Kamarck, *Economics and the Real World* (Oxford: Blackwell, 1983), p. 128.

4 Kamarck, op cit., p. 18.

5 The economist who spotted this remarkable revision was Mr Roger Nightingale, then of the city firm Hoare Govett. Reported in *The Guardian*, 5 February 1980.

6 Alfred Marshall, *Industry and Trade* (London: Macmillan, 1919), p. 7.

7 Sir Terence Burns, 'The Interpretation and Use of Economic Predictions', *Proceedings of the Royal Society*, A 407 (1986), pp. 103–25.

8 John D. Whitley, *Ex Post Forecast Analysis*, a presentation with handout at the Economic and Social Research Council Macro-economic Modelling Bureau annual conference, Warwick University, July 1989.

9 David S. Turner, *The Role of Judgement in Macro-economic Forecasting, ESRC Macro-economic Modelling Bureau, Warwick University, April 1989 (mimeo).*

10 Wassily Leontief, letter to the editor in *Science*, vol. 217 (9 July 1982), pp. 104–5, reprinted in Alfred S. Eichner *Why Economics is not yet a Science* (London: Macmillan, 1983).

11 Ludwig von Mises, *Human Action* (London, 1949) quoted in Peter Wiles, 'Ideology, Methodology and Neo-classical Economics', reprinted in Eichner, op cit.

12 Wiles in Eichner, op cit. This article orginally appeared in the *Journal of Post-Keynesian Economics*, vol. 2, no. 2 (Winter 1979–80), pp. 155–80.

Do we need a green economics?

Confusion about issues

- the economics of the greens
- growth is not necessarily noxious
- whether there is problem with finite resources
- the real problems of excessive pressure on natural systems
- possible consequences of the greenhouse effect
- evidence for and against
- measures to combat it

The shift in public policy in the major industrial countries over the threats to the world environment has been remarkably rapid. At the Toronto summit of the seven leading industrial countries in the summer of 1988, only the West German Chancellor Mr Helmut Kohl, pressed by the electoral gains made by the German Green party, championed such issues as deforestation and concern about the 'greenhouse' gases. Little more than a year later, at the Paris summit, the environment rose to the top of the agenda, taking a third of the final communiqué, and underscoring vividly the concern that the post-war path of economic development was unsustainable.[1]

There is, though, considerable confusion about many of the issues involved, in part because participants in the debate use the same words in different ways. For example, Mrs Thatcher stresses that there should be a properly 'economic' approach to environmental issues, by which she mainly means the use of the price mechanism to stop unenvironmental habits. She cites the Chancellor's reduction in successive Budgets of the tax on unleaded petrol. Mrs Thatcher's approach is to take measures to limit or stop specific activities or encourage others. It is a pragmatic, step-by-step way of dealing with problems.

This is a very different type of 'green economics' to that championed by the European Greens, who argue that conventional economics is simply unable to take proper account of the enormous changes which will be needed in our society if it is to survive the global challenges that face it. The Greens' proposals involve much more sweeping restraints on individuals' economic activity. The British Green party is typical of European green thinking. It devoted the first section of its general election policy statement to a 'green economics' which is anti-growth, anti-consumption and anti-competition: 'An emphasis on consumption leads to even more trees being cut down, even more landscape destroyed. Growth takes power out of the hands of local communities and gives it to multinational corporations which have no connection with the places where people live and work. Competition sets communities and nations against each other, and progress often leads us down untested and unsafe technological paths.'[2]

Conservation taxes would discourage the use of both renewable and non-renewable resources, so that goods with a high resource-content would cost more. Pollution charges would discourage pollutants. There would be tariffs on both imports and exports in order to promote local production for local needs. ('British butter being sold in France at the same time as French butter being sold in Britain is wasteful nonsense.') A Community Ground Rent would increase with development unless the development was regarded by the authorities as socially useful. ('In general terms, the nearer the land is to its natural state, the lower the Community Ground Rent will be.') Private banks would be phased out to be replaced by publicly-accountable community banks. Presumably, these charges and taxes would be raised to a high enough level to secure the overall objective of stopping growth.

Any such programme would mark the most significant Government intervention in the economy since war-time. Growth, after all, is merely the increase in economic activity from one period to another, most of which goes on in the private sector and is therefore a free exchange between individuals or their corporate entities – companies. It is a fair presumption that both parties draw benefit from such exchanges or they would not occur. It has been a further presumption that the Government ought not to interfere unless a demonstrably greater interest is involved. That is the root of economic liberalism. Do we really need to ban international trade in butter to resolve our environmental problems? Certainly, economic activity cannot be equated with welfare. Car crashes boost activity by increasing car repairs; a threat of invasion would boost defence spending and growth but it would not lead to an increase in welfare. Nevertheless, revealed preference – the splendid economic doctrine that tells us to judge people by what they actually do – suggests that people really do want the rising living standards afforded by growth.[3]

The full-blooded 'green economics' is not merely illiberal but is also based on two implicit assumptions which are seriously flawed. The first is that growth itself is environmentally noxious. In fact, the parts of the developed world's economies that are growing most quickly tend to be those that are least damaging to the environment. Services of all kinds – restaurants, hotels, leisure activities, banking and financial services – are the most rapidly expanding areas. They pollute little and they involve more labour and fewer raw materials than industry. The share of manufacturing within gross domestic product in the developed countries has fallen from 27.8 per cent in 1968–73 to less than 24 per cent in the first half of the eighties.[4] Within manufacturing, the fastest growing areas are electrical and electronic engineering rather than traditional 'smoke-stack' industries. General measures to halt growth might well stop these environmentally-friendly activities while leaving coal-fired power stations to continue belching sulphur and creating acid rain. After all, if people are forced to choose between cutting out an extra restaurant meal and cutting down their heating bills, it is the restaurant meal that is likely to go.

The second dubious assumption is that Government measures are required in order to encourage conservation of finite resources like tin, oil and copper, because the world is inevitably running out of them. This view harks back among others to Dr E.F. Schumacher, who plausibly argued that infinite growth of material consumption in a finite world was an impossibility.[5] It was given public prominence by the Club of Rome, whose analysis *The Limits to Growth* in the early seventies warned that the oil crisis would be only the first example of many crises of non-renewable resources.[6] That hypothesis has a long and splendid history in economics. It is said, for example, to have so obsessed the otherwise sane Victorian economist W.S. Jevons that he filled his cellars with coal. It has, however, been roundly discredited. If it were correct, the price of most raw materials would have been rising steadily throughout this period. Sadly for the Third World countries, which are the main exporters of such products, exactly the opposite has been happening. Commodity prices have seen a trend decline in real terms, which has created severe development problems in the process (see the essay entitled the growth gap on page 249).

The main reason for the falling trend of commodity prices has been the development of new technologies in the user industries which economize on resources. The advent of printed circuit boards in electronics, for example, has meant substantial savings in the amount of raw material required for a given number of connections, which has in turn dealt a severe blow to the copper market and to producers like Zambia and Zaire. Bolivia's tin mining activities have been hit by the use of plastics rather than tin in food packaging. In view of the fall in prices and in production, it hardly seems necessary to hasten the process by imposing additional measures to curb demand. If a commodity does become scarce, the rise in price is likely to encourage substitutes, alternative sources of supply, and economy of use. It is a strange fact of the seventies and eighties that the world's proven oil reserves actually increased. The rise in price ensured that discoveries outpaced use.[7]

The environmental problems which require serious and urgent action are those which involve the side-effects of particular forms of economic activity. They mainly arise because of excessive demographic or technological pressure on natural ecological systems. The over-fishing in the North Sea during the seventies, for example, risked extinguishing stocks of herring altogether, and had to be controlled and regulated by the European Community. Similar examples have been occurring in the Third World, where over-grazing or over-cropping can lead to desertification and appalling effects on local communities. Even our measures of economic activity imperfectly account for any depletion of natural (or, indeed, man-made resources). Gross domestic product, for example, includes gross investment. It does not deduct any depreciation to allow for retired capital equipment or for depleted forests or oil reserves.

First and foremost among the environmental threats, though, is the emission of greenhouse gases and the resultant global warming (figure 2). The five warmest years of the past century

Figure 2

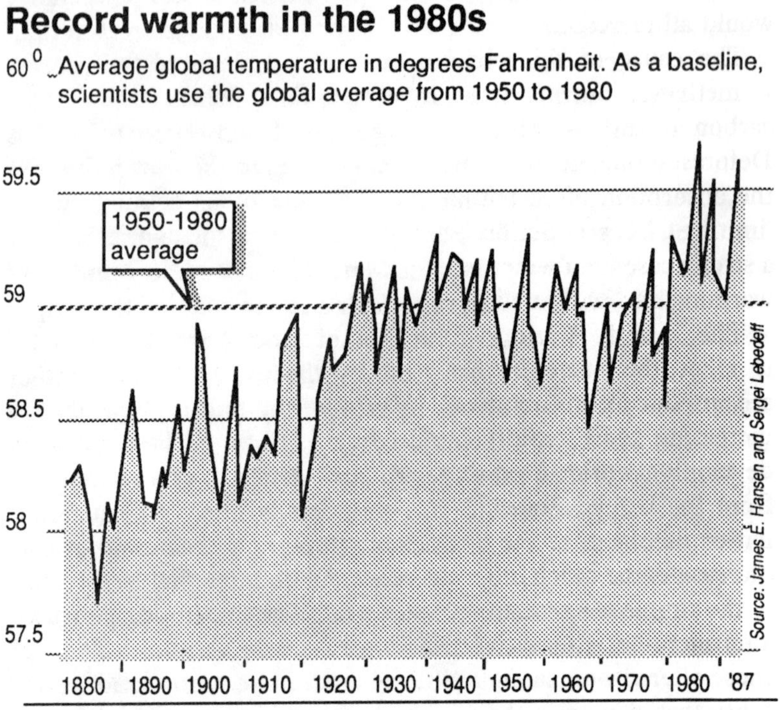

have all fallen in this decade, according to the United States National Aeronautics and Space Administration (NASA). Mr James E. Hansen, head of NASA's Goddard Institute for Space Studies, says that he is 99 per cent certain that the observed temperature increases reflect the impact of the greenhouse effect.

The Washington-based Worldwatch Institute highlights four likely effects if global warming continues. First, vast numbers of trees are likely to die, and new trees adapted to warmer temperatures are unlikely to be able to replace them rapidly. A temperature increase of 1@C per decade in the mid- to upper latitudes leads to a shift of 60 to 100 miles northward in vegetation zones. Secondly, a rise of 3@C by 2050 would melt the polar ice-caps and raise the sea level by 50 to 100 centimetres. By the end of the next century, the sea level could be up as much as two metres, leading to the swamping of delta cultures such as Bangladesh. Thirdly, the averages disguise more extreme climatic events. Stifling heatwaves, droughts and hurricanes would all increase.[9]

The cause of this climate change is the greenhouse gases – methane, nitrous oxide, chlorofluorocarbons (CFCs) and carbon dioxide – which trap heat in the lower atmosphere. Deforestation, notably the Amazon clearances, also reduces the absorption of carbon dioxide. The 1987 Montreal protocol limiting CFC production is already recognized as too lax; there is a strong case for a wider treaty governing all the aspects of global warming and with a wider coverage in the Third World.

The Third World, indeed, is crucial because much of it is at the stage of development where greenhouse gases are produced in abundance. Carbon dioxide emissions are increasing most rapidly in the Soviet Union, China and the developing world. Despite continued growth, carbon emissions from the United States, Japan and Western Europe have been flat or falling since the first oil crisis. The potential for a rapid increase in the much more potent CFCs is even greater as a result of the simple Chinese ambition of providing each household with a refrigerator. Alternative technologies are desperately needed. If those alternatives cannot be developed quickly, there is a possibility that growth in the Third World will become incompatible with protection of the environment. The developed world may be forced into what one writer, in a different context, has called a 'planetary bargain' to reduce its own pollutants sharply.[10]

The more conservative western governments – notably those of President Bush in the United States and Mrs Thatcher in Britain – continued during 1989 to highlight the uncertainties about the greenhouse effect. For example, some climatologists held that global warming would create more cloud cover, which would in turn help to deflect the sun's rays and introduce a naturally cooling element.[11] A study also showed that there had been no rise in the average temperatures recorded in the lower 48 states of the United States, although this represents merely 1.5 per cent of the global surface area, and is in contrast to the results taking the world as a whole.[12] The balance of expert opinion was agreed that global warming was under way. Indeed, Dr George M. Woodwell, director of the Marine Biology Laboratory at

Woods Hole, Massachusetts, testified to Congress that recent data had shown that the accumulation of carbon dioxide in the atmosphere is accelerating. A research station in Hawaii, which has documented a steady increase of about 1.5 parts per million of carbon dioxide each year since 1957, showed a 'surge' in 1987 and 1988. The new rate of increase was about 2.5 parts per million a year, he said, possibly due to increased warmth speeding up the decay of organic matter.[13]

The exact means of limiting noxious discharges should obviously depend on their danger. An outright ban may be the only sensible response, but if there is any leeway for a phased reduction the weapons might include charges, taxes or even an annual licence for pollution which could be auctioned. Those businesses for which the cost of moving to a less polluting technology was highest would be prepared to pay the most. This is clearly going to increase the costs of production for many businesses; cleaner types of technology will have to be developed for both products and processes. However, it is unlikely to stop economic activity. The change in costs will open up new opportunities and divert entrepreneurial attention to new fields.

Global warming faces the world with a problem in an entirely new dimension which is likely to have profound implications for international politics and the balance of power. But it is not clear that it requires the sort of fundamental, even spiritual, change in values implied by the Greens. The 'green economics' of the mainstream parties is preferable. Indeed, all the analytical tools needed to think about the environmental threat already exist in that branch of mainstream economics called welfare economics, and specifically cost-benefit analysis (CBA). CBA was designed to study and take account of the 'externalities' created by private decisions and activity, whether in the form of pollution or road traffic congestion. The only difference today is the scale of the challenge and of the likely measures that will be needed to staunch the emission of greenhouse gases. But rational and cool thinking suggests that those measures should be specifically directed at problems when they are identified, rather than at a general phenomenon – growth – large parts of which present no problem at all.

Notes

1 Communiqué of the Group of Seven industrial countries, Sommet de l'Arche, Paris, 16 July 1989.

2 Green Party, General Election manifesto, 1987.

3 The best sustained assault on growth is still in E.J. Mishan, *The Costs of Economic Growth* (Harmondsworth: Penguin, 1969).

4 OECD, *Economies in Transition: Structural Adjustment in OECD Countries* (Paris, 1989), p. 119.

5 See, for example, E.F. Schumacher, *Small is Beautiful: a Study of Economics as if People Mattered* (Blond and Briggs, 1973). Arguably, the ecological movement was started by economists, notably Rachel L. Carson with *Silent Spring* (Boston, 1962) and E.J. Mishan, op cit.

6 Donella H. Meadows, Dennis L. Meadows, Jorgen Randers and William W. Behrens III, *The Limits to Growth: a Report for the Club of Rome's Project on the Predicament of Mankind* (London: Earth Island Ltd, 1972).

7 Total world reserves rose from 5,330 billion barrels in 1970 to 6,990 billion in 1985. See Peter R. Odell, *Oil and World Power* (Harmondsworth: Penguin, 8th edn, 1986), table 4, p. 261.

8 Quoted in Lester R. Brown *et al.*, *State of the World*, 1989 edition (Washington DC: Worldwatch Institute).

9 Lester R. Brown *et al.*, op cit.

10 Attributed to Harlan Cleveland of the Aspen Institute in Lester R. Brown, *The Twenty Ninth Day* (New York: W.W. Norton, 1978), p. 300.

11 Reported by Randolph E. Schmid, Associated Press, 26 January 1989.

12 Reported by Philip J. Hilts, *Washington Post*, 27 January 1989. The results for the world as a whole come from the British Meterological Office and the University of East Anglia Climatic Research Unit. Reported by Michael Weisskopf, *Washington Post*, 4 February 1989.

13 Reported by Cass Petersen, *Washington Post*, 10 May 1989.

2 Helping Business Work Better

Why Britain's lack of training matters

Britain's productivity gap

- why a lack of training causes low productivity
- the scale of the shortfall in training
- the need for national training standards
- British managers are uneducated
- why business will not train enough

There is a curious paradox about British education and training. It is now widely recognized that Britain is a poorly educated, under-skilled country by comparison with other leading industrial nations. But at the same time, Britain's managers reported relatively few skill shortages even when the 1987–8 boom was well under way. As late as early 1987, the proportion of firms expecting a shortage of skilled labour to curb their output was about the same as at the bottom of the recession in the sixties and seventies. In other words, it was negligible.

There is an explanation of this paradox of plenty amidst the penury. It is that businesses find that they have adequate skills given relatively unsophisticated products, simple types of machinery and basic production techniques. Except at the top of a boom, when they suffer the usual cyclical problems, they find it relatively easy to get manpower. However, it is the generally unskilled nature of Britain's labour force which traps British industry into those relatively simple processes. Not enough British firms have the technical expertise or general competence to use high technology properly. It is this long-run problem which ought to be of prime concern.

As a result, the amount of output produced by each British employee is still low compared with overseas, which in turn limits our earnings and living standards. Of course, the

Table 1. International productivity levels for whole economy, 1986 (UK = 100)

	GDP per head of population	*GDP per person employed*	*GDP per hour worked*
UK	100	100	100
USA	150	141	132
Japan	106	94	67
West Germany	110	113	105
France	106	119	117
Italy	100	–	–
Canada	140	131	116

Source: HM Treasury from OECD data for GDP at purchasing power parities and employment. Figures for Italy are incomplete because of uncertainties about the size of the hidden economy.

growth of output per person – productivity – has speeded up for a variety of reasons, including the gradual erosion of trade union restrictive practices which impeded efficient use of machinery. But its level still lags. A detailed industry-by-industry study recently found that our eight top performing industries were on average 40 per cent below the American level of productivity, while our eight lowest performing industries were 75 per cent below the American level.[1] These findings referred to the end of the seventies because of difficulties finding later data, but even the improvement in productivity growth after the great 1979–81 recession cannot have closed such a large gap. Indeed, a less thorough recent estimate from the Treasury, referring to 1986, found that American output per hour worked exceeded British output by 32 per cent through the whole economy, once price differences between the two economies were allowed for.[2] French output per hour was 17 per cent higher, and German 5 per cent higher (see table 1). British output, of course, includes the highly mechanized production of North Sea oil. The gap in the non-oil economy which is crucial to our future is larger. Moreover, these figures include some questionable comparisons of productivity in services and other non-manufacturing activities. The gap in manufacturing industry is certainly larger.

Why does poor training affect the ability to produce and earn? The work of Professor Sig Prais and his team (also at NIESR) has repeatedly found that we educate our top talent relatively well. The largest skills gaps yawn at the middle skill levels.[3] This has three effects. First, it means that qualified people – such as engineers with degrees – have to get involved in sorting out relatively simple problems because the intermediate skill level is missing. This is wasteful of their expertise, and distracts them from other problems which only they could deal with. Secondly, it means that problems crop up more frequently. Production lines stop because machinery has been abused or not maintained. Line workers do not have the capacity to put simple errors right. There is a much higher proportion of idle time on the line than in more successful economies.

A third way in which low skills transmit themselves to low productivity levels is simply by ruling out sophisticated technologies, which could either not be operated at all or operated only at a relatively unintensive pace so that the investment would be uneconomic. A fourth way is by requiring a series of specialities to do a task, for example in the construction industry. In France the broadly trained building workers help ensure that output per employee is a third higher than in Britain – and building prices, task for task, a third cheaper.

How under-educated and under-skilled are we? Professor Prais's attempt to compare British and German skills levels found that 67 per cent of the German labour force had some form of vocational qualification, compared with 36 per cent of the British.[4] Moreover, the gap is not even closing. Each year, Germany qualifies between two and three times our numbers of fitters, electricians and building craftsmen. About 600,000 young people a year enter training and follow a three-year programme leading to a nationally recognized qualification. In Britain the Youth Training Scheme only became a two-year programme in the late eighties, when it began to acquire more serious training content. Moreover, the YTS certificate is in reality no more than a curriculum vitae, assessed by the teacher. Would we really be happy to let driving instructors issue their own pupils with licences, rather than having an examination conducted by an independent assessor?

A key area is engineering skills, because they are so crucial to manufacturing, which is in turn responsible for some 55 per

Table 2. Too few engineers? Numbers (thousands) qualifying in engineering and technology in UK, France, West Germany, Japan and USA (original numbers for Japan and US reduced in proportion to UK population) in *c* 1985

	UK	*France*	*Germany*	*Japan*	*USA*
Doctorates	0.7	0.3	1.0	0.3	0.5
Masters degrees	2	6	4	5	4
Bachelor degrees	14	15	21	30	19
Technicians	29	35	44	18–27	17
(Bachelors and technicians)	(43)	(50)	(65)	(48–57)	(36)
Craftsmen	35	92	120	44	n/a

Source: NIESR

cent of Britain's exports. Engineering has also been the subject of claims by the Department of Employment that Britain's skills gap has closed, much to the consternation of both independent specialists and the Engineering Council, the professional body which represents some 300,000 engineers and technologists. Subsequent work has suggested that the Department double-counted some people with intermediate-level and higher-level qualifications and also overestimated British skill levels by international standards. A separate study by Professor Prais shows that Britain is still bottom of the international league table of the five major industrial countries at every level of engineering and technological qualification except doctorates and technicians (table 2).[5]

An essential precondition of dealing with Britain's training problem is a proper bench-mark of attainment based on testing of standards, rather than the traditional British system of awarding a qualification after a certain amount of time served as an apprentice (regardless of whether the apprentice reached a proper standard in half the time, or never). The lack of a common set of qualifications building on the current haphazard system of time-serving apprenticeships, City and Guilds and other awards at intermediate level is a major impediment to the proper working of a market in trained labour. It is as if we thought it sensible to run a street market in which every fruit and vegetable trader was encouraged to operate according to different systems of weights and measures. One would be on metric, another on avoirdupois and so forth. Yet the National Council for Vocational Qualifications continues to make very heavy weather of its task, so there is as yet no nationally structured set of vocational qualifications for intermediate skills.

All of this could in time be put right. Educational standards could be raised, and the curriculum strengthened to insist on greater competence in practical maths so that vocational training need not include what is effectively remedial work. There could be a much larger throughput of trainees working to externally examined, nationally recognized qualifications. But would it be enough? There is another worrying possibility which might explain why businesses only notice our lack of skills at the top of a boom. It is that Britain's managers do not recognize that they are short of skills compared with their major competitors. Indeed, Britain's managers are very likely to be part of the problem of a generally low level of skill, education and competence in Britain. In other words, tackling the skills problem is not simply – as most politicians and officials seem to suppose – a matter of increasing the supply of skills in the areas identified by international comparisons to be most backward. It should also be about increasing the demand for those skills.

The report by Professor Charles Handy published by the National Economic Development Office[6] points out that 24 per cent of Britain's managers have City and Guilds qualifications, or A-levels, or equivalents. By implication, 76 per cent actually left school at the minimum school-leaving age, after doing O-levels or CSE. Indeed, one-fifth of the people who described themselves as managers in the 1985 Labour Force Survey had no qualifications of any description. Only 12.5 per cent had a first or higher degree.

The Handy report makes some sensible proposals for remedying our lack of managerial quality, notably general expansion of higher education, the adoption of a preliminary business qualification which would teach the basics such as identifying costs and so forth and which would be an 'add-on' to a first degree, and some form of apprenticeship linked with study as the first stage of management development. Handy also recommends establishing an official information base, statutorily backed if need be. Indeed, it is astonishing that the Training Commission (formerly the Manpower Services Commission) has only recently developed the CALLMI system to log training and needs for most of the labour force, and it will be some time before it is able to produce any sensible local results.

The Handy report, though, implicitly underlines a serious danger in the entire approach of British policy towards improving the quality of our manpower. It assumes that if we just go out and ask businessmen what they want they will necessarily know. The problem is that they will point to the immediate constraint of skill shortage, not to the long-term low level of skills around which they organize their business. Nor does this approach allow for the possibility that one of the reasons why we are a low-tech economy is because our managers are low-tech as well as our work-force. The Training Commission, the Department of Education and the sectoral employers' organizations need to monitor education and skills differences with our international competitors on a regular basis and set clear targets for closing the gap.

The second danger in present Government policy is the convenient notion that businesses can be persuaded to pay for training themselves. It may be that they should, but policy-makers cannot rely on it. Economic theory provides incontestable reasons for supposing that the degree of training actually undertaken in a free market will be below the level that would be socially desirable or 'optimal', because training carries major benefits that cannot necessarily be captured by the people who must pay for its cost. The individual gain to an employer from investing in a trained person who may leave to work for someone else is bound to be less than the social benefit. It is all too likely that the employer will rely on poaching trained workers from his rivals at times of acute shortage rather than undertake training that might benefit others. Each business tries to 'free ride' on the efforts of others, with the result that all of them end up with an unsatisfactory level of skills.

One possibility would be to ensure that employers who spent a lot of money on training could force the trained person to work for them subsequently for a period or to pay back any investment made in them: broadly the old indenture system with a let-out.

In reality, though, modern employers would be very reluctant to enforce any such contract, and they would have a very sullen and unproductive worker if they did. Many employers might still decide not to bother training, but merely to poach from firms that have trained when they need skilled manpower. There would still be no sanctions against such 'free-riders'.

Nor can individuals be relied upon to undertake training themselves. Banks are very reluctant to lend for long periods when there may be a loss of earnings, and most vocational training has to occur at least in part at a place of work. Moreover, the advantage of training does not necessarily accrue merely to the trained and to the employer. What of the advantage to the more highly qualified employee if a newly trained intermediate employee is able to take some of the chores off his or her hands? Their productivity would rise, and their pay probably will too. Training is particularly crucial in manufacturing industry, whose importance in trade is a key determinant of the ability of the whole economy to grow. There is thus a very strong case for some form of public tax or subsidy which encourages training. One possibility is the old remissible training tax levied by the industrial training boards, many of which were abolished in a fit of free-market enthusiasm by Mrs Thatcher's Government at the beginning of the eighties. Firms would pay a training tax unless they could show that they had achieved a certain pass rate in qualifications, related perhaps to the size of their average labour force.

Notes

1 Stephen Davies and Richard E. Caves, *Britain's Productivity Gap*, National Institute of Economic and Social Research, occasional paper (Cambridge, 1987).

2 *Productivity in the 1980s*, HM Treasury Economic Progress Report no. 201 (April 1989).

3 for example, Heinz Hollenstein, *Economic Performance and the Vocational Qualifications of the Swiss Labour Force Compared with Britain and Germany*, NIESR discussion paper no. 54 (September 1982).

4 S.J. Prais, 'Vocational Qualifications of the Labour Force in Britain and Germany', *National Institute Economic Review*, no. 98 (November 1981).

5 S.J. Prais, 'Qualified Manpower in Engineering', *National Institute Economic Review*, no. 127 (February 1989).

6 Charles Handy, National Economic Development Office, London, February 1987.

Britain's lack of research and development

Britain lags behind in industrial R&D

- high technology is reflected in trade performance
- public interest in R&D due to high social returns
- failure to research due to companies' policies
- interventionism and indicative planning are likely to fail
- means of influencing the market

One of the recurring worries about Britain's long-term economic performance is the lack of research and development. Without new products and processes, businesses are forced to compete on the basis of price, pushed into down-market niches in which the competitors may increasingly be low-labour-cost newly industrializing countries. This in turn is reflected in a poor trading performance, which means that spending in the whole economy is constrained to grow slowly in order to stop imports soaring. 'The acceleration of productivity growth is a notable achievement of the 1980s,' Mr Walter Eltis, the director general of the National Economic Development Office wrote in a paper in 1989, 'but during the 1990s it will need to be followed by an equally radical qualitative transformation of the range of goods that UK producers can manufacture on competitive terms.'

The facts about research and development are clear. Britain's overall level of R&D is not out of line with our main competitors, as table 3 shows. However, the picture changes if defence research, in which Britain is a major investor, is excluded. The more important research indicators for economic performance are the level of non-defence R&D (since that is where the markets tend to be) and the level of industry-financed R&D (which is where business itself expects a return). Non-defence R&D in Britain has declined from an above-average 1.78 per cent of GDP in 1967 to a below-average 1.59 per cent in 1983,

Table 3. Total and non-defence R&D as a percentage share of GDP, 1983

	Total R&D	*Non-defence R&D*
UK	2.24	1.59
Belgium	1.7	1.7
France	2.15	1.69
West Germany	2.58	2.47
Italy	1.2	1.16
Netherlands	1.89	1.86
Sweden	2.67	2.38
Switzerland	2.3	2.27
Japan	2.67	2.66
USA	2.73	1.97
Average		1.98

Source: Patel and Pavitt, *The Technological Activities of the UK* (1987), from OECD

Table 4. Trends in industrial R&D as a percentage share of industrial output, 1967–85

		Total			*Industry-financed*	
	1967	*1975*	*1985*	*1967*	*1975*	*1985*
Japan	0.92	1.28	2.11	0.9	1.26	2.07
USA	2.35	1.84	2.32	1.15	1.18	1.54
France	1.36	1.36	1.78	0.75	0.87	1.24
West Germany	1.31	1.65	2.42	1.07	1.3	1.99
Italy	0.43	0.61	0.92	0.41	0.55	0.71
Netherlands	1.45	1.45	1.5	1.31	1.3	1.22
Sweden	1.29	1.64	3.03	0.94	1.48	2.64
UK	2.01	1.72	2.01	1.34	1.08	1.32
Western Europe	1.27	1.35	1.81	0.92	1.0	1.37

Source: Pavitt and Patel in *Oxford Review of Economic Policy*, vol. 4, no. 4 (1988)

according to the University of Sussex Science Policy Research Unit (SPRU).[1] Table 4, showing industry-financed R&D, is scarcely more encouraging. Britain is again below average. The very low growth rate of industry-financed R&D has led to a steady relative decline in the UK position.

An obvious objection to these comparisons is that they measure what a country is putting into R&D rather than what it is getting out of it. However, measures of research output

Table 5. Percentage share of Western European patenting in the USA, 1963–85

	1963	*1970*	*1977*	*1985*
UK	26.3	23.9	18.4	15.8
Belgium	1.2	1.9	1.8	1.5
France	12.4	14.0	14.6	15.2
West Germany	33.9	35.9	38.5	42.2
Italy	5.0	4.6	5.2	5.8
Netherlands	4.8	4.4	4.9	4.8
Sweden	5.6	5.1	6.0	5.4
Switzerland	9.7	9.0	9.4	7.8
Denmark	1.0	1.1	1.1	1.1
Ireland	0.0	0.1	0.1	0.2

Source: Science Policy Research Unit/OTAF database

are not much more encouraging. The two leading researchers in this field, Professor Keith Pavitt and Mr Pari Patel, have used patents registered in the United States – a key market in which to protect technical advance from competitors – as an indicator of R&D output. They point out that the UK share of all European patenting in the US declined steadily between 1963 and 1985, 'and virtually halved as a share of the French and German combined total from 57 per cent to 28 per cent.' Table 5 gives an indication of the decline in the number of innovations which British companies have thought worth protecting in the United States. Nor is this a relatively recent phenomenon. Figure 3 plots Germany's US-registered patents as a percentage of Britain's back to the end of the nineteenth century. The relative decline in Britain's technological prowess has deep roots, and has continued through many different changes of regime and economic policy.

This technological decline has undermined Britain's competitive position, as one might expect. Professor Pavitt and Mr Patel compute a general measure of Britain's relative technological advantage in specific sectors by looking at the sector's share of all the patents registered in the same field in the United States, and then working out whether the sector is improving or declining compared with other British sectors. An 'index of revealed technological advantage' (RTA) above one means the sector is doing relatively well. British industries with a high

Figure 3

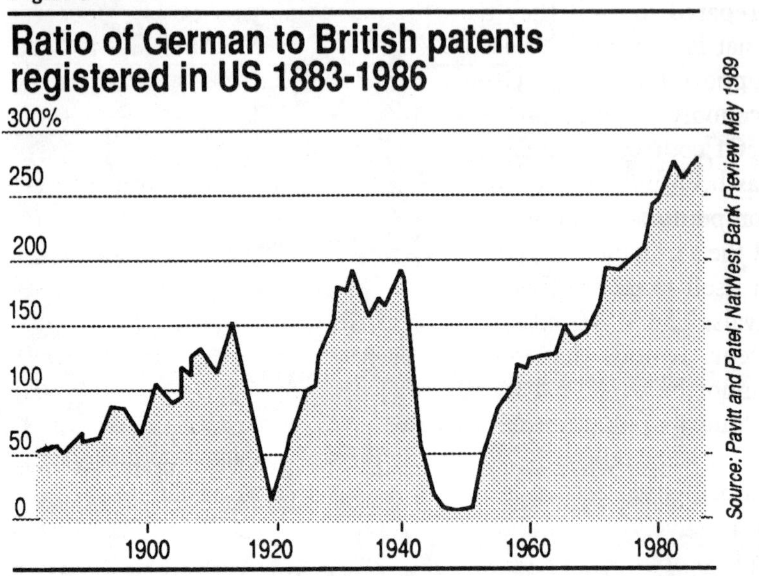

and rising RTA since the end of the sixties include drugs, food and tobacco, mining machinery and chemical processes. Those industries with a low and falling RTA include general electrical machinery, metallurgical and metal-working equipment, semiconductors, calculators and computers, and nuclear reactors and systems. The authors then find that sectors with high and rising RTA tend to be doing well in terms of relative export performance. In other words, R&D does pay off.

There may, though, be many activities which are privately profitable but which it would be rash for the public sector to encourage. Why should there be any Governmental interest in the level of research and development? Why not leave it up to the marketplace? The short answer is that R&D is a classic example of where the social returns to research are substantially greater than the private returns to the individual or company conducting it. Indeed, one study of innovations in the United States suggested that the average social rate of return on innovation in the private sector was 56 per cent, compared with a private rate of return of 25 per cent.[3] The difference between the two comprises the benefit to consumers – the consumer surplus – as they are able to buy products more cheaply than they would be prepared to do if they had to. Innovation also saves resources. That is one market-based argument for public interest in, and support for, R&D. Others stress the long-run effects on the economy's dynamism.

Of course, for much of the post-war period British industry has been relatively unprofitable compared with its international competitors. Some have argued that an increase in profitability of the sort which has occurred during the eighties will be enough in itself to rectify Britain's shortfall in R&D compared with its rivals. The SPRU research[2] suggests that this will not necessarily occur. It finds that much of the change in R&D performance cannot be explained by changes in profitability or output, but is due to policy decisions by particular firms. Indeed, much of the shortfall in R&D is due to one or two very big firms, simply because of the concentration of production and R&D in relatively few units. The deterioration in semiconductors and computers can be traced to the decisions of a handful of firms – GEC, STC/ITT and Plessey. Predictably, the largest decline in patenting activity of any British company was that of GEC, whose infamous 'cash mountain' has become a symbol of British industry's reluctance to take long-term decisions about products and processes. GEC's share of UK patents registered in the United States fell from 4.3 per cent in 1969–72 to only 2.2 per cent in 1981–4.

Some of the reasons for this lack of far-sightedness compared with our rivals overseas may lie in the relationship between industry and the financial sector, which is the subject of the next essay. However, there is no shortage of proposals for dealing specifically with the R&D problem. At one extreme, there are advocates of the sort of institutions tried during the sixties and seventies in Britain – like the National Enterprise Board and the British Investment Bank proposed by the Labour Party at the 1987 general election – which are clearly modelled on Japan's Ministry of International Trade and Industry (MITI) and on France's experience since the fifties with 'indicative planning'.

There is, though, real doubt both about how successful the overseas examples of such planning actually were, and about whether French and Japanese institutional arrangements could be transplanted to British soil. In Japan, MITI was useful in the early post-war years of industrialization because the task of catching up with overseas countries was clear. The more complex an economy becomes, the less easy it becomes to plan. MITI increasingly sees its role as encouraging co-operation over basic research. Japanese companies then compete fiercely to turn the research into commercially viable technologies. MITI failed, for example, to persuade the electronics industry to adopt one video standard: it was competition that ultimately led to the triumph of JVCs over Sony's Betamax.

In France, industrial policy is widely perceived as having failed, as the 1989 Organisation for Economic Co-operation and Development survey makes clear.[4] French industry's performance in holding world market share and repelling importers has worsened during the eighties. Indeed, the French Government has begun to shift from the policy of 'picking winners' – ploughing large amounts of money selectively into a few 'strategic' sectors and firms – towards more generalized incentives. France, of course, has a core of technocrats specially trained in the Grandes Écoles, and with a long tradition of moving between big business and the Government. If not even France can make indicative planning work, Britain certainly could not. Our previous history of 'picking winners' left us with Concorde, the abortive British Leyland merger and the GEC takeover of its main electrical industry rivals in the sixties.

Any policy to encourage R&D and the diffusion of new technology should begin by recognizing that bureaucrats and politicians are bad at playing God. (This also, by the way, appears to apply to R&D undertaken directly by the public sector.) The best hope lies in measures that change the climate within which all business works, rather than those which try to deliver rainfall on top of a particular hill. In other words, the emphasis should be on working with the grain of the market. A small but obvious change would be to insist that British public companies have a legal obligation to report their R&D and patenting efforts each year in the annual report to shareholders. The City would then be in some position to assess firms making adequate provision for their future markets. A second possibility would be to provide matching funds for industrial support of R&D undertaken at universities and research institutes, which would foster the university–business links which have been such an important feature of the most successful high technology firms here and overseas. A third would be the provision of research tax credits to firms, a scheme introduced in France in 1983 and which is said to have led in just two years to 2,000 new and often small firms reporting R&D spending. A fourth avenue is Japanese-style encouragement of core research in a particular technology available to a group of companies. For reasons of scale, this probably has to be undertaken on a pan-European basis on the lines of the EC-Commission-supported Eureka project. The fifth model is the one so successfully applied to British agriculture between the wars: the growth of extension services to spread best technological practice particularly among smaller companies which do not necessarily have the manpower or time to investigate their options.

Notes

1 P. Patel and K. Pavitt, *The Technological Activities of the UK: a Fresh Look*, Science Policy Research Unit, discussion paper no. 49 (August 1987).

2 P. Patel and K. Pavitt, 'The Elements of British Technological Competitiveness', *National Institute Economic Review*, no. 122 (November 1987).

3 E. Mansfield, 'Measuring the Social and Private Rates of Return on Innovation', *Economic Effects of Space and Other Advanced Technologies* (Strasbourg: Council of Europe, 1980), quoted in *Industrial Policy and Innovation*, ed. Charles Carter (London: Heinemann, 1981), p. 9.

4 *1988/1989 OECD Economic Surveys: France* (Paris: OECD).

An investment problem?

Slow growing investment

- the flow of investment and the stock of capital
- international comparisons of real investment levels show Britain lagging
- one cause may be an inefficient construction industry
- the influence of a market-oriented financial system
- why interest rates do not reflect risk
- the importance of rules of thumb in lending

Does Britain still have an investment problem? The question may seem bizarre after two years of exceptionally strong growth in investment of more than 8 per cent in 1988 and 5.5 per cent in 1987, but those years were the top of a boom. Over the whole cycle from 1979 to 1988, the average annual growth of investment (Gross Fixed Capital Formation) was 2.8 per cent. This was sharply better than the 0.2 per cent annual growth recorded over the period from 1973 to 1979, but it was a little below the 3.6 per cent growth rate from 1966 to 1973.

This comparison, though, is distorted both by the sharp boom in 1973, which meant that investment was depressed for many years afterwards, and by the cuts in *Government* investment spending in the last years of the Labour Government from 1974 to 1979. There is less of a contrast in the performance of *business* investment between the depressed 1973–9 cycle and the 1979–88 cycle. Moreover, investment is a flow from year to year. A certain amount is needed simply to reinstate the stock of old capital equipment which is wearing out.

It is the stock of capital which determines potential output. Yet estimates of the stock of capital are notoriously difficult. Businesses may hang on to old equipment for much longer than the theoretical life, or for much shorter periods. For what the estimates are worth, the average annual growth of the capital stock is put by the Central Statistical Office at 2.1 per cent over the period from 1979 to 1987, compared with 1.8 per cent between 1973 and 1979, and more than 4 per cent over the whole period from 1955 to 1973.

Perhaps the most important perspective on investment, though, comes from the international comparisons. The crude data at market exchange rates suggest that Britain is no longer out of line in the share of national income which it devotes to investment, a fact pointed out in a recent Organisation for Economic Co-operation and Development (OECD) country report on Britain. Ironically, though, the authors of that report had ignored the separate evidence of other researchers at the OECD into real comparisons across international boundaries of both incomes and types of spending like investment. Their results, collated in a mammoth exercise in price collecting which included getting tenders for various items of construction and

Table 6. Real international investment levels, 1985 (percentage share of GDP at purchasing power parities)

	Gross fixed capital formation and equipment	*of which Machinery*	*of which Construction*
UK	*16.0*	*8.4*	6.7
Total EEC	19.1	8.4	10.1
Belgium	17.4	7.1	9.5
Denmark	20.6	10.0	10.7
France	20.2	8.8	10.2
West Germany	21.4	9.4	11.9
Greece	17.4	5.8	11.6
Ireland	22.5	10.2	11.5
Italy	20.3	8.8	10.9
Luxembourg	22.5	10.2	11.0
Netherlands	18.4	9.5	8.9
Portugal	15.8	4.0	10.4
Spain	16.7	4.7	11.4
Sweden	19.0	8.0	10.8
Australia	23.4	10.2	11.7
New Zealand	21.1	8.6	12.0
Japan	24.1	10.2	13.9
Canada	21.5	5.8	15.7
USA	20.1	8.9	11.1

Source: OECD National Accounts Main Aggregates, vol. 1: *1970–1985, Purchasing Power Parities Supplement* (Paris, 1987)

capital equipment, make much less happy reading for Britain.

According to this research which allows for international price differences, Britain devotes a lower share of its national income to investment in real terms than any other developed country except Portugal (see table 6). However, one interesting feature of the study is that it shows that the shortfall is concentrated in construction spending, and that the gap is mainly explained by relatively high British prices for building work. The investment share of plant and machinery is far less out of line with overseas experience. This finding implies that Britain's construction industry is relatively inefficient, a conclusion which is supported by separate work showing the lack of general skills available to most British construction workers.

There may be a second, contributory cause to Britain's traditionally poor investment record, which is that investment appears to be strongly linked to the profits being made by business at the time. When profits are good, investment is good, and vice versa. The Confederation of British Industry uses this point to argue for the desirability of a profitable British corporate sector, and it is certainly right to do so. However, another more controversial conclusion is that the financial sector does relatively little to finance British investment even when businesses have relatively little cash flow themselves. After all, many of Britain's businesses operate in a world market where they are relatively immune from the ups and downs of the British economy. They ought to be able to plan ahead on the basis of expected profitability, regardless of their actual profitability today, if the financial sector were prepared to lend them the money to do so.

The evidence, though, is that the British and American financial sectors, theoretically the most efficient and competitive in the major countries, make a negligible contribution to the financing of the real investment in their business sectors. This is not important in a boom, because the companies are flush with cash. But it can make life far tougher in a recession. Why are British and American banks so tight-fisted towards industry? Basically, the market-oriented financial systems operate conservative rules of thumb which exclude relatively risky investments. The conventional wisdom is that the banks can always charge a higher interest rate to reflect any extra risk involved in their lending. In reality, however, the interest cost to a particular business simply does not go up and down to reflect the real risk of its proposed ventures, but instead reflects some sort of average of accepted risk for the system as a whole. The bank manager does not say: 'Here, you can have this loan at 51 per cent interest a year because it looks risky.' He just says no.

The institutions apply rules of thumb about acceptable risk. Ironically, many bankers have often had a soft spot for overseas lending. In the seventies, for example, it was widely believed that countries could never default: hence there was less than half a per cent difference in the interest rates paid by creditworthy France and uncreditworthy Argentina. Domestically, Anglo-Saxon banking caution was bred largely by the banks' ignorance of the industries to which they are lending.[2] Even at the height of the oil boom, one of the best British clearers had only one senior employee who had ever worked in the oil industry. Thus it is 'good' banking practice to play very safe; you match lending to small businesses to the knock-down or liquidation value of their assets. A new transit van may have an economic life to the firm of ten years, but the bank may insist, say, on repayment within two because of the rapid deterioration in its second-hand value.

Such differences in the term of loan can be important in determining whether a small or medium-sized business takes on more debt – and grows. After all, a £30,000 mortgage at 12.5 per cent spread over 25 years will cost £4,050 a year, but the same amount requiring repayments in five years will cost £8,750. It is difficult, though, to assess how different the American and British banks are. The traditional critics of the banks have pointed to the relatively low amounts of bank debt companies have contracted as an indicator of the financial system's reluctance to back business.[3] These capital gearing ratios do indeed support the critics' case. The figures, though, are a minefield of incompatibilities.

Another approach to the issue, pioneered by the Centre for Economic Policy Research project into international comparisons of corporate financing led by Professor Colin Mayer of the City University Business School, is to compare the annual flows of finance – from both banks and other sources – with the physical investment actually undertaken by businesses. Investment in financial assets – such as a company buying another company's shares – is taken out of the reckoning. The results are fascinating, and are shown as figure 4. Over the period from 1970 to 1984, the only source of finance which was important to British industry was retained profits. Companies ran down the value of shares, corporate bonds and trade credit so that they drained resources away from physical investment. Loans made a marginally positive contribution, though it was the most modest of the Big Five economies.

Ironically, the fond idea that the British stock market compensates for the shortcomings of the banking system is the reverse of the truth: both France and West Germany's relatively undeveloped stock exchanges raised a larger proportion

Figure 4

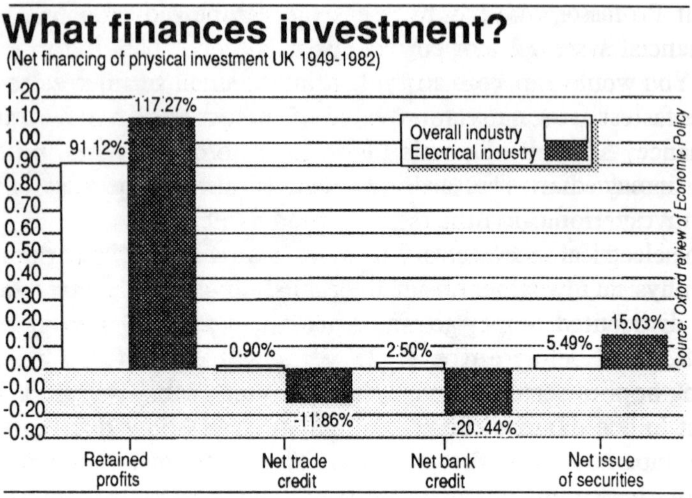

of the finance for their (higher) physical investment than ours. In London and New York the stock markets are vehicles for transferring ownership, not raising capital. Overall, companies funded 101 per cent of their physical investment from retained earnings. Britain's financial institutions, including the Stock Exchange, made no net contribution to the growth of business at all.

These figures have been criticized because of the inadequacy of the national accounts on which they are based – you may notice that they rarely sum to 100 per cent – but an exactly parallel calculation for the UK grounded instead on a database of quoted companies' own published accounts comes up with a very similar result: retained earnings funded just over 90 per cent of corporate Britain's physical investment. Moreover, the findings from company accounts[5] suggest that security issues – shares and bonds – have funded even less physical investment over the period of the recent liberalization.

All of this merely helps to establish that British companies raise less money than their competitors. It does not necessarily mean that it is the financial system which is to blame: it may simply be that British managers come up with too few worthwhile projects for financing. The evidence suggests that British managers are relatively badly educated, the British work-force badly trained. But Professor Mayer's work provides some indication that the financial system is not perfect either.

You would expect in any well-functioning financial system that the fastest growing sectors would have most recourse to external finance. After all, the banks and securities markets are meant to be 'intermediaries' funnelling savings to companies which want to invest. Ironically, the reverse appears to be the case in Britain. The electrical and electronics sector financed nearly 120 per cent of physical investment from retained earnings (i.e. it repaid debt, or distributed money to shareholders) over the period 1949 to 1982. And before anyone says 'GEC's cash mountain', this finding applies across the sector and to small and large firms, not just to one dilatory company. Just as much to the point, would the Japanese or the German financial systems allow a large firm with the leading technological edge in its sector to behave as GEC has? The answer is: 'Probably not.'

One reason why financial liberalization may not help is that it will make long-term relationships between bankers and companies even harder to forge. Why should a bank take a long view of a company, and monitor its progress closely, and invest its own staff time in learning about the company's technologies and businesses, and bail it out during a recession, if the company then turns round when the going is good and goes to a cheaper source of finance? A degree of market stickiness – the old-fashioned would say 'loyalty' – may be required to ensure that the financial institutions develop less conservative rules of thumb about lending.

In Germany, Japan and France, the development of a private sector industrial banking tradition was a major objective of public financial policy in the latter part of the nineteenth century and the early years of this century. Their policy-makers understood the key role which the financial system could play in the objective of catching up with the British and the Americans – and provided financial incentives for it to do so in the form of cheap lending to match its industrial activities. In Germany, many of the banks also acquired shareholdings in the leading industrial companies between the wars. Similar links between financial institutions and industrial companies do not exist in

Britain. It might be better for both finance and industry if they did.

Notes

1 S.J. Prais and Hilary Steedman, 'Vocational Training in France and Britain: the Building Trades', *National Institute Economic Review*, no. 116 (May 1986).

2 Yao-Su Hu, 'National Attitudes and the Financing of Industry', *Political and Economic Planning* (1975).

3 See, for example, John C. Carrington and George T. Edwards *Reversing Economic Decline* (London, 1981) and the subsequent debate between the Conservative back-bench industry committee chaired by Mr Michael Grylls MP and the Committee of London and Scottish clearing bankers.

4 Colin Mayer, *New Issues in Corporate Finance*, Centre for Economic Policy Research, paper no. 181 (1987).

5 Colin Mayer in *Oxford Review of Economic Policy*, vol. 3, no. 4 (Winter 1987).

The economics of privatization

Scale of privatization

- international trends
- usefulness in camouflaging budget easing
- 'selling the family silver'
- public and private ownership in a competitive market
- privatization and regulation of monopolies
- criteria for judging success
- poor nationalized industry performance and the case for change

The policy of privatization has come a long, long way from its first, oblique mention in the Conservative election manifesto of 1979. At that time, even the word had not yet been coined. There was explicit mention only of selling back 'the recently nationalized aerospace and shipbuilding concerns . . . we aim to sell shares in the National Freight Corporation to the general public'. A decade later, the policy is perceived by

Table 7. Privatization proceeds, 1979–93

	Income (£m)
1979/80	377
1980/81	405
1981/82	493
1982/83	488
1983/84	1,142
1984/85	2,132
1985/86	2,732
1986/87	4,400
1987/88	5,100
1988/89	7,100
1989/90	5,000*
1990/91	5,000
1991/92	5,000
1992/93	5,000

*Forecast hereafter

Source: Financial Statistics; Financial Statement and Budget Report

the Government as one of its enduring successes. By the end of 1988 seventeen companies had been privatized. This was about a third of all the industries owned by the state in 1979, a group which in turn accounted for 10 per cent of the output produced in Britain, and which employed more than 2 million people.

Over the same period, the Treasury estimates that the number of shareholders has risen from 3 million to 9 million, or one in five of the adult population, very largely due to privatization issues. This is a whole new political constituency of property-owners, as the Tories' election mailshots to people who bought privatized shares showed. (The economic significance of this spreading ownership is another matter: the shareholdings are so small that the proportion of shares owned by institutions has continued to rise despite the enormous increase in the number of shareholders. On one estimate, the institutions like the life assurers and pension funds own more than three-quarters of all equities quoted on the London Stock Exchange.) Meanwhile, the remaining utilities are on the slipway. Electricity and water are scheduled. Even the coal industry is possible. By the end of this Parliament, the gathering momentum of privatization will have dismantled Herbert Morrison's legacy of nationalized industries brick by crumbling brick.

The trend is also catching on internationally, although an International Monetary Fund study[1] argues that it is not quite as popular overseas as ministers' public relations sometimes suggests. Apart from Britain, only France has had an extensive privatization programme, although even there the proceeds are equivalent to just one year's sales in Britain. The Japanese are selling Nippon Telegraph and Telephone, and there have been privatizations in Chile, Malaysia, Niger and Turkey. However, sales in Germany and Italy have been little more than tidying-up operations.

The irony, though, is that the British drive to privatize still looks more like a felicitous accident than a carefully designed scheme to revive the economy. A major reason for the acceleration of asset sales under Mr Lawson's chancellorship from 1983 to 1989 was the happy side-effect of reducing the Public Sector Borrowing Requirement – the budget deficit caused by spending more than revenue. This released the Treasury from an uncomfortable hook by allowing a more expansionary budgetary policy than would otherwise have occurred. By a curious accounting convention, asset sales count as negative public spending, and thus directly cut borrowing. For any given borrowing target, asset sales allowed taxes to be lower and public spending to be higher. In the conditions of the early eighties, when unemployment was at record levels, anything to get the Government off its shibboleth against expansionary policies was welcome.

The criticism that the Government was 'selling the family silver', in Mr Harold Macmillan's splendidly emotive phrase, was always wide of the mark. Indeed, it is very hard to see in economic theory why there should be any difference to the Government if it finances its deficit by getting cash in exchange for issuing bonds – promises to pay interest in the future – or if it finances its deficit by selling assets – which are entitlements to a stream of income in the future. If the capital markets are working efficiently, it should be impossible to tell which is the better course of action to take. This is a closely related result to the famous theorem of Franco Modigliani, for which he won the

Nobel prize for economics. He pointed out that the market value of a firm does not depend on the particular mix of equity (shares) or debt (say, bank finance) in its funds. If firms found that it was cheaper to raise money through borrowing than through the issue of shares, the relative cost would begin to change until it became equal. The Government's net worth – its assets minus its debt – is also the same whether it finances a deficit by borrowing or by selling assets.

The real economic arguments about privatization should revolve around whether the companies work better in the private or in the public sector. The public claims about the relative economic efficiency of privately owned companies, or the benefits of rolling back the frontiers of the state, are not as clear-cut as ministers like to argue. The more the theorists write about the subject, the plainer it becomes that the simple idea that many of the former nationalized industries could operate independently of Government scrutiny is so much eyewash. The real choice is between actually owning the businesses, and regulating them tightly. The Government is simply not going to be able to wash its hands of most of the privatized industries.

The key determinant of whether the Government can take its hands off the tiller is whether the companies are operating in a competitive market. If they are, then it can safely let the management get on with it. Companies like Jaguar or Amersham International must perform, or they will lose market share, sales and profits. If they do not perform, there are plenty of companies big enough to make a takeover bid. Even the threat of takeover may encourage the management. Like most ordinary joint stock companies, they face competitive pressure in the markets for their products, for their inputs, and for their capital.

With this type of company, theory suggests that the switch from public to private ownership makes most sense. Any conflict between social and private objectives is likely to be smaller in competitive markets than in monopoly ones. A competitive market means that the prices of goods and services will be fairly set to reflect demand and supply, which ensures that resources are efficiently allocated. Private ownership may in turn encourage another type of efficiency – internal or X-efficiency, which is the more efficient production of a given good or service for fewer inputs of labour, land and capital.[2] The private owner, or his manager, has more incentive to save costs than a public sector manager who will receive no extra reward if he does.

Nevertheless, the evidence that privately owned companies perform better in competitive markets than publicly owned ones is not conclusive. Vickers and Yarrow[3] quote a study of the performance of the privately owned Canadian Pacific against the competing, publicly owned Canadian National railway. It concludes: 'Public ownership is not inherently less efficient than private ownership' and that the 'oft noted inefficiency of Government enterprises stems from the isolation of effective competition rather than public ownership per se'. Other work in North American markets where public and private enterprise compete, is inconclusive. Overall, Vickers and Yarrow conclude that private ownership is probably more efficient, when operating in a competitive market, simply because more of it survives.

If the company is operating in a market over which it has substantial control because of lack of competition, then the arguments about ownership and efficiency are quite different. Internal efficiency – reducing costs to produce a given bundle of output – may be increased if ownership changes, but only if private owners establish better monitoring of performance. However, if the monopoly company is able merely to raise prices to its customers, it is quite possible that it will not even bother to make extensive gains in internal efficiency. After all, it has less incentive to do so. Indeed, establishing high pay in an industry is one way of preventing new competition from entering the market. There are certainly plenty of examples of private sector monopolies which have not traditionally benefited from internal efficiency, including Mrs Thatcher's current *bête noire* of the independent television companies.

The sensible response of policy is to introduce as much competition as possible into the market, either by splitting up public corporations or encouraging new competitors. Yet the Government, until its recent proposals on electricity, has been

Table 8. Productivity growth in the UK public sector, 1979–88 (annual percentage rate of increase)

	1979–88	*1979–83*	*1983–88*
BAA	1.6	0.0	2.8
British Coal*	2.9	0.6	4.6
British Gas	3.3	−0.2	6.2
British Rail	1.3	−0.4	2.7
British Steel	12.9	8.4	12.4
British Telecom	2.4	2.0	2.5
Electricity	1.4	−1.6	4.0
Post Office	3.7	3.6	3.3
Average	3.7	1.6	4.8

*Adjusted for effects of the 1984–5 coal strike
Source: Bishop and Kay, *Does Privatisation Work?* (1988)

very slow to recognize the case for competition as opposed to a change in ownership. British Gas was left intact, and British Telecom has had to contend only with Mercury. A much more sensible solution might have been to split the industry up, as the Americans did with AT&T and the so-called regional 'Baby Bells'. If competition is not introduced, or if it cannot be introduced because the industry is effectively a natural monopoly like the water businesses, then the Government choice is between public ownership and regulated private ownership. That is where we are with the existing privatizations, notably water.

The impact of privatisations on the economy will take time to assess, but it is not going to be easy to do so. Productivity changes may be one proxy for internal efficiency. The evidence so far is that different rates of productivity growth in the public sector companies bear little relationship with being on the slipway to privatization (table 8). Matthew Bishop and John Kay conclude that 'gains in British Coal and British Steel (where privatization has not been in prospect until recently) and the electricity supply industry have matched those in British Gas and the poorest performance since 1983 comes from the flagship of privatization, British Telecom'.[4] However, a conclusive study would have to compare similar industries in the public and private sector.

Figure 5

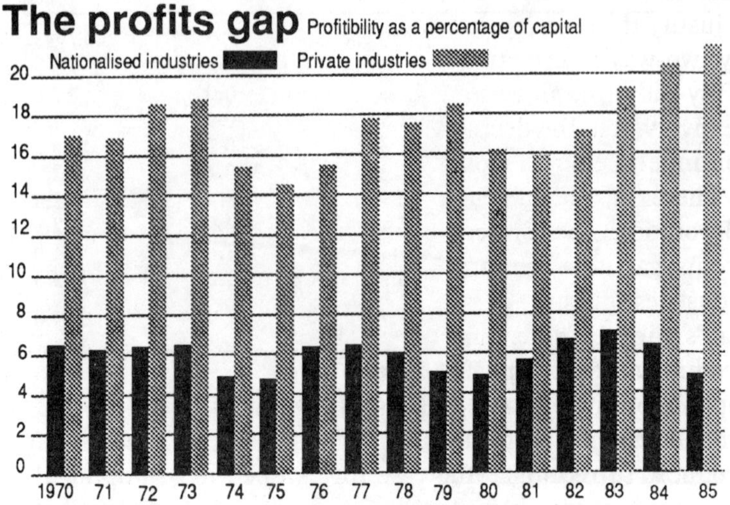

Gross trading profit or surplus as percentage of net capital stock at replacement cost.
Private industries are industrial and commercial companies. Source: Vickers & Yarrow

Another measure is profitability. There has been a large difference between the profits as a percentage of the replacement cost of capital – the rate of return – of the public and private sectors. In 1985, for example, industrial and commercial companies earned 21.3 per cent against 2.6 per cent for public corporations (figure 5). But the closing of the profits gap with private business is not necessarily a good indicator of increased efficiency, since it may come about due to more vigorous exploitation of monopoly power to levy high prices. There are, as a Lloyds Bank report[5] makes clear, plenty of loopholes in British Telecom's regulation and pricing rules.

Nor will it be enough to see whether the prices charged to consumers have risen more slowly than before. One danger of a regulated regime is that the company 'captures' the regulators so that they become ineffective; however, there is also the opposite danger that excessively strict regulation of output prices – or the fear of excessively strict future regulation – leads to under-investment in plant and equipment. This, indeed, was one of the original reasons proposed for utility nationalization: the rate of return required by the private owners in assessing investment possibilities was perceived to be higher than the social one. (This argument is used by the Labour Party to justify the renationalization of British Telecom, which will not lay two-way information technology cables to every household.) Willy-nilly, the Government or its agencies are going to have to be involved in the decisions of those privatized companies which continue to enjoy a monopoly.

There is, though, not much doubt that Britain's public corporations performed poorly through the seventies. The profits gap was too large to be explained by the nationalized industries pursuit of social objectives (for example, British Rail's subsidizing commuter services to avoid city congestion). Productivity growth was also low, and the rate of return on capital abysmal. A sharp change in regime was certainly called for and even the preparation for private ownership seems to have produced substantial results. It may be that big corporations, like economies in some Schumpeterian or Mancur Olson view of the world, benefit from occasionally being shaken by the scruff of the neck. Fifty years on, renationalization may be needed to put them all on their toes.

Notes

1 Richard Hemming and Ali M. Mansoor, *Privatization and Public Enterprises* (Washington DC: International Monetary Fund, 1988).

2 The concept of X-inefficiency was coined by Harvey Leibenstein, professor of economics at Harvard. See, for example, Leibenstein, *Beyond Economic Man* (Cambridge, Mass.: Harvard University Press, 1976) and *Inside the Firm: the Inefficiencies of Hierarchy* (cambridge, Mass.: Harvard University Press, 1987).

3 John Vickers and George Yarrow, *Privatisation: an Economic Analysis* (Cambridge, Mass.: MIT Press, 1988) quoting D.W. Caves and L.R. Christensen, 'The Relative Efficiency of Public and Private Firms in a Competitive Environment: the Case of Canadian Railroads'. *Journal of Political Economy*, vol. 88 (1980), pp. 958–76.

4 Matthew Bishop and John Kay, *Does Privatisation Work? Lessons from the UK* (London: Centre for Business Strategy, London Business School, 1988).

5 *Lloyds Bank Annual Review, Privatization and Ownership*, ed. Christopher Johnson (London, 1988).

Do mergers make sense?

Reasons for mergers

- the difference between social and private benefits
- how mergers happen in spurts and bull markets
- tax and financial technology reasons for the recent merger boom
- the evidence for the results of mergers
- the case for more restrictive merger policy
- the dangers of removing the merger threat from management
- the banks and employees as alternative monitors of performance

The late eighties saw the largest boom in corporate bids and mergers for twenty years. Household name after household name – Guinness, Rowntree, Allied Lyons, Habitat – kept the financial pages singing with argument and counter-argument. What were the reasons for the 'merger mania', and what were its effects? Does it prove, as many have anxiously argued, that British merger policy needs to become more restrictive?

It is important to distinguish between mergers which are advantageous to the firms involved, and mergers which bring advantages to society as a whole. Start with two types of merger which have dubious social benefits. Firms may be able to reduce their joint tax bill if one of them has offsets against corporation tax it is unable to use. Firms may also give themselves greater market power by reducing competition, and hence becoming able to push up prices and make larger profits for a given level of cost. In both cases, there are private benefits to the firms involved at the expense of the rest of the community.

There are also, though, mergers which benefit the whole economy. One firm may have a management team which is better than another. The sum of the parts may genuinely be larger than if they remained separate. Another good reason for mergers is if the two firms can reap economies of scale in production or by cutting overheads. Such mergers improve the efficiency with which resources are allocated. This is likely to be an increasingly strong motive as firms adjust to the 1992 single market in the European Community. However, many of the mergers which attract most public opprobrium also fall into this category. Plant closures may be involved if the industry is contracting. But it is surely much better for two firms to merge and close their least efficient plants (some of which may be in each firm) rather than have one firm drive the other out of business entirely.

Another motive for merger may be financial gains from diversifying out of a business which is, for example, particularly cyclical or concentrated in vulnerable foreign markets. Thus the combined entity may be able to borrow more cheaply, and hence reduce the financial costs of its operations. The bidder may have perfectly honest information about the victim not available to other market participants and hence not reflected in the market price of the victim. This is probably an important reason for agreed mergers, which are still the vast bulk of takeover activity. 'Thus Hanson Trust was able to recoup almost two thirds of the costs of acquiring the Imperial Group through subsequent sales (including Courage) whilst retaining subsidiaries which accounted for 55 per cent of Imperial's profits,' say Professor Brian Chiplin and Dr Mike Wright.[1]

There may also be, in the case of the financial conglomerates, some sort of 'bicycle effect': their past growth encourages the stock market to award them high share prices relative to the rest of the market. Thus their price is high relative to earnings, reflecting future expectations of more earnings. That in turn means that a takeover of a smaller firm with a low price relative to earnings immediately justifies a higher share price for the predator. The earnings are worth more to a firm with high price–earnings ratio than they are to a firm with a low one.

The trouble with this phenomenon – discovered successively by Clore, Slater-Walker and today's takeover barons – is that the pace of acquisitions has to go on accelerating to keep the share price high relative to the market. At some point, of course, sheer size stops the process and the bicycle becomes wobbly. Nevertheless, all of these effects have existed since Pericles, if not before, and fail to explain the crucial observation in figure 6 that takeover activity in the UK appears to happen in short, sharp

Figure 6

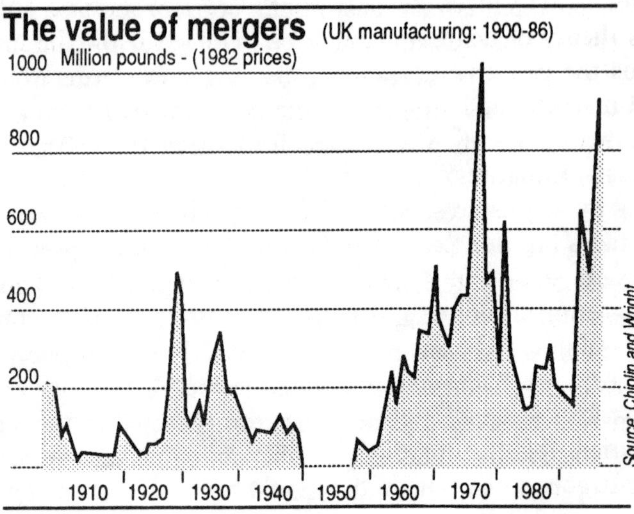

bursts, and mainly during big bull markets like the late twenties, late sixties and late eighties.

We therefore have an analytical problem: the reasons for takeovers are constant, but the takeovers are not. So the interesting question about takeovers is not so much 'why?' as 'why now?'. In the United States some analysts have attributed the takeover boom to a change in financial technology – the ready availability of credit through the invention of 'junk bonds' by Mr Michael Milken of Drexel Burnham Lambert, who is now facing charges concerning some of the mergers he helped to finance. 'Junk bonds' are merely promises to pay for a given period of time a given interest rate – usually between 3 and 5 per cent higher than the rate on US Government promises to pay (or Treasury bills). They are secured on the assets of the takeover victim, assuming that the bid is successful. In addition, a new breed of arbitrageurs – the most famous of which is the now imprisoned Mr Ivan Boesky – were prepared to take speculative positions in companies and hence make them easier targets for predators.

In Britain, neither factor has been as important as it was on Wall Street. True, merchant banks appear to have moved from being passive midwives of mergers to active marriage-brokers.

But the most intriguing explanation for the spate of British takeover activity over the last few years is Professor Mervyn King's theory of tax-driven mergers.[2] His model of the market explains the two crucial factors: why it is that mergers happen in bull markets, and why they happen in bursts.

The reason is essentially that it is cheaper to buy assets on the stock market than to invest in new ones: it is cheaper to grow by acquisition than to grow organically. The corporate sector faces taxation on its earnings which reduces the value of the income stream of its assets compared with the same assets used by unincorporated businesses – people. Thus companies' market value tends to be lower than the replacement cost of its assets. And why does this particularly encourage mergers in a bull market? Because bull markets are caused in part by the expectation that future profits will rise. Investment becomes more attractive. But higher future profits also mean higher future taxes: the proportional difference in cost between buying companies on the market and buying assets may stay the same, but the absolute difference will increase markedly.

If Professor King is right (and he certainly tells the most convincing story about the past) then the late eighties takeover boom was already set to fade, quite regardless of the wave of scandals and the October 1987 stock market crash. One of the reasons for the late eighties British bull market was the reform of company taxation, which sharply reduced the tax rate on the returns from old capital just as those returns were soaring. But the tax reform also brought the tax rates faced by incorporated business and unincorporated businesses much more closely into line. The tax incentive for mergers has been progressively reduced as the 1984 reforms have taken effect. The ratio of the value of a company on the stock market to the replacement cost value of its assets – the ratio known as the Keynes–Tobin q – has risen from 0.68 before the corporate tax reforms to some 0.92 after them, according to Professor King.

Should anything more be done to affect the climate for mergers? Your view of the beneficence or otherwise of takeovers depends a lot on whether you think companies in general are merging for the nice reasons given above – greater efficiency and so forth – or the nasty ones – pulling a fast one on consumers.

The evidence which shows that share prices for shareholders in both predator and victim companies tend to rise is distinctly unimpressive from a social point of view: increased market power which allows higher prices relative to costs will boost profits and share prices, but cut economic efficiency and lead to overall losses for the economy.

Those who are on balance prepared to give the benefit of the doubt to the corporate wheeler-dealers argue for a level playing field: just bring the rates of tax for businesses and people into line so that there are no artificial inducements to merger, and let them get on with it. Those who are a little more suspicious of the social benefits from merger activity will want to go further. Of course, some mergers are sensible. Sometimes big really is beautiful. (Who out there would really advocate splitting up the national grid?) But the onus of proof might usefully be shifted to the predator to show the likelihood of genuine social gains in terms of higher efficiency (rather than higher profit which may result from lower efficiency).

After all, the evidence from studies that have looked for higher profits after mergers is inconclusive, and the evidence for higher share prices for the acquiring companies' shareholders is also ambiguous. But the clincher is that the work which looked for genuine gains in efficiency (through reduced costs) could not generally find them.[3] There is also an argument, put by the Confederation of British Industry, for more effective restrictions on bids by foreign companies which are not able to be taken over themselves. The most important example was the successful takeover in 1988 of Rowntrees by Nestlé, a Swiss company whose charter effectively prohibits any hostile takeover bid. This is not necessarily a xenophobic case. Indeed, it would be foolish if it were. British overseas assets are far greater than foreigners' assets in the UK. It is a case for ensuring that the managements of part of British industry are not isolated from the pressures to perform which exist because of the threat of takeover.

Indeed, this is a crucial reason for treading very warily in making mergers any more difficult. Who will then be responsible for keeping managers on their toes? The one advantage of a free market in corporate takeovers is that managers in threatened companies do have to perform at something, even if the things they perform at – short-term profits – may on occasion be socially flawed and may underestimate the importance of investing for the future. The alternative may be even worse if managers merely fall asleep. There is, of course, some long-term control on managers through the market for their products and services: ultimately they will fold up if they do not produce things that consumers want. But there may be a very long period between now and nemesis if there is no other mechanism for disciplining managers. If takeovers are made much more difficult, something else needs to keep managers awake.

This is not a plea for pension funds or other such financial institutions to take a longer-term or more detailed interest in their shareholdings rather than selling up when the going gets rough. There may be a few notable exceptions such as M&G, but in general shareholders will not. Fund managers do not have the expertise for close monitoring, and have little incentive to develop it. In no other country have they ever developed it. Nor, of course, do small shareholders. In reality there are only two serious candidates for the role of management-watching – the banks and the company's own employees. The advantages of encouraging the banks to develop an industrial and commercial tradition – as their counterparts in Germany, France and Japan have – are legion. They would be able to act as a pressure on sleepy management, because they would have the expertise to know when things were going wrong. This is one reason why industry is efficient in these countries despite the lack of any tradition of contested or even agreed takeover bids. That expertise would also encourage the banks to lend more and longer-term, thus making capital formation in Britain both easier and less linked to retained earnings (see the previous essay).

A second route – and maybe an even more fundamental one for the longer term – is through employee participation. After all, the greatest single repository of knowledge about a management's own efficiency is the work-force that it bosses about. There is not a pub in the land which does not ring with stories of managerial folly (and occasionally managerial success). A successful economy needs to find ways of legitimising that capacity to spot folly, and channelling it into constructive improvements. At present, employee suggestions are too often treated as evidence of rank insubordination against the chosen hierarchy. Suggestion boxes are fine as far as they go, but giving employees a real stake in the firm or the profits of the firm does more at a stroke to make that interest constructive and legitimate than anything else. Just ask the National Freight Corporation – or the John Lewis Partnership.

By all means let's make the merger-go-round a little more difficult. But don't stop there. We will need to dream up some other ways of keeping our managers on their toes as well.

Notes

1 Brian Chiplin and Mike Wright, *The Logic of Mergers*, Hobart Paper no. 107 (London: Institute of Economic Affairs, 1987).

2 Mervyn King, *Take-over Activity in the United Kingdom* (London: London School of Economics, 1987, mimeo).

3 See K. Cowling *et al*, *Mergers and Economic Performance* (Cambridge: Cambridge University Press, 1980), quoted in Chiplin and Wright, op cit.

3 Tax, Incomes and Equality

Taxation and inequality since 1979

A sea-change towards inequality

- international comparisons of tax burdens
- tax burden over time and burden solely of income taxes
- increased inequality in pre-tax earnings
- increased inequality due to benefit changes and the profits boom
- the inequality of incomes and wealth

The former Chancellor Nigel Lawson claimed in a pamphlet in 1987 that 'for the first time in our adult lives, Britain is a low tax country'.[1] However, he subsequently gave the game away when he was cross-questioned by interviewers. He was asked to justify the statement when many of the lower-paid are paying more tax, and replied that their real incomes had gone up. That marvellous example of the political *non sequitur* was designed to obscure a series of complex trends in taxation, incomes and wealth which have resulted in an unprecedented sea-change towards greater inequality during the Thatcher years.

The results of a series of interesting Treasury parliamentary answers,[2] along with other official figures, are shown in figures 7–10. They highlight five messages about tax, income and wealth distribution during the Thatcher years since 1979. First, we are still neither a low- nor a high-tax country by international standards. Secondly, the tax burden, after rising sharply for most of the population in the early years of the Government despite its objective of tax cuts, is still above where it was in 1979. Thirdly, even taxes on income are up for most people. Fourthly, these policy changes have compounded a dramatic shift to inequality

Figure 7

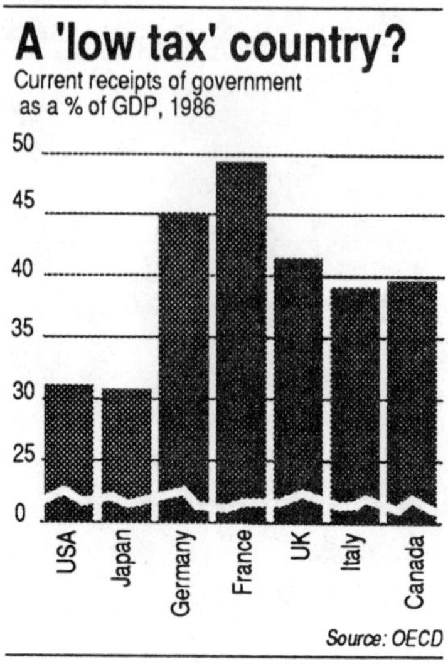

Figure 8

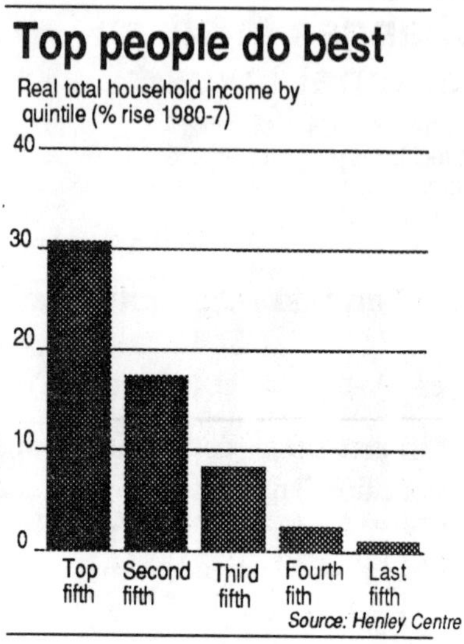

in pre-tax incomes. Fifthly, the shift in incomes has in turn encouraged less equal wealth distribution for the first time since the twenties.

First, figure 7 shows that we are not by international standards a particularly low- or high-tax country. There was in fact a sharp rise in taxes in the early Thatcher years, which has been only partially reversed by tax cuts after 1984. The European Commission calculates that the share of our gross domestic product going in Government receipts of all kinds will actually have risen by 1.8 percentage points between 1978 and 1988, even after the budget tax cuts. Part of this is due to the windfall revenues from North Sea oil, but non-oil taxes have also risen as the Government has cut its borrowing and spent more on unemployment, old people and defence.

The second conclusion from the figures is that total taxes paid – from income tax through to the rates – have risen for most of the population. For someone on male average earnings, the rise is from 38.5 per cent of gross income in 1978/9 to 40.5 per cent in 1988/9. The shift is made up of a 0.8 percentage point rise in the rate burden due largely

Figure 9

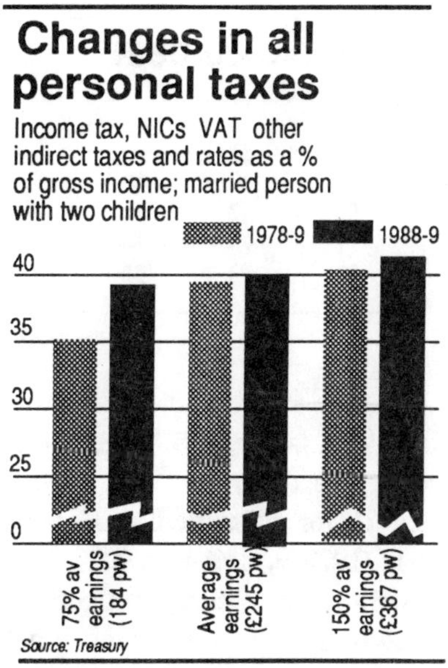

Figure 10

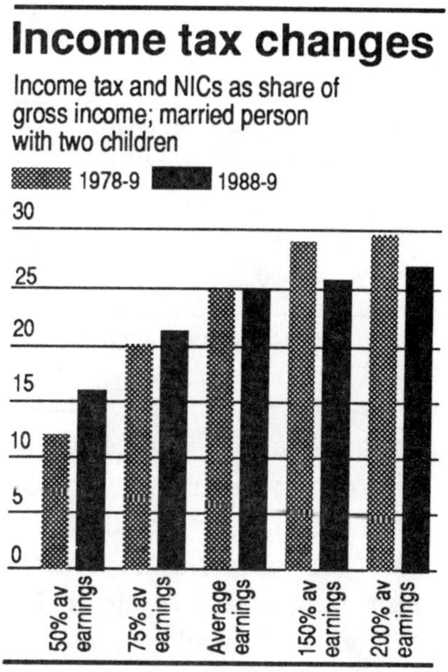

to the cut in central government grants to local authorities; a 2.3 percentage point rise in employees' National Insurance contributions (NICs) whose rate has increased from 6.75 per cent to 9 per cent; and a 2.4 percentage point rise in Value Added Tax (VAT) whose standard rate nearly doubled in the 1979 Budget from 8 per cent to 15 per cent. Income tax was down 2.8 percentage points thanks to an 8p in the pound cut in the tax rate, and non-VAT indirect taxes on drink and so on were down 0.6 percentage points.

The third conclusion is that even if we confine our attention to taxes on income alone – income tax and NICs – the changes do not justify the claim that we are a low-tax country. At average earnings, there has been a very small fall in the share going in income taxes from 20.9 per cent of gross income to 20 per cent. This is essentially because the cut in income tax rates has been offset by the rise in NICs, the abolition of the reduced rate band, and the fact that tax allowances have only just about kept up with earnings. If the Chancellor were not to raise allowances each year in real terms – over and above

Table 9. Personal wealth: distribution among adults of marketable wealth, 1966–85

	1966	*1979*	*1984*	*1985*
Percentage of wealth owned by most wealthy 1 per cent of adults	33	22	21	20
5	56	40	39	40
10	69	54	52	54
25	87	77	75	76
50	97	95	93	93

Source: Inland Revenue statistics

price inflation – income tax would take a larger and larger slice of growing earnings, the usual economic definition of a rising tax burden. The income tax threshold (for a married man) was 31.8 per cent of average earnings in 1978/9, and was 32.2 per cent of average earnings in 1988/9. Many of those with incomes below the national average are paying more in income taxes. The number of households paying a higher burden of income tax and NICs than they did in 1978/9 is about 3.7 million out of a total 17.2 million single people and married couples liable to income tax. (This excludes the self-employed and those with unearned income.) That is, by anyone's standards, a significant number.

Is it fair to count NICs as a tax? Mr Lawson has argued that National Insurance contributions are 'not strictly a tax matter', implying that they should not be counted as tax on income because of the contributory principle whereby they are used to fund the NHS and pensions. This doctrine may be expedient, but it is not correct. In reality, NICs are just another part of the tax system. As Sir Geoffrey Howe rightly said in the first Budget of this Conservative administration in June 1979: 'It is the basic rate (plus of course the National Insurance contribution) which represents the deterrent effect of tax on additional earnings.' He pointed out that the basic rate (including National Insurance) was 4p in the pound higher than when the Tories had last left office in 1974.

The drop in income taxes gets bigger as income rises and the effect of the 8p cut in the basic rate becomes more valuable, but the cuts become truly impressive only above the level at which the 40 per cent higher rate has replaced the previous nine higher rates going up to 83 per cent for earned and 98 per cent for unearned income. This is a rarefied point of the income distribution. Only about 1.25 million households, or some 4 per cent of the total, fall into this category. Taxpayers typically had to earn more than £25,075 in 1988/9 to be liable to higher rate tax of 40 per cent (if they were married with no children; it was less for single people). The gains for these high-income earners are nevertheless huge. Someone earning 500 per cent of average male earnings – £1,223 a week – paid around 35 per cent of gross income in tax and NICs compared with 49 per cent ten years before.

The fourth conclusion from the figures is that the inequality of income has increased sharply in Britain during the eighties. Clearly, the changes in the tax and benefit system have played a part in this trend, but in fact changes in pre-tax income have been important too. The tax system has compounded the misfortunes of the low-paid in the jobs market, where the real rise in their gross earnings (i.e. the rise after allowing for inflation) has been negligible compared with those further up the income scale. Thus the annual official New Earnings Survey taken in April each year shows that the real rise in gross pay for the highest-earning 1 per cent of male workers was 60 per cent between 1979 and 1988 against 38 per cent for the highest-earning 10 per cent and only 12 per cent for the lowest-earning 10 per cent. For women the discrepancy was less marked, with the highest-paid 10 per cent getting a real 46 per cent rise, against an 18 per cent rise for the lowest-paid 10 per cent.[3]

The reason for this skewing in gross earnings, which has also taken place in the United States, is a shift in demand from the low-skilled to the high-skilled, greater pay flexibility, plus a rise in unemployment particularly concentrated among the low-skilled. The effect of more unequal gross pay together with a more unequal tax system is dramatic. The highest-paid 1 per cent of male earners in the official survey saw a real increase in their take-home pay of 73 per cent between 1979 and 1988. The equivalent increase for the bottom 10 per cent was 13 per cent.[4]

These figures based on earnings from employment understate the rise in inequality. Among poor people, anyone in a job has been relatively lucky. Most of the people in the bottom 30 per cent of the population by income are people who are not in work either because they are pensioners, or unemployed, or disabled. The state pension, unemployment and other benefits have been raised in line with prices, not with the higher increase in earnings. Moreover, there is evidence that the prices of the goods bought by the poor have risen more rapidly than those bought by the rest in recent years, partly because of the rise in council rents under Mrs Thatcher. One study found that the prices of goods and services bought by the bottom 10 per cent of the income distribution rose by nearly 6 per cent more than the prices faced by the top 10 per cent between 1974 and 1982.[5] At the top of the income distribution, the post-tax earnings figures also understate the boon to the well-off during the Thatcher years. The recovery of profits and dividends has led to enormous unearned income gains concentrated on the best-off.

Unfortunately, no definitive answers can be provided about the distribution of total personal incomes after 1984/5, the year of the data in the latest study published in November 1987 by the Central Statistical Office.[6] This study used to be published annually, but the Government decided, apparently on the grounds of economy, to publish it only once every three years. The result is that we will not be able to assess the effects of the profits boom and the abolition of top tax rates in the 1988 Budget until November 1993. The latest information shows that the pre-tax income distribution continued to widen sharply up to 1984/5. The main trends are plotted in figure 11. The CSO study shows that the gap of post-tax incomes also widened sharply. The highest-income 10 per cent increased their share of total income from 23.4 per cent in 1978/9 to 26.5 per cent in 1984/5. The poorer half of the population received 24.9 per cent, against 26.2 per cent in 1978/9.

One implication of those figures, as LSE researcher John Hills has pointed out,[7] is that the living standards of the poorest fifth of the population have been squeezed. Average

Figure 11

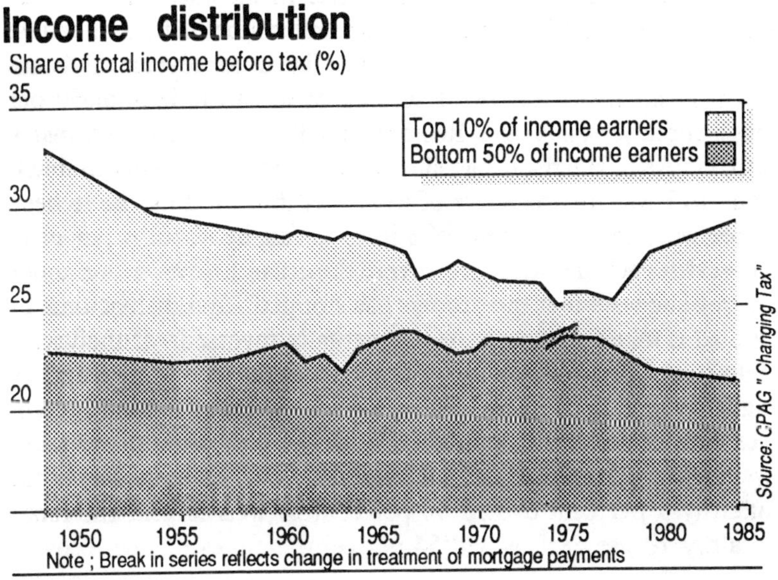

real incomes grew by 7 per cent, but the share of the poorest fifth fell from 6.1 per cent to 5.6 per cent. 'This suggests,' he argues, 'that their real income after allowing for all taxes and cash benefits fell by 2 per cent between 1979 and 1985: despite economic growth, the poorest were worse off in absolute as well as relative terms.' This conclusion has been fiercely contested by ministers, but there is little doubt that the poorest income groups have participated relatively little in the growth of prosperity during the Thatcher years. For those reliant solely on state benefits – the elderly without occupational pensions and the unemployed – these have been remarkably lean years. As in the United States, there has been a growth of a new 'under-class' effectively excluded from the mainstream of national economic life.

The fifth trend has been encouraged by the new inequality of incomes, but has also taken on a life of its own. It is the sharp increase in the inequality of wealth – the stocks of assets like houses, shares and other claims on future incomes which people own. The increase in profits has also led to a sharp increase in share prices, which has given a particular fillip to those already owning shares. The rise in incomes has boosted house prices, which in turn has particularly helped tose already owning houses. The net result has been to reverse a trend towards greater equality of wealth which had been apparent since the interwar years. Research by Professor A.B. Atkinson and Dr Alan Harrison has shown that the trend between 1924 and 1972 was for the share of total wealth owned by the richest 1 per cent and 5 per cent of adults to fall by about 4 per cent of wealth each decade.[8] However, the Inland Revenue's annual survey suggests that the process has stopped – if only marketable wealth is taken into account – or actually reversed – if the wider definition of wealth to include occupational and state pension rights is included.[9] The 1985 figures show that the wealthiest 1 per cent of the adult population owned a fifth of all marketable wealth, while the poorest half owned only 7 per cent. The most wealthy 5 per cent owned 40 per cent of wealth, and the most wealthy 10 per cent owned 54 per cent.

Notes

1 Nigel Lawson, *Tax Reform: the Government's Record* (London: Conservative Political Centre, 1988).

2 See for example parliamentary answers to Mr Gordon Brown and Mr Nigel Griffiths: *Hansard*, 17 May 1988.

3 Section 4 on inequality in Richard Layard and Stephen Nickell, *The Thatcher Miracle?*, Centre for Labour Economics, discussion paper no. 343 (London School of Economics, March 1989).

4 Layard and Nickell, op cit.

5 Vanessa Fry and Panos Pashardes, 'Distributional Aspects of Inflation: Who Has Suffered Most?', *Fiscal Studies*, December 1985.

6 'The Distribution of Income in the United Kingdom', *Economic Trends* (London: Central Statistical Office, November 1987).

7 John Hills, *Changing Tax: How the Tax System Works and How to Change it* (London: Child Poverty Action Group, 1988).

8 See A.B. Atkinson, J. Gordon and A.J. Harrison, *Trends in the Distribution of Wealth in Britain, 1923–1981*, TIDI Discussion paper no. 70 (London School of Economics, 1986).

9 Inland Revenue Statistics, January 1988.

Do tax cuts make you work harder?

The disincentive effect of high tax rates

- Treasury evidence on whether people can work harder
- work-inducing versus laziness-inducing effects of tax cuts
- the effect of taxes on spending should be included
- top rate taxpayers a more extreme case
- American and British evidence on whether top rate tax cuts pay for themselves
- a base-broadening option which the Chancellor ignored.

'High taxes,' Adam Smith wrote, 'sometimes by diminishing the consumption of the taxed commodities, and sometimes by encouraging smuggling, frequently afford a smaller revenue to Government than what might be drawn from more moderate taxes. When the diminution of revenue is the effect of the diminution of consumption, there can be but one remedy and that is the lowering of the tax.'[1]

In the later part of the eighteenth century, when Smith was writing, most taxes were indirect taxes on commodities. But his perception applies in principle to direct taxes on income too, and it was the inspiration behind Professor Art Laffer and America's so-called 'supply-side' economics, behind President Reagan's massive tax reductions of 1981 and behind the radical top-rate tax cuts of the British Conservatives in Mr Nigel Lawson's fifth Budget in 1988. Like Reagan, Lawson slashed tax rates on each extra pound that the well-off carn in an attempt to provide incentives to work harder. In both cases, the claim was that the cut in tax rates would actually *raise* more revenue.

The theory is clear, and incontrovertible. There will be some tax rate on additional earnings – the so-called 'marginal' rate of tax – which will discourage work effort. It may also encourage illegal tax evasion. An industry of accountants will grow up to discover and exploit legal tax shelters for rich clients. Initiative and enterprise will be directed at avoiding the taxman, rather than creating new wealth. The relationship between tax rates and tax revenues is shown in figure 12 – the famous 'Laffer curve'. But the curve, you will note, has no numbers on it. The

Figure 12

The Laffer curve

(Revenue (R) as a function of the Tax Rate on Labour Income (tl), given the Tax rate on Income from Capital)

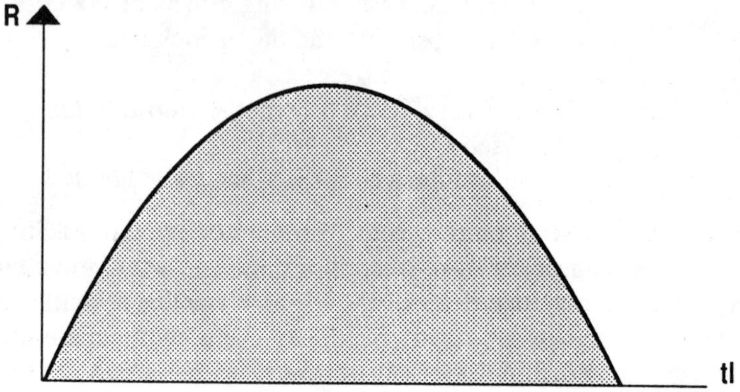

Source: Fiscal Studies, October 1988, from Canto Joines and Laffer (1983)

controversy arises over exactly what this revenue-maximizing top tax rate actually is. At what point does the tax rate on extra earnings become so high that you would actually raise more revenue if you cut it? And what sort of response might there be to a cut?

The evidence depends very much on whom one is looking at. For most tax payers there is little reason to believe that tax cuts will pay for themselves. The Treasury itself commissioned an extremely costly, in-depth study which finally reported in 1986, amid much embarrassment to the Chancellor when it was leaked in the press.[2] It had been designed at a time of rising concern about the effect of high tax rates on middle-income earners – particularly the skilled working-class – to see whether the pre-1979 basic rate of income tax of 33 per cent plus 6.75 per cent National Insurance contributions rate really acted as a disincentive. The study discovered that most people could not work harder even if they wanted to, because the opportunities for overtime were limited. In other words, labour supply was more determined by employers' demand than by employees' willingness to work.

This study, indeed, gave yet another reason for believing what standard economic theory was anyway telling policy-makers. There are always two effects from a cut in tax rates: there is a work-inducing incentive effect because you can keep more of each extra pound you earn, but this is offset by a laziness-inducing income effect because you get more money for doing nothing extra. Would you really work harder if you won the pools? Most tax economists argue that the cuts in the basic rate of income tax from 33 per cent before the Conservatives' first Budget in 1979 to 25 per cent by the 1988 Budget have had minimal effects on work effort precisely because the income and the incentive effects balance out. The only qualification to that conclusion suggests that low-paid, part-time and women workers may be more sensitive to changes in their tax rates.

There is a third reason for believing that the incentive effect for most people has been minimal, as Mr Enoch Powell MP pointed out in 1979. A large part of the cut in the basic rate of income tax was offset by a rise in employees' National Insurance contributions and a near doubling in VAT. Indeed, the policy was initially to switch the tax burden from direct to indirect taxes to improve incentives. Mr Powell pointed out that people were unlikely to be so foolish as to ignore what their post-tax income would actually buy. If people are motivated by material things, it is not merely by cash but by what cash can purchase. The marginal rate of tax for most people in 1979 was thus 33 per cent plus 6.75 per cent of incomes, plus 8 per cent standard VAT on the remainder if it was spent on goods subject to VAT. In other words, it was 44.6 per cent. The marginal rate for most people in 1989 was 25 per cent basic rate plus 9 per cent, plus 15 per cent standard VAT on the remainder. It was 43.9 per cent. Nobody is going to get excited by a 0.7 percentage point cut in marginal rates.

There may, of course, be other reasons for wanting to cut taxes. There is the good liberal reason that people should be left more of their own money to spend. The evidence merely suggests that the incentive argument is woefully oversold. But what of higher rate tax payers? Clearly, the higher the marginal rate of income tax, the greater the likelihood of serious disincentive effects. Who would undertake extra work if the state took 100 per cent of the extra income? The 1988 tax reform included 2p off the basic rate, but the Chancellor saw this as a necessary political price to pay for cutting the top rates much more dramatically. The Budget aimed fair and square at the top 4 per cent of the population who pay higher rates. These are the people, the Chancellor said, who can start businesses and make money and create jobs.

Mr Lawson firmly believed that these cuts in top tax rates would actually pay for themselves within the lifetime of a parliament – that is, by 1991–2. In other words, the apparent £2 billion annual cost of abolishing all the tax rates above 40 per cent which is entered into the 1988 Budget documents is a mirage, because it assumes that behaviour will not change. Indeed, Mr Lawson claimed that the entire real increase in tax revenues since 1978/9 – Labour's last year – had come from these top taxpayers despite, or perhaps because of, the cut in top tax rates in the Conservatives' first Budget in 1979 from 83 per cent to 60 per cent. Secondly, these top rate taxpayers contributed a third as much again in real terms as they did in 1978/9. Thirdly, the top 5 per cent paid 24 per cent of total income tax in 1978/9, but this had risen to 29 per cent in 1987/8. Even after the abolition of the 45p to 60p rates, this was expected to be 27 per cent, he said.

However, is that increase in revenue really evidence of a change in behaviour because of cuts in top tax rates or is it the result of other factors entirely, such as the rise in profitability and dividends, the ending of incomes policy in the late seventies and a resulting switch among the high-paid from being paid with perks to being paid in cash, and an increase in demand for those with scarce skills? Real gross earnings – before tax – for the top 10 per cent have soared by more than a fifth, while those at the bottom have hardly had any rise at all (see the previous essay).

The honest answer is that this area is a minefield. At the time of the 1988 Budget, the only respectable studies which had tried to separate out rises in revenue as a result of reduced tax rates from rises in revenue because of other causes were American. Professor Lawrence B. Lindsey of Harvard dissected the 1981 Economic Recovery Act, which slashed tax rates by 23 per cent over three years and cut the top personal rate from 70 per cent to 50 per cent. Professor Lindsey concluded that the cut in the top tax rate was indeed costless to the Government, because the top 170,000 US taxpayers in 1982 ended up paying $26.6 billion under the new law instead of $26 billion under the old one. He also found that there was some increased revenue to offset the expected losses from lower-earning groups of the US population. In total, the avoidance-reducing and incentive-increasing effects of the Reagan tax cuts offset about one-sixth of the expected losses if behaviour did not change. His guess from early work reported to a conference in London was that the top revenue-maximizing tax rate in the US was 52 per cent.[3] However, a later paper put the top rate at between 40 and 43 per cent.[4]

This is American evidence, not British. Lindsey's work allowed for many of the obvious factors boosting top incomes and tax payments which might have had nothing to do with the cut in tax rate (such as the increase in dividend payments), but he has been criticized for assuming that the remaining rise in earnings of top income groups in the United States after the tax reform was caused by the tax cut, rather than by some independent cause (such as a new demand for scarce skills). The only British study of this thorny question, completed after the 1988 Budget, examined the 1979 cut in top tax rates to 60 per cent and concluded somewhat agnostically: 'We can account for the entire growth of aggregate tax revenues without reference to incentive effects . . . however, we are not able to account for all the growth in the share of revenue paid by the highest income taxpayers, particularly by the top 1 per cent.'[5]

Any reduction in marginal tax rates is likely to reduce the average tax rate, and hence make the whole tax system less burdensome to the well-off. One criticism of the Lawson reforms must be that he went too far, given the shaky nature of the evidence for the revenue-maximizing top rate. After all, an Inland Revenue study at the time of the 1988 Budget showed that Britain's top rate of tax was lower than that in any other major industrial economy, including the United States once state taxes in the major states (like California or

Figure 13

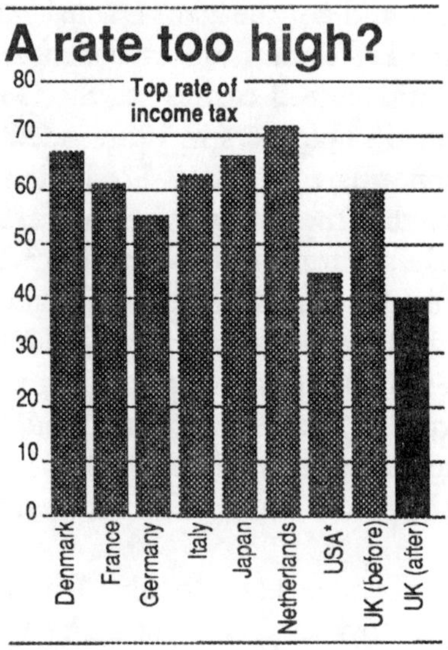

Top rate threshold as a % of average manual earnings

Denmark	113
France	720
W Germany	338
Japan	3,665
Italy	1,675
Netherlands	660
USA	290
UK	444

* Top Federal rate and Californian rate
Source: Inland Revenue

New York) are added to the Federal income tax (figure 13).[6] Subsequently, Canada has cut its top rate to 29 per cent and New Zealand to 33 per cent, but Britain is still relatively low. Secondly, Mr Lawson could have done much more to claw back some of the income gains to the better off which would, ironically, have improved their incentives to work harder. The incentive effect would still have been improved by the marginal tax rate cut, but the disincentive pools-win effect of windfall gains could have been limited by restricting tax breaks and tax shelters.

This is sometimes called 'base-broadening', because the tax base is broadened and the tax rate reduced but the revenue remains the same. The Reagan tax reform was far more radical in reducing tax breaks than the Lawson reform. The same applies to the sharp cuts introduced by the New Zealand and Australian Labour governments. The only tax perk which Mr Lawson trimmed in 1988 was the value of company cars. This caution is only partly because the British system had fewer breaks to begin with. After all, the cost of mortgage tax relief for owner-occupiers, generally people in the top half of the income distribution, is worth around £5.5 billion a year or nearly 3p on the basic rate. Short of full abolition of mortgage relief, Mr Lawson could also have cut top tax rates but turned mortgage interest relief into tax credits of equal value to everyone. Mortgage relief on £1,000 of interest payments is worth £250 to the basic rate payer, but £400 to the higher rate payer. But the Prime Minister vetoed any change in the subsidy for owner-occupiers, a key Conservative constituency.

Notes

1 Adam Smith, *An Inquiry into the Nature and Causes of The Wealth of Nations* (1776). In this case, the quotation is from p. 414 of the University of Chicago Press edition (1976).

2 C.V. Brown *et al.*, *Taxation and Family Labour Supply in Great Britain*, the final report of a project on direct taxation and short run labour supply funded by HM Treasury (Stirling University, Department of Economics, September 1986).

3 Lawrence B. Lindsey, *Individual taxpayer response to tax cuts, 1982–4* (Cambridge, Mass., 15 October 1986, mimeo).

4 Lawrence B. Lindsey, *Taxpayer Behaviour and the Distribution of the 1982 Tax Cut*, National Bureau of Economic Research Inc., working paper no. 1760 (Cambridge, Mass., October 1985); Lindsey, *Estimating the Revenue Maximising Top Personal Tax Rate*, NBER, working paper no. 1761 (November 1985); Lindsey, 'Individual Taxpayer Response to Tax Cuts, 1982–1984', *Journal of Public Economics*, vol. 33, pp. 173–206.

5 Andrew Dilnot and Michael Kell,'Top Rate Tax Cuts and Incentives: some Empirical Evidence', *Fiscal Studies*, vol. 9, no. 4 (November 1988).

6 *Comparisons of Direct Tax on Employment Income* (London: Board of Inland Revenue, Somerset House, London WC2, December 1987).

The reform of local government finance

Characteristics of the poll tax

- three reforms to local government finance
- business winners and losers
- areas which will win and lose
- people who will win and lose
- the examples of Hackney and South Buckinghamshire
- poll tax designed to curb profligate authorities
- the snag of the voting system
- possible erosion of control of public spending

The poll tax, or the community charge as its friends call it, is a remarkable measure. The sheer derring-do of environment ministers in proposing a replacement of the rates from which very substantial numbers of people will lose is compounded by the fact that they are bound to notice. Unlike VAT or even income tax, which are paid in regular, small doses, the community charge will thud onto doormats no less painfully than the rates.

Nor will the poll tax tap a more attractive tax base. However extortionate the rates charge in an area may be, the tax is virtually impossible to avoid because buildings and land do not disappear. However, the community charge is a straightforward tax per head on individuals who can walk and run. At the very least, such a shifting tax base is difficult to record. In some areas with a lot of young people in rented accommodation, the poll tax is almost bound to lead to shrinking official populations. In others with more settled and older people, official populations – and electoral registers – may rise because of the new local authority incentive to keep an up-to-date record.

The most remarkable feature of the poll tax and the other reforms is their distributional consequences. The combined effect of the three changes now on the statute book – the poll tax on individuals, the uniform business rate including a revaluation of business rateable values, and a grant system based largely on assessment of needs – is to set up a series of lethal interactions which are going to create some very hard cases indeed.

Take the small shopkeepers, a group of people which has supplied the most loyal Tory voters for two decades. If the Scottish experience in 1985 is anything to go by, the promised reassessment of businesses' rateable values (RVs) will reduce the rates bill for manufacturing firms and increase it for retailers. (The rateable value multiplied by the rate is what people actually pay.) If your shop happens to be in an area which has traditionally set a relatively low rate – in a district council in the Tory South East, for example – then the odds are that your shop will lose out not merely because retailers generally will lose out, but because your low-rated area will now be subject to the higher, uniform national rate poundage.

Whole areas will also be winners or losers. Under the old finance system, Whitehall made a grant to local authorities which had low rateable values to ensure that they could maintain a similar level of service to elsewhere. This particularly benefited the North – but this grant is to go. Areas with a lot of businesses, like inner London, at present benefit from their

Figure 14

Poll tax winners and losers

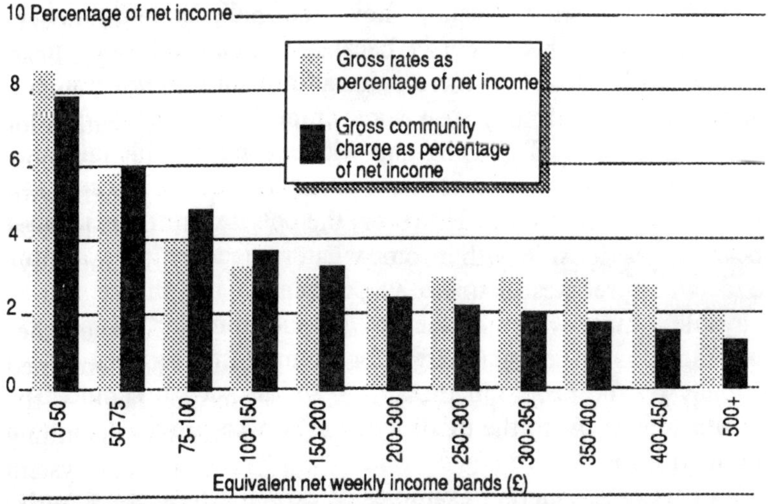

Relationship of rates and full community charge (before rebates) to net household income by equivalent income band

high commercial rate income. But they will also lose because they will only get an equal share of the total raised by the national business rate.

However, these effects look like small beer compared with the distributional consequences of the poll tax itself. It sets up an enormous shift of the local tax burden from small households – like that of the single pensioner – to large ones – like the family with adult children. Don't be misled by figures showing that the poll tax does not much affect the net income of households in different income bands by comparison with the rates. This is true, but trivial, since those households vary enormously in their needs and hence their outgoings.

One person earning £500 a week net income is substantially more prosperous than a five-adult household earning £500 a week (which may also have children), yet both are counted as households in the same income band. In reality, there is an enormous shift in the incidence of local taxes from small households to large ones. It is possible, of course, to make some allowance for household size by effectively ranking households by income per head. This concept – of ranking by net equivalent income – is used in figure 14, taken from an annex of the 1986 green paper.[1]

The graph shows clearly how the poll tax will benefit the better-off. This is partly because of the shift from small to big households, but there is an additional regressive effect. Rateable values usually bear some imperfect relationship with the consumption of housing and with income. As incomes and wealth rise, people tend to want larger and better houses, and tend to pay higher rates. However, the poll tax quite consciously bears no relationship with income whatever (except at the bottom end, where rebates of up to 80 per cent of the charge will be payable). Indeed, one of the key justifications for the poll tax is that it is an equal charge for community services drawn equally by the people in the area – and as such it should help to sensitize them to the quality of the service provided by their local authority.

Let us take concrete examples of how the local government finance reform will redistribute the tax burden. Start by taking two local authorities with diametrically opposed characters:

Hackney in London, which is a by-word for inner city deprivation, and South Buckinghamshire, which is typical of the leafy Home Counties. Mr Tony Travers of the London School of Economics calculates, from Government figures for 1987/8, that South Bucks would have gained £180 per adult from the combined effect of the new grant and business rate, while Hackney would have lost £391.[2] That was the redistribution from area to area which would have occurred in 1987/8 once the full system was operating (without transitional cushions and buffers).

Now look at the extreme winners and losers within each area, again assuming that the full system was operating. A three-adult household – say, two earners, plus an aged dependent – in a Hackney home with two-thirds the average rateable value was paying £362 in rates, but would have paid £2,073 with the community charge. The extra cost would have been £1,711, which means that the household would have had to find an extra £2,592 of gross earnings merely in order to get the extra post-tax income to pay the community charge. Even if the household had a full rebate of 80 per cent, the extra cost would have been £342 a year or £518 on gross income.

Now contrast the retired spinster, still living in the extensive family home in South Buckinghamshire. The house has double the average rateable value for the area. In 1987/8, she was paying £1,505 in rates but would have paid only £207 a year in poll tax. The benefit was equivalent to an extra £1,966 of gross income to be taxed at the standard rate with NICs. She is also likely to benefit disproportionately from a sharp rise in house prices, simply because a tax on the value of property has been lifted. The shift from the rates to the poll tax is a shift from a tax on property to a tax on people; it thus reduces the extra cost of buying a bigger house – it cuts the marginal cost of housing – and will tend to increase the price, particularly of larger houses.

How can the Government justify such an extraordinarily regressive change? First and foremost, ministers argue that it is not important for any one part of the tax system to be progressive, so long as the whole system is. This is clearly true. After all, we put up with taxes on cigarettes on health grounds even though they are disproportionately paid by the low-income earners who smoke most. Nevertheless, it seems sensible to avoid such changes where they are not strictly justified on other grounds. And in the case of the poll tax, it is simply not practicable to compensate the wide diversity of winners and losers by changes in other parts of the tax system, as Stephen Smith of the Institute for Fiscal Studies argues.[3] It is bound to create a large number of hard cases.

Nor will it achieve the one effect which the Government most wants to achieve, which is to use low-income voters to discipline high-spending local authorities. The theory is that the community charge is actually paid by the people who receive the local government service, so that the consumer is able to establish a much more direct relationship with the provider. In Conservative demonology, local authorities up until now have been spending the money of people with few votes (rich ratepayers) or no votes (businesses) on people who hardly pay any rates because of rebates (council tenants, poor pensioners and so on). It is always easy to spend other people's money.

However, recent research has suggested that the community charge will not be paid by the beneficiaries of local authority services any more than the rates. The children of relatively well-off families tend to be the ones who stay on at school after 16, when education becomes most expensive. The well-off also use roads and leisure services more than the low-paid. Four out of ten households still have no access to a car. Yet the poll tax levies the same charge from everyone. The mismatch between those who pay and those who receive will in fact be slightly worse than under the rates system.[4]

Moreover, the Government's efforts to bring to heel such profligates as the inner London Labour boroughs face one fatal flaw. The electoral system is simply too unresponsive to allow the voters to eject many controlling parties of local authorities even if they wanted to. If ministers wanted to make councils responsive to their electorates, it would have been simpler merely to change the voting system. After all, Labour wins 65 per cent of the council seats in Brent for only 46 per cent of the vote, and it would take a 10 per cent swing from Labour to Tory for it to lose control. In other words, the Labour share of the vote would have to fall to 36 per cent for it to lose its majority, which is virtually unimaginable.[5] Nor is Brent out of the ordinary. Many of the inner London Labour councils most criticized for high-spending were elected with a minority of the votes – including Lambeth and Southwark. The poll tax would have to shift voters' preferences on a truly gargantuan scale to make many of these bastions change hands.

It is nevertheless true that a deliberate effect of the reform is to make the rate of poll tax extremely sensitive to local spending. The rates currently meet about half of local government spending, with the rest coming in grants from Whitehall. Under the new system, the national business rate will supply a proportion of the money which previously came from the local rates. Only the final quarter of local spending will be paid for by the community charge. The result of this arithmetic is to change the relationship – the gearing – between local spending and local taxation. At present, an extra 1 per cent on local council spending adds on average 2 per cent to the rates. Under the new system, an extra 1 per cent on spending will add an average 4 per cent to the poll tax.

In theory, this will make all right-thinking local authorities much more parsimonious. However, the same arithmetic also means that the community charge is very sensitive to the scale of the Whitehall grant. This in turn will raise all the traditional political temptations. There are a lot of marginal Tory seats in areas which stand to lose from the poll tax, not least the North West. One of the main victims of the reform may turn out to be the Treasury, which will have to dish out large extra grants to alleviate the political consequences. What is more, local authorities may put the poll tax up anyway, and spend the extra money. After all, they are unlikely to be blamed for its introduction. This was one reason why the former Chancellor, Mr Nigel Lawson, opposed the tax so adamantly. Ironically, the poll tax may prove a mixed blessing for the control of public spending.

The best that can be said for the poll tax is that many of the alternatives also look unattractive. The rates system was gradually becoming more and more absurd because no

Government had plucked up the courage to update the rateable values which were the key base of the system. As a result, RVs were still based on the value of property in 1973. The revaluation in Scotland in 1985 showed very substantial changes in values, which is one of the reasons why ministers were determined not to extend the revaluation to England and Wales.

Nevertheless, it is hard to believe that we could not devise a better principle of taxation than the one which was previously abandoned in this country in the middle ages. The Layfield committee, which reported in 1986, recommended a mixed system of local government finance which would add a local income tax to the rates. The rates could be reformed so that they are based on the value of the land, and no longer act as a disincentive to development (as described in the next essay). A local income tax would be readily understandable, and operates successfully in several parts of the world.

Needless to say, the idea of an extra income tax did not endear itself to a Government which had made income tax cuts the centrepiece of its economic appeal to the electorate. The bottom line was that the Prime Minister had repeatedly promised to abolish the rates. And she finally did.

Notes

1 *Paying for Local Government*, Green Paper (HMSO, 1986).

2 These calculations were supplied directly to the author by Mr Tony Travers of the Greater London Unit at the London School of Economics, on the basis of Department of Environment figures.

3 Stephen Smith and Duncan Squire, *Local Taxes and Local Government*, Institute for Fiscal Studies, report series no. 25 (May 1987).

4 Glen Bramley, Julian Le Grand and William Low, *How Far is the Poll Tax a 'Community Charge'? The Implications of Service Usage Evidence*, Welfare State programme, STICERD, discussion paper WSP/42 (London School of Economics, April 1989).

5 Mr Owen Thomas of the Electoral Reform Society supplied these figures to the author.

The merits of the land value tax

Co-existence of house price boom and inner city blight

- higher wage inflation because of house price rises
- causes of failure of land market
- taxing land values would increase supply
- special characteristics of taxes on economic rent
- distinction with after-the-event taxes

Consider two phenomena which are curious precisely because they have occurred alongside each other. The first is the extraordinary increase in British house prices in the late eighties, which has been so marked that many owner-occupiers in the South East will have managed to make more cash from the capital gain on their homes than they earned at work. The second is the continuing reality of blighted inner city wasteland. The co-existence of boom and blight is one of the compelling pieces of evidence for suggesting that the property market does not work properly.

This failure has a distressing impact on the urban environment in which more than a third of the population live. The latest survey concluded that 4.9 per cent of the surface area of inner London was vacant, a proportion which rose to 11.9 per cent in the case of the worst placed British city, Glasgow. Moreover, the amount of outright dereliction – where land was so damaged that it could not be used without further treatment – was growing substantially and appeared to be worst in the highest land priced areas. In Greater London, outright dereliction increased sixfold between 1974 and 1982.[1] The effects of wasteland in an inner city are to depress property values in the area, and extend blight. Gradually, the whole neighbourhood begins to look run-down, and the quality of life of all its inhabitants suffers. Land use problems also help to cause inner city job losses, because the trend of manufacturing companies to need more floor space per worker has driven them out to greenfield sites. Bringing vacant land back into social uses is a necessary condition of inner city revival.

The malfunctioning of the property market also has a series of important ramifications for the macro-economy. For

Figure 15

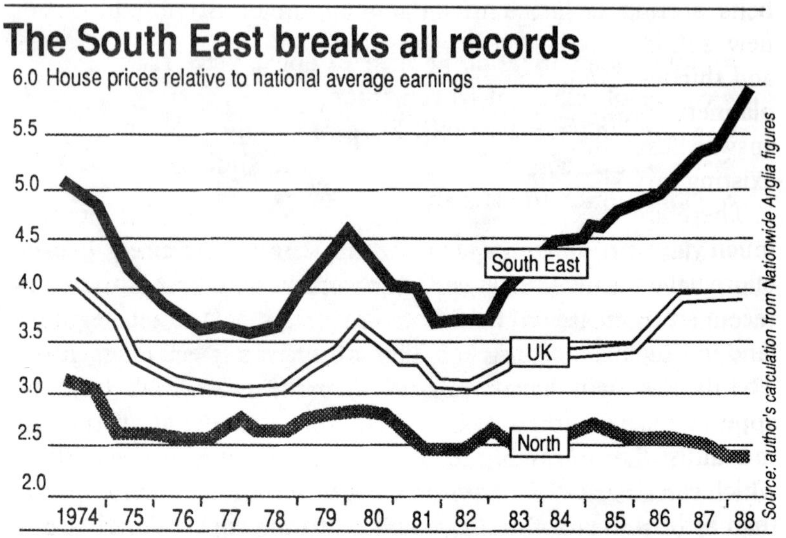

example, the extraordinary rise in house prices was one of the key factors encouraging people to borrow and spend, which in turn created the problems of trade deficit and inflation. It was caused by a sharp increase in demand as a liberalized financial system made credit more freely available, but it could not have occurred without problems with land supply. Research has also suggested that the virulence of the house price boom in the most prosperous parts of the country – in London and the South East – acted as an obstacle to skilled labour moving to the region and competing with the locals for jobs.[2] The result was to bid up wage rates still further and to cause the Government to clamp down on the activity of the whole economy because of the evidence of over-heating in one part of it.

The house price boom is really a boom in the value of the land on which houses are built. The actual cost of construction does not tend to vary very much more than the general rise in prices. What caused the cost of an average London home to soar from under £50,000 in 1984 to more than £110,000 in 1988 was the rising cost of land. As Will Rogers is said to have pointed out: 'Land is a good investment. They ain't making it any more.' One solution to the problem, much favoured by the builders, would be to relax planning restrictions in the green belts around British cities, enabling them to construct large new suburbs and satellite towns as they did in the twenties and thirties. Understandably, however, both local residents and planners are opposed to the extension of urban sprawl. The real answer lies in more intensive development of the land within the existing city spaces.

There are enormous difficulties in pinning down exactly how much vacant and derelict land there is, because of the inadequacy of official data and the partial nature of land registers. However, a recent study suggested that there were 210,000 hectares of vacant land in England alone, most of it in the main metropolitan areas.[3] The habitual length of time for the development of derelict land appeared to be 12 to 20 years. Nor, the authors pointed out, is this unused land owned merely by the public sector, a problem which can be dealt with largely by administrative measures. More than a third of the total appears to be privately owned.

Why do owners hang on to vacant land, even when the price of it is soaring? First, there is no cost to the owners in retaining it, which makes it easy for them to nurture unrealistic price expectations. Secondly, they are entitled to use their property in whatever was its last use, so that they have no incentive to sell at a lower price for an alternative cheaper use (say, residential instead of offices). Thirdly, land zoning for a particular use produces an element of slow-moving bureaucracy. Fourthly, there is still only piecemeal public information about the ownership, value and use-rights of land parcels. The Land Register is not a complete record of ownership, and it was only due to be open to public inspection in the winter of 1989/90.

There may also be more fundamental forces at work causing the market to fail. Not only do owners incur no cost when they fail to use their land, but they can often look forward to capital gains. There is no land speculator in the sky who sells when land prices rise; the phenomenon of rising prices encourages hoarding if it also encourages the expectation that prices will rise further. In this case, a price rise actually discourages supply and encourages demand – the reverse of the usual position. Moreover, the rise in price of an asset like land can provide backing for new credit to enable further purchases and development. As soon as a property is let, its value becomes effectively fixed by the value of the agreed rents. (This is one reason why the developer Harry Hyams kept London's enormous Centre Point office building empty for so long. As rents rose, so the building's value rose, and his borrowing limits rose.)

Equally important in the inner cities is a problem of collective reassurance. If parcels of land are owned by several proprietors, each may only be prepared to develop their land if there is some assurance that others will do the same. The value of the development will depend on other developments: a critical mass is necessary. Dispersed ownership may be a cause of market failure.

Part of the Government's answer has been urban development corporations, but they have tended to be aloof organizations with little accountability. A more liberal solution is a tax on vacant land which would increase the incentives to bring it into use.[4] Development would be encouraged by the private sector, rather than a public corporation. A tax on vacant land might avoid many of the clashes with local communities which appear to have been thrown up by the UDCs, which are often accused of being bureaucratic and out of touch. It would also encourage more pluralist solutions. However, a tax which would have exactly these advantages and others has been on offer for years: a site value tax, or a site value rate, or a land or rental value tax.

The essential principle is the same whatever the name. The basis of the tax is the value of the site in the use allotted to it by the planning authorities, rather than the total value including whatever is built on the site now (as with the present rating system). Thus an empty site zoned for a ten-storey office building is taxed at the same rate as a site with a ten-storey office building. There is then a powerful economic incentive to use the site to the full: the owner uses it, or sells it to someone who will. This effect is borne out by construction activity in areas as far flung as Victoria in Australia and Pittsburgh in Pennsylvania which have introduced site value taxation.[5] It thus helps to eliminate wasteland and it creates a range of jobs. It also encourages the full use of under-used land, also a prominent feature of many city centres. The land value tax makes land cheaper to develop – and holding land more expensive.

Indeed, such land value taxes are one of the few types of taxation which most economists agree do not distort economic decisions. Land is unlike either capital or labour in that there are (broadly) no costs in supplying it, and it is in fixed supply. In these circumstances, the land price or rent is determined entirely by the demand for it – not by variations in supply. In a competitive market, a land tax leaves rents paid by users unchanged. If the owners try to pass the tax on, the renters simply stop using some land. The owners would then have the incentive to bid the rents down again. After all, their supply of land has not changed. They may now receive, say, half of the previous rent, but it is still better than none. A tax on economic rent by definition does not affect supply, because economic rent is the surplus over and above the payment needed to retain land, labour or capital in its present use. (The same principle applies to the payment of pop singers or footballers, though their 'rent' is more transitory.)

Needless to say, landowners have never been too keen on the land value tax. Moreover, it may not be ethical to tax excessively someone who merely happens to hold their assets in land and who may have bought it very recently. However, the morality of taxing *gains* in land value seems very clear and could surely justify an initially moderate land value tax. After all, particular pieces of land acquire their value not because of the effort or diligence of their proprietor (for we are not taxing buildings on the land) but because of the efforts of the whole community. Property prices in an area rise when it is connected with the underground, or when the road network is improved, or when a new amenity is introduced, or just because other people are developing land in the same area.

The principle that such 'betterment' as a result of social activity should be taxed is as old as the hills. The most famous champion of the land value tax was Henry George, who thrust the issue onto the radical agenda in both the United States and Britain at the end of the nineteenth century, where it remained for fifty years.[6] The principle that land values which accrue because of social improvement should be taxed appeared in an English law of 1662; in 1807 a law was passed in France whereby owners of property bordering on new roads, quays, or squares were liable to pay compensation when the public works contributed to the greater value of the property.[7]

On a similar basis, the Conservative Government has also bargained with developers in Docklands to pay a part of the cost of infrastructure from which they will benefit. More formally, there was the development land tax introduced by the Labour Government on the gains by developers when land was allowed to be used for a more profitable purpose. However, such after-the-event taxes do not have all the beneficial properties of the site value tax because they impose a charge when the developer does something, and not when the developer does nothing. They thus discourage development, whereas the land value tax encourages it. The land value tax's incentives are the right way round.

Another advantage of the land value tax, from the point of view of the tax man, is that it is unavoidable. Land does not move to the Channel Islands, or have costs to offset against tax liability, or disappear in the night. Certainly, the administrative chore of establishing a proper land register with the permitted uses of each type of land and its value would take time, but has been shown elsewhere (and indeed here, in a pilot study of Whitstable)[8] to be manageable. By comparison with the poll tax, a reform of the rating system to de-rate buildings – which would in effect be a site-value rate – would be equitable and economically attractive. It would also have, in time, substantial macro-economic advantages by making the sort of boom which Britain suffered at the end of the eighties much less likely.

Notes

1 Robert N. Chubb, *Urban land markets in the United Kingdom*, Department of Environment Land and Property Division (HMSO, September 1988).

2 John Muellbauer, *The Housing Market and the UK Economy: Problems and Opportunities*, Nuffield College, Oxford, January 1987 (mimeo) and revised version December 1988.

3 Michael Chisholm and Philip Kivell, *Inner City Wasteland: an Assessment of Government and Market Failure in Land Development*, Hobart Paper no. 108 (London: Institute of Economic Affairs, September 1987).

4 Chisholm and Kivell, op cit.

5 Fred Harrison, *The Power in the Land* (London: Shepheard Walwyn, 1988).

6 See the classic work of Henry George, *Progress and Poverty* (1880), reissued as an Everyman edition (London: Dent Dutton, 1976).

7 Charles Gide and Charles Rist, *A History of Economic Doctrines* (London, 2nd edn, 1948), pp. 593–4.

8 *Site Value Rating: Report on Research Exercise Carried out in Whitstable* (London: The Land Institute, 1974).

4 The Economics of the Welfare State

The Education Act and the economics of information

Economic ideas behind the Education Act 1988

- the theory of parent sovereignty
- problems arise if one person's choice limits another's
- the importance of information in the market-place
- misleading effects of crude comparison of examination results
- adjustments for social background

The 1988 Education Act is the first example for many years of social policy inspired by economic thinking. Until Mr Kenneth Baker's bill, economic ideas had largely been confined to self-evidently economic fields: privatization, taxation, cutting overall public spending and so forth. Mr Baker's legislation is therefore something of a breakthrough.

Its economic ideas are competition and choice. It is the consumer who rules the market place, by deciding what and how much to buy. If demand exceeds supply, the price of the goods rises, and the suppliers have an incentive to produce more – or another supplier will. Thus the rise in price in a competitive environment encourages more output, and allocates more resources to meet the consumers' preferences.

Mr Baker openly advocates consumer-parental sovereignty in education. As he said when arguing the case for his bill: 'We need to inject a new vitality into that system. It has become producer-dominated. It has not proved sensitive to the demands for change.'[1] First, schools have to take as many pupils as they took in the peak year of 1979: there will be no artificial entry limits imposed to ensure that bad schools get enough pupils to stay viable.

Secondly, a majority of parents who vote in a ballot is enough to allow a school to opt for direct government funding, bypassing the traditional means of funding through the local education authority. It is fairly clear that such a school will eventually be able to establish its own admission policy. Such schools will be able to respond directly to their parents' wishes and encourage others which stay with local authority funding to become more responsive too. Parental choices will thereby determine funding, even though they are not paying themselves. The Baker Act will set up an internal or surrogate market within the education system.

The theory is very clear and very old. It is also very correct when it is applied to most goods and services. Markets are an efficient way of allocating resources to produce things that people want, because the price mechanism so splendidly transmits signals about scarcity. No central planning mechanism could possibly do as efficiently what the market does everyday in co-ordinating millions of separate decisions to buy and sell. Even Mr Mikhail Gorbachev's economic adviser says so.

The trouble is that the theory also tells us that a number of other conditions have to be fulfilled if markets are to work properly, and the economics of Mr Baker's Act may not be quite as clever as they look.

The first point is what one might call the adjustment problem or the collective nature of choice. If you are buying a washing machine, your decision to buy Zanussi rather than Hotpoint is a marginal one. The Hotpoint factory will not go bust: the people who want to go on buying Hotpoint will be able to do so, without noticing anything. Indeed, they may even find they get better value if prices fall a little to encourage demand. In other words, the act of choosing does not change the nature of the choice on offer and may even improve it. Where there are large numbers of buyers and sellers, one of the key conditions of so-called 'perfect' competition, then there is a presumption that markets deliver the best outcome.

Schools, however, are different. First of all, there are relatively few 'sellers'. The act of choosing one school rather than another may in general be marginal: it may not affect other parents' choice. But it is more likely to do so today when the number of pupils has fallen far from its 1979 level. Many authorities already operate admission limits to spread out pupils between, say, six schools to ensure that each one is able to offer a viable sixth form with reasonable choice of A-levels – and to ensure that a handful of schools do not suffer over-crowding. If parental desertions mean that a particular school is no longer able to offer the less mainstream subjects up to A-level standard, what remains of the choice of the parents who did decide to opt for that school?

The second way in which the situation of schools differs from the well-functioning market is that the product – schooling – is not divisible. In the case of food, for example, you can buy baked beans at Tesco and cross the road to buy bagels at Sainsbury's. If your local bakery loses quality, you can bail out and choose another one instantly. But you cannot take Latin lessons in one school, and Greek in another. Moreover, there are real costs to the children in changing schools. Who protects the children whose choice is suddenly much less attractive?

Those hard cases may seem unlikely to happen, but there certainly need to be more safeguards than there are in Mr Baker's Act to ensure that they do not. One possibility (as he has mooted) is for unpopular schools to get more money. Another is that children who lose out by being locked into declining schools (because successful schools are bumping against their 1979 limits) should be compensated. But the problem does not stop there, for the possibility of schools which have opted out of the local authority system increasingly operating a selective system may also destroy comprehensive systems and with it the choice of those who do not want their children to be streamed irrevocably at 11.

In both cases, the operation of the market is not marginal: it destroys choices for some as a result of others exercising choice. It cannot satisfy the basic condition of economic welfare, which insists that a change is categorically beneficial if everyone is either the same or better off. In these circumstances, economic theory tells us that market outcomes do not necessarily raise social welfare or even provide most people with the nearest approximation of what they want. The outcome cannot be predicted with certainty, although a good guess would be that if the Prime Minister has anything to do with it, parental choice and opting out will become the stalking horse for a system of selection.

This is a shame, for it is not hard to imagine some sort of educational reform which would make schools more responsive to parents' wishes and give them more incentive for self-improvement (which may not be the same thing) without leading to the wider, destructive consequences which may be the result of Mr Baker's Act. If it is possible to pay teachers special supplements for maths, why not supplements for exam results or other desirable objectives? Economic incentives could be introduced without the likely blunderbuss effects of school closures.

This leads on to the second major problem of the Baker Act – the problem faced by many motorists who ask themselves after their car has been serviced at the garage: 'What have they really done under the bonnet, and how do I know that the garage really changed the oil?'. The greatest enemy of any properly functioning marketplace is lack of information.[2] Thus one of the earliest roles of Government, along with national defence and the maintenance of internal order, was quite rightly the establishment of weights and measures. In many cases, notably today with car repairs and servicing, the consumer is simply unable to judge the standard of the work. The consumer is therefore unable, in the nature of the product, to reach informed decisions trading off price against quality.

The same is now true of schools. Even the welcome publication of test results for children at 7, 11, 14 and 16 – the proposed bench-mark tests under Mr Baker's Act – will not fill the gap. They are as if the camp cook of a polar expedition was pitted in competition with the chef of a three-star Parisian restaurant. Not surprisingly, the restaurant would win if the final result was the only measure, and no allowance was made for the difficulty of the cooking conditions or the availability of materials. In economic terms, exam results measure output rather than value added: the construction company that builds a house from scratch is more skilled and adds more value than the one that bolts together prefabricated panels. Yet the final house may be the same.

Table 10. League table of exam results

	Position in league of 96 authorities	
Local education authority	*on Crude results**	*on Adjusted results***
Barking	92	79
Barnet	2	2
Bromley	9	96
Cleveland	49	9
Harrow	1	1
ILEA	91	56
Liverpool	78	4
Manchester	89	10
Norfolk	69	93
Northamptonshire	74	94
Somerset	63	86

*Based on Parliamentary answer, February 1985
**From the Sheffield University league table (1986) by Dr John Gray and David Jesson

Source: Gray and Jesson, op cit.

Thus it is surely a lesser achievement for a school to attain a 90 per cent pass-rate if it has a catchment area of university families than one of poorly-housed first-generation immigrants. Crude results (as in the ministerial league table) can be totally misleading.[3] A child may stand a better chance of higher qualifications at a school where apparently fewer children achieve them. Imagine a school with an entirely middle-class intake where half the children pass two A-levels. Now imagine a school where only 10 per cent of the intake is middle class but three-quarters of those pupils pass two or more A-levels. On the comparison of crude results, given the poorer performance of working-class children, it is almost certain that the middle-class school looks better. But in fact a middle-class child stands a better chance of doing well at the apparently worse school.

The provision of like-with-like information about school performance is crucial. For example, on the straightforward league table of school certificate grade, Bromley comes out ninth out of 96 English authorities.[4] But you would expect its score to be high

Table 11. Top and bottom education authorities on the Sheffield league table

Top ten	*Bottom ten*
Harrow	Bedfordshire
Barnet	Brent
St Helens	Haringey
Liverpool	Rochdale
Coventry	Isle of Wight
Sutton	Essex
Newcastle	Norfolk
Wirral	Northamptonshire
Cleveland	Oldham
Manchester	Bromley

Source: Gray and Jesson, op cit.

because it is a middle-class area. When social and other factors are allowed for in a statistical model, it appears that it ought to be doing far, far better. Less advantaged education authorities are outperforming it. Thus in the Sheffield University league table calculated in 1986, Bromley comes bottom (tables 10 and 11). This authority also ranked last in the Department of Education and Science's 1984 study.[5] Table 10 shows the extraordinary difference which allowing for social background can make to the standing of particular authorities. No less dramatic than the fall of Bromley is the apotheosis of Liverpool and Manchester, which soar up the tables.

The availability of such information to parents on a school-by-school basis would probably do more for educational standards in this country than any other single reform: the pressures for change would rapidly mount as one group of parents wanted to know why the school on the next block was so much better. The only authority to have sponsored such a school-by-school study and make its results available – for which three cheers – is the much-maligned Inner London Education Authority.[6] Its rankings took account of factors which influence results but which are outside the control of the school, such as a measure of ability in intake and the proportion of school children who were claiming free school meals as a measure of poverty. Ironically, the ILEA was abolished under Mr Baker's Education Act.

The best testimony to the power such comparisons would give to parents is the fact that the independent sector's establishment does not provide even crude exam results or university entrance in a comparable, collated form: the copious guide books will tell you the length of the swimming pool rather than exam results, let alone results compared with the state sector after allowing for social background and advantages. At the very least, Mr Baker is missing an opportunity to facilitate sensible comparisons between maintained and independent schools. (Do Jeremy and Fiona really want to spend £1,800 a year when the chances of getting Hugo into university are only 10 per cent better?) At worst, he is being deliberately discriminatory. As Labour's spokesman Jack Straw said: 'Why should the national curriculum apply by law to my children but not apply by law to his children?'

Mr Baker is also hobbling his own competitive schemes from the start, for any market without informed consumers is not going to function properly, even if the previous objections to his reforms are waved aside. Economic ways of thinking have a lot to offer many parts of our national life which they have not yet touched, including education. That is particularly the case if the limits of markets are also clearly understood and allowed for. Otherwise, Mr Baker's reforms will merely serve to give the whole enterprise a bad name.

Notes

1 Speech, 1 December 1987; press notice, Department of Education and Science.

2 See, for example, Richardson, *Information and Investment*.

3 See, for example, John Gray, David Jesson and Ben Jones,'The Search for a Fairer Way of Comparing Schools' Examination Results', *Research Papers in Education* (Slough, 1986).

4 Parliamentary answer, *Hansard*, 12 February 1985, cols. 126–7, quoted in John Gray and David Jesson, 'Exam Results and Local Authority League Tables', *Education and Training UK 1987*, ed. Anthony Harrison and John Grettan (Newbury, Berks.: Policy Journals).

5 *DES Statistical Bulletin*, 13/84, quoted in Gray and Jesson, op cit.

6 Inner London Education Authority, *Actual and Predicted Examination Results in Schools: Research and Statistics* (1987).

Reforming the National Health Service

Economics of insurance systems

- demand for health care controlled by suppliers
- the NHS budget constraint
- the underfunding debate
- perverse incentives and waste in present system
- the Government's reforms make GPs the consumers
- competing hospital suppliers
- difficulties with pay and quality
- the danger of demotivation

The Government deserves one cheer for what it has not done in its National Health Service reforms.[1] It has not thrown out the principle of a mainly tax-funded service freely available to all. It deserves a second cheer for the imaginative ideas designed to improve the way the NHS allocates its resources. This 'internal market' will indeed be the most sweeping reform of the NHS for 40 years – and it makes sense. The third cheer, though, will have to wait until the Government commits the resources needed to fund the NHS.

When the NHS policy review began under the aegis of Health and Social Security Secretary John Moore there was a fair chance that the radical right would run away with it. As it is, little remains of its ideas. The minister who took over, Mr Kenneth Clarke, is committed to the principles of the service. The one vestige of a move to private insurance is some tax relief for private care for pensioners. There is a danger that this will become the thin end of a long wedge when people begin to ask why there should not also be tax relief for people under retirement age. But most analysts believe that the relief is unlikely to take off, because the medical private sector is generally not interested in treating an age group where the incidence of serious disability rises sharply. Indeed, one of the main reasons for the introduction of Medicare – the public scheme – in the United States was because the private sector failed old people.

Any serious move to an insurance system for the bulk of the population would be economically calamitous, quite apart from any arguments about values and rights of access for all. A private insurance system is a recipe for an escalation of costs, with little overall benefit. The reason lies in health care's curiosity as a 'product'. Patients cannot decide that they would like to buy more or less as if health care was Persil. People do not deliberately break their own legs, get involved in car crashes, or need hernia operations. The patient's role is confined to complaining about an ache or a pain. From then on, you are in the hands of the professionals.

In short, the demand for health care is unusual because it is largely controlled by the doctors who supply it. The dangers in any such market are enormous. Imagine what the demand for Rover cars would be like if it was left up to the people who produce them. The health professionals will tend to discover ever more glamorous forms of care, and ever more glorious excuses for high pay. In the United States there is very little check on either. The insurer pays up. Both the patient and the doctor are happy to ensure the highest possible standard of service. The losers are the generality of people who see their premiums soar.

The result? The United States spends twice as much of its far higher national income on health care as Britain does. Because many are not insured, the US also suffers higher infant mortality and lower life expectancy. Many doctors, of course, love it. They earn 5.1 times the national average wage, compared with 2.4 times in Britain.[2] A great advantage of the NHS is a feature most people moan about: the fact that the Government sets an overall total for spending, and we have to muddle along within it. That 'budget constraint', along with universal access, is a crucial ingredient which ensures that we get extraordinary value for money.

There are, though, two serious remaining problems: underspending on health care as a whole, and inefficiency in the way the money is spent within the service. The White Paper has nothing to say about underfunding, because the Government does not accept the case that there is any underfunding. The only promise of increased resources in the White Paper is an extra 100 consultants, which adds a princely 0.6 per cent to the total of some 17,000. Yet study after study has shown that the NHS needs a real annual rise in resources of some 2 per cent a

Figure 16

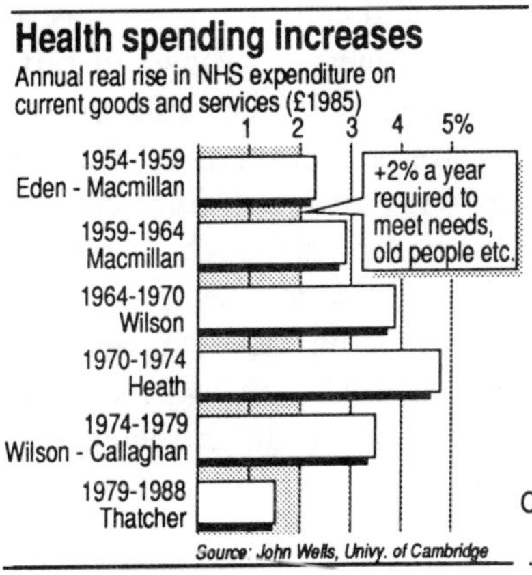

Figure 17

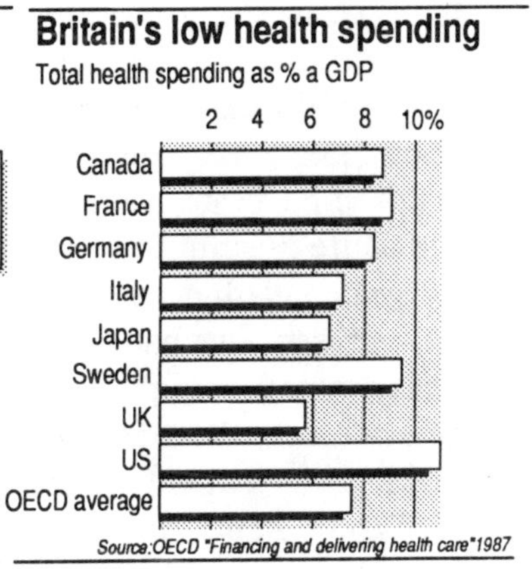

year to meet the demands of an ageing population, new health technology and some policy aims.[3]

The Government claims that it is generating part of that real increase from cost savings within the NHS – so-called 'efficiency savings'. However, this is fiercely contested by many who work within the NHS, who merely see old-fashioned cuts. The Government is certainly not funding the necessary real increase from tax: calculations from the national accounts by the Cambridge economist John Wells[4] show that the record of the Thatcher administration is the meanest of any since the NHS was founded, as figure 16 shows. The result is that health spending has declined as a share of national income, in contrast to almost every other country. A recent international comparison from the OECD demonstrated that we spent less on health care than any other major country (figure 17).

With that sort of record, it is understandable that the reaction to the Government's reform proposals should be one of suspicion. Much will also depend on how the plans are implemented in detail. However, a first reading suggests that there will be an improvement in the incentives within the service, and therefore in its efficiency. At present some of the incentives of the system are perverse.

For example, a hospital which is good – i.e. low-cost and efficient – at providing a particular operation is now discouraged from taking patients from another health authority. If it receives any recompense, it will only be with a long time-lag. And its own local patients will have to wait longer. In other words, the existing structure of the NHS does not reward efficiency or encourage particularly effective parts of the service to expand. The White Paper points out that the average cost of treating acute hospital in-patients varied by as much as 50 per cent between health authorities. There are wide discrepancies in the drug-prescribing habits of GPs. In some places drug costs are nearly twice as high per head of population as in others. At the extremes, there is a twenty-fold variation in the rate at which GPs refer patients to hospital.

The White Paper proposes to set up a surrogate market within the NHS, which builds on the ideas proposed in the path-breaking study by Alain C. Enthoven but which in some crucial respects goes even further than he advocated.[5] Since the nature of the marketplace means that patients do not have the expertise to choose between one type of service and another, their GPs will act as their agents, buying services from hospitals depending on cost and availability. GPs will thus have an incentive to economize on waste. At the outset, the Government proposes that only the biggest 9 per cent of all GP practices covering a quarter of the population should operate such budgets.

The second key change is to allow hospitals to set up as independent trusts within the NHS. Clearly, the main aim is for the 320 acute hospitals with more than 250 beds (and budgets of more than 10 million a year) to run themselves. Hospitals will be able to compete with one another – and expand those services at which they are particularly cost-effective. They will also be able to set their own pay rates, thus implicitly rewarding those teams that bring in new 'business' from the GP budgets. In effect, they will act as the 'supply side' of the NHS to the GPs' 'demand side'.

The grand strategy of the White Paper is broadly in line with what many health economists had been arguing for some time, but a lot will depend on the details. Professor Alan Maynard of the Centre for Health Economics at York University argues that the ability of hospitals to set their own pay could undermine the whole system by bidding up pay rates and causing a wage and cost explosion. However, it is hard to see why this should occur so long as the Government is strict in applying overall limits to spending: hospitals will only bid up pay because they are more successful in cutting other costs, improving productivity and attracting more patients.

A more corrosive influence could be patients who offer to 'top up' the money available in their GP budgets so that they can go for an operation now rather than in two months' time, after the end of the current financial year. At present the Government says it will allow no such thing. (It will only allow extra payments for so-called 'hotel' services like having a private room, not for medical ones.) But the temptation will be there, with two pernicious effects. First, it would undermine the principle of health care regardless of means. Secondly, by relaxing the overall budget constraint it would open the door to exactly the sort of cost-escalation seen in the United States.

Dr Nicholas Barr, the London School of Economics specialist who wrote *The Economics of the Welfare State*, persuasively argues that a key issue in the reforms will be quality.[6] It is impossible to introduce incentives to greater efficiency by saving costs – as the reforms do – without also putting downwards pressure on quality. In a normal marketplace, this problem is dealt with by the consumer making a trade-off between the two. But in the health market, as we have seen, the consumer is not in a position to make trade-offs because of ignorance of treatments, and as soon as the service is funded by a third party the consumers' interest is anyway in having the highest quality of care to be obtained.

The central question then becomes how to ensure that high clinical standards are maintained despite the incentive to economize on costs which the reforms introduce. The type of peer review entailed in medical audits is one route, though occasionally flawed by mutual back-scratching. Another less desirable route to ensure quality may arise from the Government's proposed legal reforms. If lawyers are entitled to be rewarded by a slice of winnings, there could be an increase in US-style medical litigation – and a less desirable increase in doctors' negligence insurance premiums.

The Government is also going to need the wisdom of

Solomon to get its criteria for allocating GP budgets right. Clearly, money that is given to GPs should be varied to allow for the likely needs of their patients, or their own self-interest will dictate that they turn away the patients known to be the most expensive to treat. They may take to setting up surgeries on the second floor of buildings with no lifts as a way of discouraging the unhealthy from applying. Budgets will have to be weighted by the number of old people, and will probably also have to include some flexibility to allow for chronic illness and extremely expensive conditions, otherwise GPs will still have an incentive merely to treat the uncomplicated.

There is also a serious danger in an excessively hard-headed and economic approach to the reform of an area like the National Health Service. After all, the NHS is unlike many areas of private sector business where the pursuit of private gain is at least an important motivation, if not the crucial one. Many employees of the NHS work for it with a sense of considerable vocation and pride – and despite exceptionally low material rewards for the level of their skills and responsibilities. They need to feel that their efforts – indeed, sacrifices in many cases – are at least rewarded by the high opinions and esteem of their employers. The risk of the Government's parsimonious approach is that it will succeed in so reducing the morale of the NHS's practitioners that the end result, despite the reforms, is a far worse service. In economic terms, there would be a sharp loss of internal or 'X-efficiency' as a result of demotivation.[7] Arguably, something similar happened to teachers as a result of the Government's education policies.

The prize of success, though, could be sweet. The management systems which will be needed to identify costs will also clearly identify whether patients are being turned away because of inefficiency in the system – or overall underfunding. Mrs Thatcher may not like the answer. The stimulus to good husbandry could in turn help to re-establish the consensus for much-needed real increases in funding.

Notes

1 *Working for Patients*, Cmnd 555 (HMSO, 1989).

2 *Financing and Delivering Health Care* (Paris: Organisation for Economic Co-operation and Development, 1987).

3 See, for example, Ray Robinson and Ken Judge, *Public Expenditure and the NHS: Trends and Prospects*, King's Fund Institute for Health Policy Analysis (1987). The Government itself admitted as much in a leaked paper on long-term spending prospects in 1980.

4 Mimeo supplied to the author.

5 Alain C. Enthoven, *Reflections on the Management of the National Health Service*, Nuffield Provincial Hospitals Trust (1985). Enthoven's 'internal market' involved trading between district general managers: the White Paper suggests that GPs have their own budgets and act as surrogate consumers.

6 Nicholas Barr, Howard Glennerster, and Julian Le Grand 'Working for Patients: the Right Approach?', *Social Policy and Administration*, vol. 23, no. 2 (August 1989), pp. 117–27.

7 See Harvey Leibenstein, op cit. in note 2 to 'The Economics of Privatization', the fourth essay in chapter 2.

Dealing with regional inequality

Income and unemployment differences

- drawbacks of unemployment as measure
- migration a sign of failure
- employment opportunities
- causes of regional diversity
- effects of national policies
- the faults of regional policies
- new proposals

Britain's North–South divide became a source of intense controversy shortly before the 1987 general election, when the Labour Party made it one of its main themes. The cynical pointed out that Labour's own electoral base is increasingly to be found north of a line from the Wash to the Bristol Channel. Some argued that it was meaningless to talk about a North–South divide since there were poor areas in the South and rich areas in the North. The genteel prosperity of Harrogate and the problems of the run-down channel ports figured largely in the evidence.

Nevertheless, it seems clear to most analysts who have examined the figures that there is a regional dimension to Britain's economic problems. Aggregations have to be made if there is to be any understanding of the real world, or it would merely become a succession of impossibly complex and random events. The figures which aggregate economic data on a regional basis show higher unemployment and lower incomes in the areas outside London and the South East, and sometimes reveal spectacular problems of local and regional decline. There is little reason to believe that these problems will disappear of their own accord in any reasonable timescale.[1]

Start with a look at incomes. According to the official figures, the difference between the richest and the poorest region of Britain in terms of income per head is now the widest for more than a decade.[2] Almost all the poorer regions have grown more slowly than the richer ones. Income per head in the richest region – the South East – is 44 per cent higher than incomes in the poorest British region – Wales – and 53 per cent higher than in Northern Ireland. This compares with an equivalent difference in incomes a decade before of 29 per cent and 40 per cent. The gap between income in the capital and outside is even more extreme, with London income now 57 per cent higher than those in Wales and 67 per cent higher than those in Northern Ireland.

There must, though, be an important caveat here. These figures do not allow for differences in prices in different regions. They assume implicitly that people pay the same prices for the same goods and services. We know that this is not the case for housing, where rents and land values are sharply lower outside the richer regions. It is also likely that the prices of many goods and services are lower in poorer regions than in richer ones. This particularly applies to services whose principal cost is labour (like hairdressing, restaurant meals, transport services) rather than goods which can be traded between regions and countries. This phenomenon, which is a major reason why the figures exaggerate the gap in the standard of living between different countries, will certainly apply between regions too. The real gap will be a good deal narrower, but there is no study to suggest by how much.

These differences in income per head are also less pronounced for those in work. Lower average incomes in poor regions arise in part because more people are out of work. As figure 19 shows, unemployment remains higher outside

Figure 18

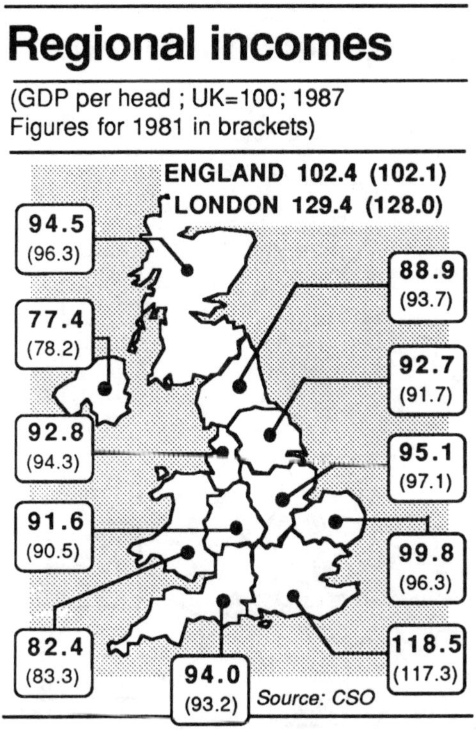

southern England. These figures if anything understate the gravity of the problem because unemployment is far from being a good measure of regional distress.[3] It is the result of a whole series of adjustments – including migration from the poorer to the richer regions. For example, there was a net migration out of the northern regions, Scotland and the West Midlands of 71,000 in 1986, a fairly typical year which merely continued a trend. Net migration from these relatively poor areas cancelled out their natural population rise over the period 1981–6. In the case of most of the poor regions, outward migration began with the first oil shock in 1973–4 but appears to be accelerating. The North West, the largest northerly region, lost population at an annual average rate of 0.3 per cent between 1981 and 1986. This compared to an annual average rise of 0.3 per cent in the decade to 1971. Yorkshire and Humberside is declining by 0.1 per cent a year compared with stability between 1971 and 1981, and a rise

Figure 19

Regional unemployment

Unemployed as percentage of workforce
Oct 1989 (1979 in brackets)

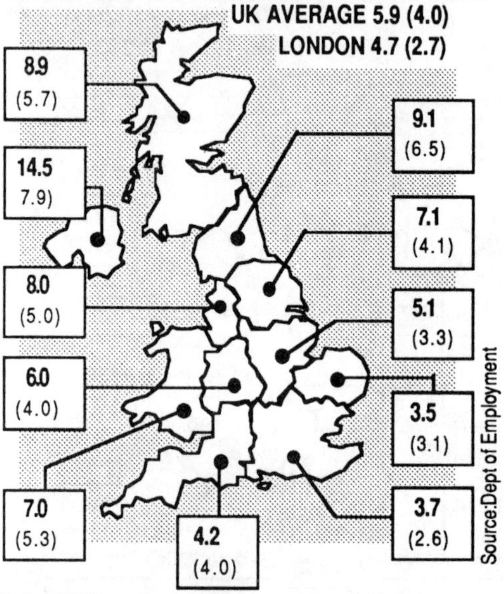

Note: 1979 average figures consistent with current figures; seasonally adjusted

of 0.5 per cent a year between 1961 and 1971. The population of the North is shrinking by 0.2 per cent a year.[4]

Without migration, which is generally seen as a sign of economic weakness in an economy, the unemployment rates in the poorer regions would be even higher in the short term. A better measure of regional dynamism than the figures for unemployment is given by employment. The results of the 1984 Census of Employment were finally released in 1987, and showed a far more dramatic skewing of job prospects in the regions than was suggested even by the unemployment figures. The calculations based on the Census showed that there was a net loss of 745,000 jobs in Great Britain between June 1979 and June 1986.[5] But the job losses were concentrated north of a line from the Wash to the Bristol Channel, and the gains were below it. The South East, South West and East Anglia gained a net 356,000 jobs, while there was a net loss of 1,107,000 in the rest of the country. Only one region outside the southern three saw a rise, and that was the East Midlands, with a modest 6,000. If the self-employed are excluded, the figures showed that a mere 6 per cent of the job losses were in the three southern regions, and 94 per cent in the Midlands and the North. The regional pattern appears to have been remarkably persistent in the downturn and in the upturn. Broadly, the regions that showed the sharpest job losses have also experienced the slowest growth of jobs since that point.

Why do regions suffer such diverse fates? The Government's advisers argue that a contributory cause has been pay inflexibility, including in some industries the settlement of pay according to national rates regardless of local labour-market conditions. Nevertheless, separate evidence from the Census suggests that the accident of industrial structure has as much if not more to do with the regional differences. One of the features of the figures was that the decline in manufacturing employment was even larger – at 1.9 million from the peak in 1979 to 1986 – than previously supposed. This was offset by a revised and larger increase in services, but that was not much consolation to the northerly regions. Far more of their labour forces are involved in manufacturing. For example, manufacturing jobs account for 35.8 per cent of jobs in the West Midlands, compared with an equivalent share of only 20.6 per cent in the South East. They were therefore particularly hard hit by the recession, which was concentrated in manufacturing industry because of the sharp overvaluation of sterling. Manufacturing is a highly tradable sector, and it was simply priced out of its markets. Southern England also benefits from its disproportionate share of the fastest-growing industry – banking, insurance and finance.

Part of the answer to regional problems is therefore to pursue macro-economic policies (for interest rates, tax, public spending and the exchange rate) which do not bear particularly heavily on a single sector of the economy. At one point this was regarded as an advantage of monetary policy as against the apparently more discretionary effects of Government tax and public-spending decisions. However, the uneven impact of the

1979–81 monetary squeeze highlighted the arguments for using macro-economic levers in a balanced way.

Regional problems are also much less than they would naturally be, thanks to national policy instruments which reduce regional inequalities automatically. A progressive tax system which raises more revenue from people with higher incomes and higher spending will clearly raise a disproportionate amount of money from the richer parts of the country, while the public-spending side of the Government's accounts is meant to be shared around equally. In the case of unemployment benefit, there is a direct compensation to regions with high unemployment rates. Thus rich parts of the country run budget surpluses, which fund budget deficits in poorer parts. One study found that public finance flow benefited Wales by 7.8 per cent of regional product, Scotland by 6.1 per cent and Northern Ireland by 16.1 per cent. The public finance outflow from the South East was worth 4.8 per cent of regional product.[6]

Despite these flows, most British Governments since the war have also run a specific regional policy designed more actively to reduce the discrepancies of unemployment and income. An important economic justification is that regional policy can help to reduce inflationary pressures in booming regions if some of the slack is taken up in depressed ones: reducing the mismatch between regions should enable a higher level of output and employment in the country as a whole, without sparking off wage inflation. On some occasions, Governments have encouraged labour to move to the growing regions, but this was often politically unpopular and may have had fewer effects than supposed. The skilled find it most easy to move – and when they do the depressed region may be less attractive for prospective employers. Nor do migrants necessarily reduce unemployment by the same number, since they take their spending power with them, and this is bound to reduce the sales of local businesses.[7] Furthermore, such migration aggravates the problems of congestion and overcrowding in the South East, which are also an important motive for regional policy. Most regional measures have therefore been directed at encouraging people to stay in the depressed regions by providing more jobs. That also makes sense politically, because people generally prefer to stay in their region of origin, and economically, because of the substantial sunk costs in providing a viable community.

Under Mrs Thatcher, however, regional spending has more than halved in real terms, in part because the Government argues with justice that previous regional policy measures proved to be costly failures. Assisted areas cover about 35 per cent of the working population. In so-called 'intermediate areas' the Government can make money available for specific projects and companies. In 'development areas' there can also be selective assistance but there is also a 15 per cent automatic grant towards new plant and buildings up to a limit of £10,000 per job created. This is substantially more restrictive than the previous system, where the limit per job was £35–40,000, allowing very large subsidies for capital spending. Indeed, there were stories of companies setting up to gain the cheap capital equipment – and then selling it off at a profit after a few years. But the new and the old systems continue to encourage relatively investment-intensive production.

Surely a more sensible approach to reducing regional inequalities would be to make labour more attractive to hire, since this would specifically direct policy at what the Government is aiming to keep in the regions: labour. One possibility would be employment subsidies paid on the additional members of a work-force in a given year, though such measures have in the past attracted criticism from the EC Commission on the grounds of unfair competition within the Community. Another possibility is to reduce some part of the tax on labour. One proposal is for variable rates of income tax, with especially low rates in the most depressed regions. Part of the benefit would almost certainly be passed back to the employer, making him more willing to hire labour. Another alternative, with very similar effects, would be regional reductions in employers' National Insurance Contributions. The effect would be to concentrate help on the local people rather than their machines.

Notes

1 For a good summary of the arguments, see David Smith, *North and South: Britain's Growing Divide* (Harmondsworth: Penguin, 1989).

2 Regional accounts in *Economic Trends*, no. 421 (London: Central Statistical Office, November 1988).

3 See, for example, Graham Gudgin, Barry Moore and John Rhodes,'Employment Problems in the Cities and Regions of the UK: Prospects for the 1980s', *Cambridge Economic Policy Review*, vol. 8, no. 12 (December 1982).

4 *Regional Trends* (London: Central Statistical Office, June 1988).

5 *Department of Employment Gazette*, January 1987.

6 *Report of the Study Group on the Role of Public Finance in European Integration*, vol. 1, Commission of the European Communities, general report (the 'MacDougall Report') (1977), table 4, p. 33.

7 For a discussion, see *The Economic System in the UK*, ed. Derek Morris (Oxford, 2nd edn, 1979), p. 532.

What type of benefits?

Means-testing pensions

- whittling away at pensions
- selectivity versus universality
- opposition to selectivity
- poverty trap and take-up
- using the tax system to avoid drawbacks
- need for selectivity among pensioners because of ageing population

The scrape that the former Chancellor, Mr Lawson, dived into in 1988 over old age pensions highlighted a dilemma running through any reform of the benefits paid by the state. Should they be paid selectively to those in need, which involves some form of test of the recipients' means, or should they be paid universally regardless of means, which is much more expensive but obviates the need for any test?

Such is the sensitivity of this issue among benefit recipients and future benefit recipients – which is most of the population – that the Chancellor had to deny firmly that he was going to apply a means test to the old age pension, which is now paid universally to anyone of retirement age who has made their National Insurance contributions, and is uprated each year in line with the movement in the Retail Price Index. He said that he was going to introduce instead a new benefit for poor pensioners which would be means-tested. As an extra benefit, there could be no cause for any protest.

However, the policy of means-testing a new pension may not in fact turn out very differently from a policy of means-testing the existing pension. The present practice of merely linking pensions to the rise in prices would simply not have been sustainable in the medium term, because the pension is becoming a steadily shrinking proportion of earnings. The alternatives facing the Government were either to provide something extra for pensioners who have no other means of support apart from the state pension, or to raise the pension for everyone. Without a new benefit, political realities would have dictated that eventually the pressure for a large uprating in pensions would become irresistible.

After all, the single pension has fallen from nearly a quarter of average earnings in 1979, when the link with earnings was broken, to little more than a fifth today. Another ten years of real income growth combined with no pension growth will have made the state pension an increasingly feeble instrument. In effect, it is being phased out as a serious form of income support in old age. Some 1.25 million out of 9.75 million pensioners already rely on additional income support, and they have had virtually no real increase in living standards over the period since 1979. In other words, nearly one in five of our elderly are part of that underclass of the long-term unemployed and the low-paid who have been shut out of the prosperity of the Thatcher years. Mr Lawson's new benefit was probably always intended merely to draw off the pressure for something more expensive.

This is not as dishonourable a position as the Opposition suggests. The slogan 'universal benefits good, selective benefits bad' is a silly gut reaction. Mr Lawson rightly pointed out that the average real income of pensioners rose by 23 per cent between 1979 and 1986. Most of the newly retired are benefiting from the State Earnings Related Pension Scheme and from the spread of occupational pensions. Real interest rates have been at historically high levels, which particularly benefits the elderly because it boosts the return on their savings. Is it really sensible to relieve the needs of a small fraction of pensioners at the cost of benefiting the well-off majority? For the right wing of the

Conservative party, the question of public expenditure savings is paramount. However, selectivity raises broader issues too.

It is, indeed, the key question in the economics of welfare benefits, for it affects not only the pension, but universally paid child benefit, and social security and unemployment benefits. There has always been an honourable seam of opposition to selective benefits because of the history of the means test during the slump of the thirties, which was a particularly demeaning investigation into family circumstances to ensure that the claimant merited the award. A second strand of criticism focuses on a side-effect of selective benefits which are withdrawn as income rises – the fact that this adds an additional disincentive to work. About 545,000 low-income families face effective tax rates on extra income of 70 per cent or more because they not only pay tax and National Insurance contributions, but also lose their income-related benefits.[1] The sort of high effective tax rates to be found in the poverty trap were regarded by the Government as an intolerable disincentive for the well-off. Surely, the poor deserve no worse.

The advantage of universal benefits like child benefit is that they are not withdrawn as income rises, and hence cannot act as a disincentive to work. The disadvantage, though, is their cost. The cost of helping a minority of pensioners through universal pensions – like the cost of helping a minority of poor families through increases in universal child benefit – becomes so great that Governments give up attempting to use these instruments to attack poverty. After all, the last Labour Government conspicuously failed to launch a serious attack on poverty, and left the pattern of income inequality broadly unchanged. Relying on universal benefits to relieve poverty implies politically unacceptable income tax rates. It just does not happen.

However, the traditional Labour objection to selectivity – means tests – may be falling by the wayside. It is true that the take-up of means-tested benefits is very low because people are ignorant of their rights and dislike claiming. For example, Family Credit is said to be claimed by only some 30 per cent of eligible families. It is true, too, that selectivity has often been a camouflage for cutting benefits. But both drawbacks can be tackled. New technological possibilities have opened up because of the computerization of the Inland Revenue. The Institute for Fiscal Studies has long argued persuasively that the take-up problem can be eliminated by providing universal benefits but clawing them back from the well-off by changing their tax codes.[2] We can at last combine the advantage of universality in ensuring take-up with the advantage of targeting those in need. A far greater attack on poverty can be achieved for politically realistic sums of money. Income tax rates for most people can stay within bounds, even though rates of tax and benefit withdrawal for those on low incomes must be higher, the more generous is the assistance.

Sadly, it is quite inevitable that a generous system of income support will lead to relatively high effective marginal tax rates somewhere in the income distribution. If benefits are withdrawn, the tax rates on recipients are very high. If the benefits are generous and not withdrawn, the tax rates on everyone have to be high. Indeed, this is the central and key problem with any form of negative income tax or basic income guarantee scheme which would give a minimum income to everyone – and then merely tax whatever they earned on top. If the income support is set at a high enough rate to be reasonable and generous, the increase required in the basic rate of income tax in order to fund the universal income support is enormous. Even to pay everyone the supplementary benefit level and a little extra would require the basic rate of income tax to rise to more than 40p in the pound. Even partial schemes which retain means-tested local housing supplements for those in need – a crucial caveat given the variance of rents – imply a flat rate income tax of some 38 per cent.[3]

Poverty is only ever likely to be tackled generously if benefits are selective, albeit applied through an integration of the tax and benefit system and clawed back automatically from those who do not need them. But concern about the impact of the poverty trap applies with less force to pensioners, because fewer of them work. There is also a very important reason why we should over time be moving towards a more selective payments of state income support to pensioners, which is the steady rise in the proportion of the population which is going to be over retirement age (as shown in figure 20). In Britain, the so-called dependency ratio

Figure 20

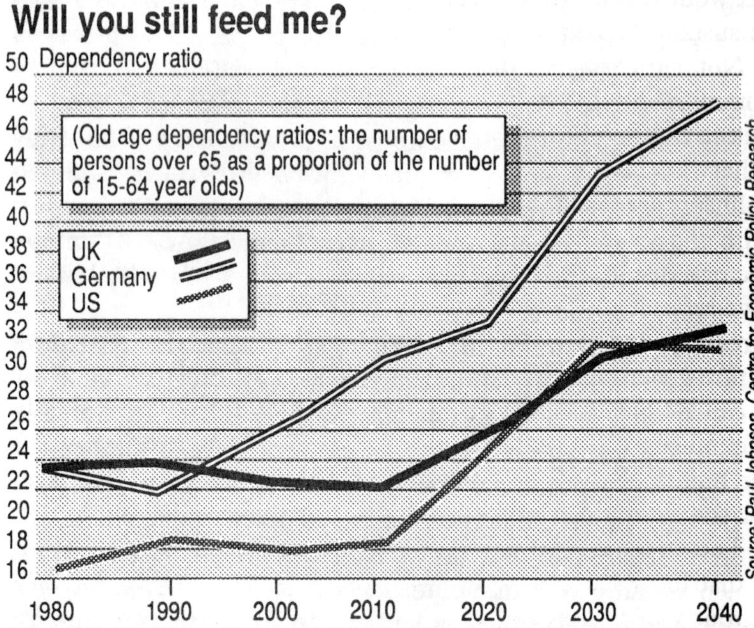

– the ratio of people over 65 to those of working age between 15 and 64 – is forecast to rise from 23.5 per cent in 1980 to 29.7 per cent in 2025.[4] Demographic forecasters have been wrong before, mainly because of difficulties in forecasting birth rates. This time the prediction looks more certain, if only because it arises from two phenomena which have already occurred, and which are gradually working their way through. The reason for the sharp rise in the 'dependency ratio' is the scissors effect of the lengthening life-expectancy of the old combined with the decreased birth rates of the post-war period of prosperity.

This demographic shift is, according to Paul Johnson of the London School of Economics, unprecedented in economic history.[5] Even the Black Death culled equal proportions of each age group, diminishing the total but not throwing the generations out of balance. The OECD has calculated that real earnings per worker need to grow by more than 0.8 per cent a year in Britain up until 2030 merely to pay for the real 1980 levels of health and pension benefits. In West Germany, where the demographic scissors is among the most severe, the payroll tax would need to rise from 18.5 per cent to 42 per cent by 2030 to sustain the current pension system.

Not surprisingly, the UK Treasury is keen to reduce its commitments to the pensioners of the Baby Boom generation. Selectivity is one way it can extricate itself from what could otherwise be a major problem of public expenditure control. Johnson argues, though, that society as a whole is presented with the same problem even if the Treasury ducks the public sector's role in resolving it. If today's baby-boomers save for their own retirement through pension funds, rather than relying on the Treasury, they will still build up enormous financial claims on future generations of working age. You cannot actually produce a can of baked beans today for eating in 2010. You merely accumulate pieces of paper which are IOUs for the future. A far higher share of national output will have to go to provide for the elderly, leaving a lower share for those in work.

This assumes, though, that we are essentially talking about a distributional problem within an overall total of national output which does not vary because of the demographic shift. One solution which always eases distributional problems is to increase the size of the cake, which may in part come about by relaxing the retirement rules so that more people continue working for longer. Another is to build up claims on other countries which then keep us in our collective retirement, but the whole world cannot do this and the debt crisis shows that international obligations are not always reliable. Another is to boost the size of the working age population through higher fertility (make childbirth less expensive to working mothers) or immigration (Hong Kongers?)

The demographic shift is likely in itself to change important aspects of economic behaviour, not necessarily in a direction which makes it easier to support the baby-boomers when they become geriatric. If today's baby-boomers eventually save more, will that lead to increased investment and hence a greater long-term capacity to meet their needs? Or will their desire to increase savings merely lead to a cut in demand as consumption falls, in turn leading to lower investment and lower incomes until savings are back in line with investment? The economics of the demographic shift are still in their infancy, but will require some hard thinking and some hard choices, not least in the system of pensions.

Notes

1 John Hills, *Changing Tax: How the Tax System Work and How to Change it* (London: Child Poverty Action Group, 1989), p. 29.

2 A.W. Dilnot, J.A. Kay and C.N. Morris, *The Reform of Social Security* (Institute for Fiscal Studies and Oxford University Press, 1984).

3 This is the BI2000 scheme advocated by Hermione Parker in *Instead of the Dole* (London: Routledge, 1989).

4 United Nations projections quoted in Paul Johnson, Christoph Conrad and David Thomson, eds., *Workers versus Pensioners: Intergenerational Justice in an Ageing World* (Centre for Economic Policy Research and Manchester University Press, 1989), p. 29.

5 See for discussions Johnson *et al.*, eds., op cit., and Peter Scott and Paul Johnson, *The Economic Consequences of Population Ageing in Advanced Societies*, Centre for Economic Policy Research paper no. 263 (London, July 1988).

Measuring public spending

The importance of public sector pay

- volume measures
- cash planning
- spending in cost or 'real' terms
- the example of the NHS
- a turning point in pay trends
- why spending rises are perceived as cuts
- differing fortunes of departments
- the political control of spending

The Treasury has been cheating. Dig as you might in the slurry of information contained in the annual public expenditure documents, there is a seam of crucial facts about Britain's public spending which refuses to come to light. Nowhere in the 500 pages of the Autumn Statement and associated booklets is there information about what public service workers have been paid, how their pay has changed, and what is in prospect. Since this information has an essential bearing on many public debates, not least the situation of the National Health Service, this is a lamentable state of affairs.

Public spending, after all, accounted for some 39 per cent of national income, or some £199 billion in 1989/90. But some £51 billion of that is pensions and other social security payments, and another £17 billion is debt interest payments.[1] Of what remains – the cost of the goods and services provided by the public sector – pay accounts for nearly two-thirds of the total. This lacuna of information about pay is crucial because, within a given spending total, the trend of pay costs is the single most important determinant of the real service which is provided at the end of the day. What appears to be a generous real increase in the cash allocated to a spending programme can look far less generous if pay has been rising far more quickly, as increasingly occurred in the late eighties.

It used to be different. Before 1980, the Government used to publish so-called 'volume' figures for overall public spending, and for each service. They purported to measure the actual volume of inputs – the number of pencils supplied to the schoolroom, paint put on the walls and tanks delivered to the army. They thus stripped out the effect of pay rises from year to year, and indeed the effect of price rises for particular goods in that area. The Government even used to plan in these volume terms.

The problem with volume planning, in the inflationary seventies, was that each department presumed that it had the right to a given volume of inputs regardless of its rise in costs. Thus a particular missile system might rise in price by, say 40 per cent where the general inflation rate was 15 per cent. Or a particular group of public sector workers might get a highly favourable pay deal, which meant that the cost of the service they provided soared. Planning in volume meant that the purchase or the service still went ahead, with the exchequer picking up an inflationary tab.

The first step away from this daft system, which effectively underwrote any inflationary increase in wages or prices, was cash limits. They at least introduced a budget for each area set in cash

Table 12. Inflation is the key: revision of Government inflation estimates January–November 1988 (percentages)

	Overall price rises assumed Jan 1988	*Overall price rises assumed Nov 1988*	*Likely public services cost rises*
1987/88	4.2	5.3	7.5
1988/89	4.5	6.25	7.2
1989/90	3.6	5.0	6.8
1990/91	2.9	3.5	6.3

and which was consistent with the volume plans at the predicted inflation rate. If costs accelerated, then the department had to go back to the Treasury for approval to spend more. This was the system operated by the Labour Government from 1975, when it tried to unwind the very sharp increase in spending which had occurred in the inflationary years of 1973–5. It succeeded in reducing spending in real terms by 3.8 per cent in 1976/7. With the incentive of the 1976 sterling crisis and the International Monetary Fund loan, it kept a tight rein until losing office in 1979.[2] Then, under the Tories, we went right over to cash planning. The objective was to cut the level of public spending in real terms. Volume figures were entirely expunged from the White Paper in order to make it easier to squeeze spending hard. Ministers threw out the baby with the bath-water.

For the last few years, the White Paper has at least included one table setting out the spending on each department after allowing for the general rise in prices through the economy – the so-called GDP deflator. This measure used sensibly to be called 'cost terms', because it measured what was happening to spending in the pounds used by the taxpayer (corporate as well as individual). If spending rises by 1.9 per cent in cost terms (as it was predicted to do in 1988/9, on the optimistic basis of a general rise in prices of 4.5 per cent), then the amount raised in taxes or borrowing would have to go up by 1.9 per cent as well. It represents the real cost to the taxpayer.

The danger of calling this 'real terms', as the Treasury's public relations machine does, can best be seen in the Health Service. In the financial year 1986/7, the cash increase allocated

Figure 21

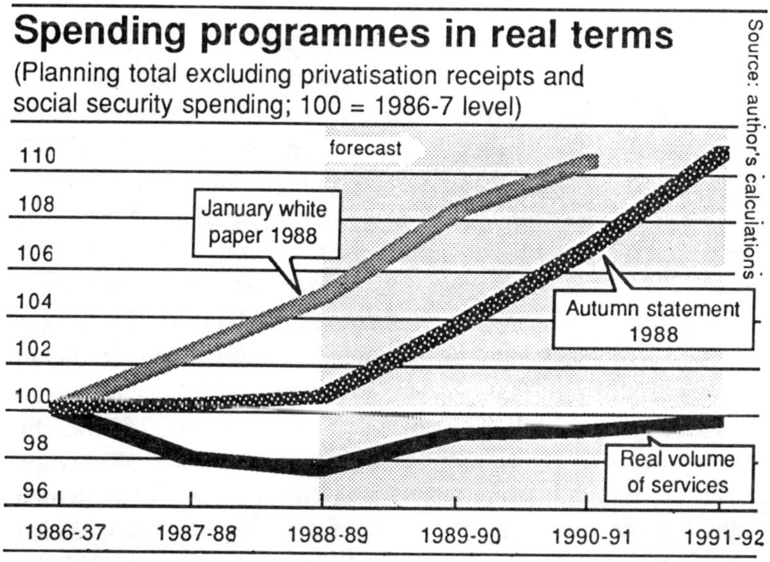

to hospital and community health service current spending – the hardest pressed area of the NHS – was 7.2 per cent [3] This was an increase 'in real terms' – i.e. in cost terms, after allowing for general inflation – of 4.1 per cent. However, the inflation rate within the hospital service was no less than 6.9 per cent because of pay rises and other items. Thus the rise in the volume of inputs – the number of nurses, kidney machines and so forth – was precisely 0.3 per cent. This is what the old volume measure would have shown were it still published in the spending plans.

Does this represent the real increase in services to patients? We are certainly getting nearer to the truth than we are with either cash or the Treasury's 'real terms', but we are not quite there yet. After all, this is a summary measure of the volume of inputs, not of output. If each nurse became slightly more efficient; if each doctor handled more operations; if each bed were used more frequently because new techniques allowed more rapid discharges from hospital, then there would have been a sharper growth of output than input. In short, there are increases in productivity in the public sector as well as the private sector (despite the convention used by statisticians that non-marketed spending output is assumed to be the same as the value of the inputs).

In some areas of spending it is possible to go further and work out a reasonable approximation of what has been happening to output overall. Thus cost saving measures in the hospital service are claimed to have generated about £158 million in 1986/7, or enough to add 1.5 per cent to the resources available to the service was thus 1.8 per cent, just short of the 2 per cent which is widely recognized to be necessary to cope with the ageing of the population, medical advances and policy priorities. Nevertheless, a note of caution is due. Some NHS workers argue that such 'efficiency savings' are merely a euphemism for cuts.

There are thus, in theory, four distinct ways of measuring public spending, each of which has its uses: cash, cost or 'real' terms, volume terms and real output. Of these, the most difficult to measure is real output. The Government therefore has a perfect excuse for the partial nature of its information on output. It has no such excuse for its failure to include information on volume. The sharp acceleration in inflation during 1988 underscored the danger of relying solely on cash planning: what were reasonable real rises in some spending programmes suddenly became cuts. Table 12 shows how the Government's inflation assumptions went up in the course of just one year. Figure 21 shows the implications for the real level of spending.

There is also a long-run argument for supplementing cash planning with volume indicators. If the gap between public and private sector pay begins to close, the implications for services will be serious unless the Government increases the cash allocated to spending. Assume that the Government merely allows public sector pay to grow in line with private sector pay, and that they both grow in real terms at the same pace as the economy; i.e. at about 2.5 per cent a year. Two-thirds of the cost of the NHS is pay, so that there would have to be a real rise in the funding of the NHS of nearly 1.7 per cent each year just to allow its employees to share in the rise in general prosperity, leaving the actual number of nurses and doctors unchanged. This is the so-called 'relative price effect': the relative price of goods and services with a heavy labour input and little or no capacity for productivity improvements will tend to rise over time.

In this context the provision for the NHS budget to rise by 2 per cent 'in real terms' in 1989/90 is not munificent. Moreover, the Government may be lucky to get away with public sector pay merely rising in line with the average. Public sector pay in 1980/81 was just about at its normal historical relationship with private sector pay, since that was the year when the Clegg comparability awards were paid. As table 13 shows, private sector pay steadily outstripped public sector pay.[4] In fact, a gap of 10 per cent opened up over the years between 1980/81 and 1986/7. In 1988/9, it was widening again and was probably more than 9 per cent. Even if, as the Treasury argues, Clegg was too generous, it was not that generous. Indeed, the Government was beginning to pay for its determination not to have a regular comparability body settling public sector pay. In 1989, it suffered a wave of industrial unrest in combination with serious difficulties in filling some public sector posts.

The labour-intensive nature of much of public spending is one

Table 13. Public and private sector percentage pay rises, 1972–9

	Average earnings (whole economy)	*Private sector pay*	*Public services pay*	*Public services pay relative to average*
1972/3	13.6		9.7	−3.9
1973/4	12.5		9.2	−3.3
1974/5	23.1		22.4	−0.7
1975/6	23.8		27.7	3.9
1976/7	13.4		12.3	−1.1
1977/8	9.0		5.8	−3.2
1978/9	13.9		9.9	−4.0
1979/80	16.9		17.3	0.4
1980/1	19.4		23.5	4.1
1981/2	11.8		9.4	−2.4
1982/3	8.8	9.5	6.5	−2.3
1983/4	7.7	8.5	5.5	−2.2
1984/5	6.5	6.75	5.5	−2.2
1985/6	8.6	9.25	6.4	−2.2
1986/7	7.5	7.5	7.75	0.25
1987/8	8.2	7.0	9.0	0.8
1988/9	8.9		7.75	−1.15

Source: NIESR, *New Priorities in Public Spending*; *National Institute Economic Revue*, May 1988; *Department of Employment Gazette*

of the reasons why there has been, for most of the Thatcher years, a widespread perception of cuts despite the steady growth in the overall total of spending, measured in real terms to the taxpayer. Public sector pay rose by less than private sector pay, but it was still going up faster than the general rise in prices. Since pay was a large part of spending, that inevitably meant that the price of public spending was rising faster than the general inflation rate, so that apparent 'real' increases were often not real increases.

The second reason for the misperception was the dramatic shift in public expenditure priorities which occurred under Mrs Thatcher. The overall total went on rising, but some departments lost out while others did remarkably well from the change of regime. Britain honoured its commitment to increase defence spending in real terms by 3 per cent a year despite the widespread flaunting of the same commitment by other European NATO members. Even after a couple of years of squeeze at the end of the decade, defence was up in real terms by 17 per cent between 1978/9 and 1989/90. Home Office spending – on items like prisons, the police and law and order – soared by 63 per cent in real terms. One department also saw an unintended real increase due to spending on unemployment benefit and social security. Although benefits were raised by barely more than inflation, the sharp rise in unemployment in the 1979–81 recession left a legacy of bloated spending on benefits which carried way over into the nineties. Even in 1989/90, real spending on social security was up by 36 per cent.

Other programmes were squeezed or sharply cut to make way for these large increases, and in order to hold to the Government's modified policy of keeping the growth of spending below the growth rate of the economy so that spending as a share of GDP declined steadily from post-recession highs. Housing, for example, was down 79 per cent in real terms between 1978/9 and 1988/90. Other Department of Environment spending was down 13 per cent. The Department of Trade and Industry was spending 68 per cent less in real terms. And the budgets for health and education grew relatively slowly given the demands placed upon them.

From the Government's point of view, this pattern of public expenditure growth was politically unfortunate. The sharp rises took place in areas like defence which do not have a high public profile, unlike health and education. The sharp increases in law and order spending were in response to a growing crime problem, which was much more dominant in public perceptions than the measures the Government took to correct it. (When the crime wave did begin to abate at the turn of the decade, it was probably more due to the shrinkage of the number of young people – the most criminal element in any population – than to the Government's efforts.) And the rise in social security was largely involuntary, and something for which the Government hardly wanted to take credit.

Nevertheless, the varied fortunes of different departments during the eighties scotch the notion that Governments cannot control Whitehall. Ironically, one of the most popular television programmes of the period was *Yes, Minister*, in which politicians were depicted as the unwitting instruments of a manipulative civil service. The Government's success in holding down public spending testifies to the inaccuracy of the image. The question, after a decade of strict public expenditure control, is whether the Government really needs to obfuscate the issues by failing to supplement cash planning with other indicators. It would certainly be a mistake to abandon cash planning, but ministers can hardly expect an informed public debate if vital information about costs and prices is deliberately withheld.

Notes

1 Autumn Statement, November 1988 and Public Expenditure Analysis, January 1989.

2 See Joel Barnett, *Inside the Treasury* (London: Andre Deutsch, 1982) p. 78 on the introduction of cash limits.

3 See Ray Robinson and Ken Judge, *Public Expenditure and the NHS: Pay Prospects* (London: King's Fund Institute for Health Policy Analysis, 1987).

4 Chris Trinder in *National Institute Economic Review*, August 1987 and May 1988; successive issues of *Public Domain*, published by the Public Finance Foundation and Peat Marwick Maclintock.

5 The Economics of the Slump

Monetarism and other golden rules

Search for the grail

- the costs of monetarism
- monetarism defined
- the lack of a link between broad money and spending
- similar failings in narrow money
- drawbacks in a target for total money spending
- drawbacks in targeting the exchange rate
- the desirability of judgement

Economists only make a show of being dismal. In reality, they are romantic people, constantly hunting for some holy grail which will unlock the secrets of the complex beast they try to understand. The grail is a simple, golden rule which policy-makers can follow in order to avoid either inflation or recession. Economists have elevated in turn the gold standard, the money supply, the exchange rate and total money spending as the answer to all our ills. There will no doubt be more. At the inflationary end of the late eighties consumer boom, the times were propitious for another revival of an old favourite among the golden rules – monetarism.[1]

There is much more at stake than the arcana of monetary policy. The extended experiment in monetarism which was ushered in by Mrs Thatcher's election victory in 1979 had serious and unintended consequences (which are described in the next essay). The depth of the recession between 1979 and 1981 was in large part because monetary and fiscal policy were excessively tight, which in turn was a result of attempting (though failing) to hit targets for the money supply. Despite that failure, inflation came tumbling down. On two scores, monetarism was found wanting. First, the costs in lost output and jobs were far more grave than its adherents anticipated. Secondly, there was no apparent link between money growth and inflation.

The simplest starting point for the monetarist doctrine is the Fisher equation, named after the great American monetary economist.[2] This states that the stock of money (M) multiplied by the number of times each unit changes hands in a period (or velocity, V) equals total money spending in the economy. This is true by definition since V is calculated by dividing total money spending by the amount of money. Secondly, money spending is equal to the price level or average price of transactions (P) times the amount of output or transactions (T). This again is true by definition. We therefore have the incontrovertible proposition that $MV = PT$.

What defines a monetarist is that he, or she, goes on to assert three further ideas. First, the money supply can be determined by policy-makers: it is outside the system or 'exogenous'. Secondly, there is a stable and predictable relationship between the money supply and total money spending. In other words, V is predictable. It need not be constant. It may vary with interest rates or other variables, but it will be predictable. Thirdly, the monetarist argues that the level of output in the economy is in the long term determined by real factors such as human skills, the propensity to save and invest and so forth. It is not affected by monetary factors.

The corollary of the second and third premises is that one variable on each side of the Fisher equation is stable. This in turn means that any change in one of the other variables on either side – either M or P – must lead to similar changes in the other. If prices rise, then they will pull up money. If money rises, it will push up prices. Thus to control prices, the essential ingredient is to control money. For Professor Milton Friedman, who did so much to revive monetarism in the seventies and eighties, inflation is always and everywhere a monetary phenomenon in the sense that money growth actually causes inflation.[3]

This is roughly where the Conservatives had arrived in the spring of 1980, when the Government had just set four years' worth of declining monetary targets for the money supply as measured by sterling M3 (notes, coin and bank accounts). That summer, there was an explosion of M3 which should, if the theory was right, have led to an explosion of spending and inflation. But, far from accelerating, both total money spending and inflation began to slow down sharply. Nor was the historical evidence for a close link between money and inflation as strong as Friedman had supposed in his *Monetary History*.[4] Friedman never replied to a devastating critique of his work by two British econometricians, and which was sponsored by the Bank of England in 1983 (a sponsorship which did not endear it to the Government).[5]

Any measure of broad money – essentially credit money which includes deposits in banks and sometimes building societies – has been growing rapidly in most countries over the last ten years, mainly because of an increased preference for readily available cash – liquidity – as income rises and because of the willingness of a liberalized financial system to provide it. As figure 22 shows, broad money has grown exceptionally rapidly throughout the eighties. Anybody arguing for the setting of targets for a broad money indicator like M4 (which adds building society accounts to M3) must do so against this background of disappointment.

This is not to argue that money does not matter. Certainly, money matters. Certainly, credit money matters. The boom in the housing market between 1984 and 1988 showed all the signs of a credit-driven speculative bubble which needed pricking, and there were also signs at the end of 1987 that the sharp growth of demand and output was becoming unbalanced. There was too much domestic demand, and not enough effort going into exports. But it is one thing to say that money matters, and quite another to say that its relationship with either spending or inflation is stable enough to warrant setting a target for it. At no point in the late eighties did M4 accelerate so decisively that it provided a firm warning of overheating in the economy. For the record, the growth of M4 between the fourth quarters of 1983 and 1984 was 14 per cent; in 1985, 13 per cent; in 1986, 16 per cent; in 1987, 16 per cent; and in 1988, 15 per cent. Total money spending grew over the same periods by 6.6 per cent; 9.1 per cent; 7.2 per cent; 10.4 per cent and 10.3 per cent.

Indeed, one of the strongest advocates of broad money targets, Mr Tim Congdon, implicitly concedes the difficulties in setting them when he says: ‘First, institutional changes in

Figure 22

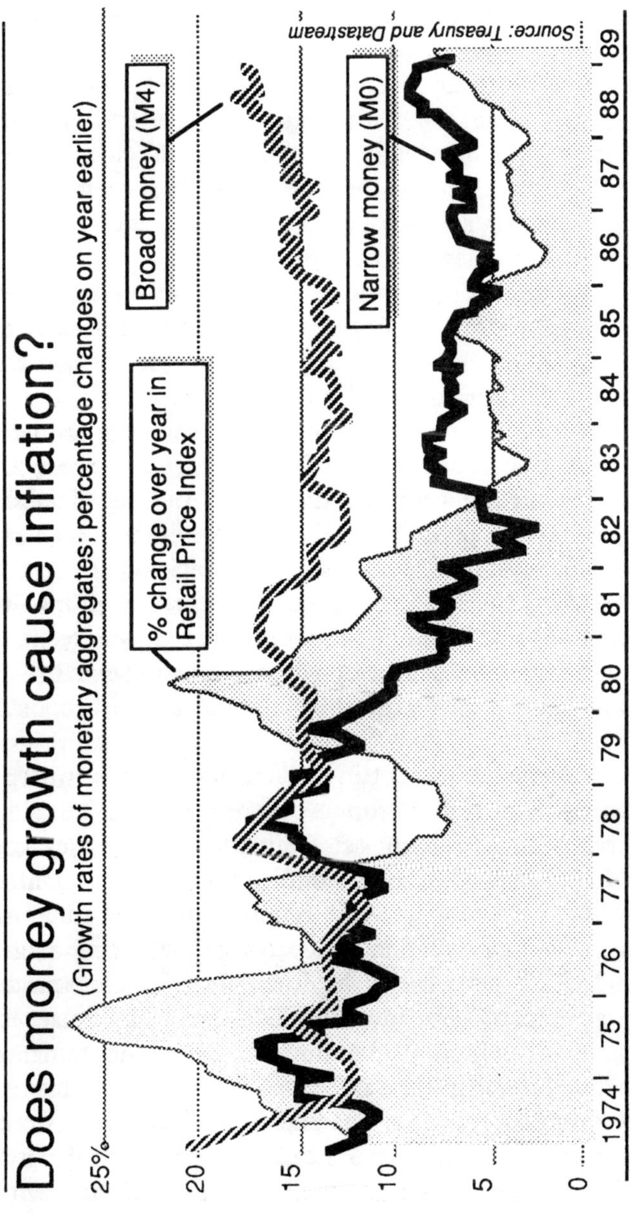
Does money growth cause inflation?
(Growth rates of monetary aggregates; percentage changes on year earlier)
25%
20
15
10
5
0
% change over year in Retail Price Index
Broad money (M4)
Narrow money (M0)
Source: Treasury and Datastream
1974
75
76
77
78
79
80
81
82
83
84
85
86
87
88
89

the financial system do not invalidate the setting of broad money targets. Instead, the right procedure is to calculate the probable effect of such changes on the demand for money and to adjust the target accordingly. Second, although it may be difficult to estimate how much any institutional change alters desired money balances, it is inconceivable that institutional change can cause the demand for money to become infinite.'[6] It seems that broad money is not such a golden rule after all, and that a certain exercise of judgement is required even here.

Nor is there a clear and predictable relationship between inflation and narrow money – M0 or notes, coin and bankers' cash held at the Bank of England, but excluding bank and building society accounts. Few of its proponents claim more than that M0 is a good guide to current spending in the shops. At best, it is regarded as an indicator of trends rather than the cause of monetary laxity or tightness. And the Treasury has still to publish a paper providing some evidence even for this. Narrow money failed, for example, to pick up the inflationary pressures which arose at the time of the first oil shock (whereas broad money had accelerated beforehand). So the reality is that there is no measure of money – either broad or narrow – which offers a stable and predictable relationship with spending or prices.

The experience of setting monetary targets was so disillusioning that some proponents retreated to an altogether more reasonable position: set targets for total money spending instead.[7] In that way, one would obviate the difficulties of a stable link with money while retaining the essential emphasis on the idea that inflation is always a phenomenon of excess demand. The practical difficulties, though, are scarcely less formidable than those involved in pursuing monetary targets. The figures for money spending – or gross domestic product in current prices (money GDP) – are currently published very nearly three months after the end of the quarter to which they refer, which is such a long time lag as to render them an unhelpful guide to policy. In fact, the Government currently sets targets for money GDP now (along with its targets for M0). However, it clearly takes very little notice of them. In the 1988 Budget, the Chancellor aimed at a growth of money spending of 7.5 per cent. The outturn was more like 11 per cent.

There are also theoretical difficulties. The first is that excess demand may leak out into imports without boosting money GDP, whose definition is total domestic spending plus exports minus imports. Yet any surge in imports, of the sort which occurred in 1988, eventually has to be corrected either by a period of very slow demand growth or by a sharp fall in the exchange rate which will boost import prices and inflation.

Why not, then, set a target for the growth of domestic demand in money terms? The first problem, although perhaps an unlikely one given the history of the British economy, is that it might be undermined by an unexpected rise in net exports which led to overheating of the economy.[8] The second and more realistic problem is that even a target for domestic demand presents problems if there is a sudden, external change in inflation such as an oil shock. There may also be a sudden surge in domestic inflation due to a misjudgement of demand policy, or due to some misperception in the labour market. Why should a pre-determined path be set for reducing that inflationary impetus, regardless of its size or its strength? In practice, policy-makers would simply overrule their targets, as the Chancellor increasingly has, or suffer an exceptionally severe recession in the mistaken cause of squeezing the growth of money demand back within its target, and reinforcing their anti-inflationary credibility.

The final candidate for the grail is the exchange rate, but full membership of the European Monetary System (or any other fixed but adjustable system of exchange rate parities) should allow for some flexibility. To rule out any exchange rate change, regardless of circumstances, merely in order to reinforce the Government's credibility in controlling inflation, seems perverse. It implies, for example, that the existence of any trade deficit should be tackled solely by restricting the growth of demand below its growth in other countries in order to curb imports and boost exports, without any help from a devaluation. Inevitably, the tradable sectors of an economy would bear the brunt of any anti-inflationary policy, which is objectionable on two grounds. First, it is inequitable since the half or more of the economy which cannot trade internationally bears no part of the disinflation. Secondly, it is likely to undermine the longer-term performance of the tradable sectors and hence limit the growth of demand and output which is consistent with maintaining broad balance on international payments.

The reality is that there are no simple rules which will work to guide economic policy in all likely and unlikely circumstances. Indeed, Professor Charles Goodhart has expounded a doctrine which states the pursuit of any monetary target will so alter its nature as to render it misleading for the purpose.[9] The doctrine can be widened to suggest that the pursuit of any target will tend to outlive its own usefulness and trap the unwary.

There is ultimately no substitute for the exercise of judgement. The politician may prefer to dress up the need for judgement in the guise of multiple targets – as in the case of the Conservatives' policy aims for M0 and money GDP, taking account of the exchange rate. But the reality is that multiple targets merely mean that discretion is required in choosing between them when they are in conflict. There is no real alternative to trusting to the instincts of the politicians who control the economy, and voting them out if they mismanage their role, as they have done in the past and will certainly do again.

Alternatively, like the Germans or the Americans, we can establish institutions like the Bundesbank and the Federal Reserve Board, shielded from overt political pressures, to exercise some of that discretion for us. There are dangers here too, in case the institution falls into the hands of Arthurian knights who are gripped by a seductive delusion. But what we cannot do – or rather should not do – is follow a simple rule and all go on holiday. It does not work.

Notes

1 See, for example, Tim Congdon, *Monetarism Lost and Why it Must be Regained*, Centre for Policy Studies, study no. 106 (London, 1989).

2 See Irving C. Fisher, *The Purchasing Power of Money* (New York: Macmillan, 1911).

3 The most famous summary of Friedman's monetary views is in his presidential address to the American Economic Association, 29 December

1967,'The Role of Monetary Policy', *American Economic Review*, no. 58 (March 1968), pp. 1–17.

4 Milton Friedman and Anna J. Schwartz, *Monetary Trends in the United States and the United Kingdom* (Chicago: University of Chicago Press for the National Bureau of Economic Research, 1982).

5 David F. Hendry and Neil R. Ericsson, *Assertion without Empirical Basis: an Econometric Appraisal of 'Monetary Trends . . . in the United Kingdom'* (London: Bank of England, 1983).

6 Congdon, op cit.

7 The best short case for this position is in Samuel Brittan *How to End the Monetarist Controversy*, Institute for Economic Affairs, Hobart Paper no. 90 (London: Institute for Economic Affairs, 2nd edn, 1982). It originates with James Meade in J.E. Meade, *Stagflation*, vol. 1: *Wage-fixing* and David Vines, Jan Maciejowski and James E. Meade, *Stagflation*, vol. 2: *Demand Management* (London: George Allen & Unwin, 1982).

8 A way of avoiding some of these objections, while preserving the essential idea of targets for money GDP, was put forward in Andrew Blake, Nicos Christodoulakis, James E. Meade, David Vines and Martin Weale, *Macro-economic Policy: Inflation, Wealth and the Exchange Rate* (London: Unwin Hyman, 1989); the authors advocate targets for the exchange rates and national wealth or savings.

9 Or more properly: 'Any observed statistical regularity will tend to collapse once pressure is placed upon it for control purposes.' See C.A.E. Goodhart, *Monetary Theory and Practice: the UK Experience* (London: Macmillan, 1984), p. 96.

Monetarism applied

The 1979–81 experiment

- the recession compared
- the hopes of the Conservatives
- world recession, North Sea oil and the trade unions
- differences with Healey policy
- the scissors of rising costs and collapsing demand
- the 1981 Budget and the 364 economists
- reasons for the upturn
- the gathering pace of pragmatism

The decisive economic event of recent years was the 1979–81 recession. It was such an extreme experience that it provided a wealth of information about how an economy reacts under acute stress. In a very real sense, it was an experiment in monetarism. Neither of the two economic schools of thought which had fought over the future of policy before 1979 was able to claim total victory. For the monetarists, there was no doubt that the costs of reducing inflation were far greater than they had supposed and that the role of the money supply was tenuous. The Keynesians, particularly the 364 economists who signed a protest about the 1981 Budget, had to accept that budgetary policy was of more limited influence than they had predicted. Out of the rubble of 1979–81 emerged a new economic modesty.

The costs of the monetarist experiment were exceptionally high. Unemployment doubled within three years, and went on rising steadily until July 1986, even with several convenient changes in the official definition of unemployment. Gross domestic product fell in absolute terms by 2.2 per cent in 1980 and by 1.1 per cent in 1981 despite the sharp growth of North Sea oil output. One sector in particular was hammered: manufacturing output fell by 18 per cent in real terms between the second quarter of 1979 and the first quarter of 1981. There had not been a similar collapse in industrial output since 1920–21. The overall scale of the recession dwarfed both 1929–31 and the recession in other industrial countries.

Such a disappointing outcome was far from Conservative thoughts in the run-up to the 1979 election. 'Of course,' Sir Geoffrey Howe, the then Shadow Chancellor, said 'we should not want to proceed in such a way as to produce what some people would call a dramatic short term recession.'[1] During the election campaign both Mrs Thatcher and Sir Geoffrey stressed that there was nothing inevitable about rising unemployment. 'We must make sure,' the future Prime Minister said 'that the next five years are not as bad as the last.' This was not cynicism. They genuinely believed that the costs of reducing inflation by monetary means would be small, as most British monetarists had argued.[2]

The extent to which the Government was taken unawares by the slump is shown by its own assumptions about unemployment, used to plan social security spending. The left hand column of Table 14 contains the publication dates of each set of assumptions, while the years to which the forecast refers

Table 14. How the Government's unemployment assumptions went wrong: forecast average adult unemployment in Britain for each financial year, 1979–84, excluding school leavers

	1979/80	*1980/1*	*1981/2*	*1982/3*	*1983/4*
Nov 79 Actuary's report	1.25	1.6			
Mar 80 White Paper	1.25	1.6	1.8	1.8	
Nov 80 Actuary's report		1.7	2.3		
Mar 81 White Paper		1.81	2.5	2.7	2.7
Dec 81 Actuary's report			2.6	2.9	
Mar 82 White Paper			2.6	2.9	
Actual unemployment	1.26	1.82	2.6	2.9	3.0

are shown along the top. Thus in March 1980, the public spending White Paper said that adult unemployment would reach 1.8 million in 1982/3. By the time of the 1982 White Paper, the forecast had been revised upwards to 2.9 million. By the standards of post-war economic history, an unexpected addition to unemployment of an extra 1.1 million people was a disaster.

The anatomy of the slump is inevitably complex, but some of the most common explanations of the time are clearly wrong. The role of the world recession, for example, was much exaggerated. Britain's industrial production began falling nearly a year before the fall in production in the Big Seven economies, while the OECD's figures also show that the world recession in most countries involved only a slowdown of growth from year to year, not the absolute drop experienced in Britain. Real GDP in the major seven (G7) industrial countries rose by 0.9 per cent in 1980 and by 1.7 per cent in 1981. Only in 1982 was there a small 0.7 per cent decline in G7 GDP, mainly due to the recession in the United States.

This poor relative output performance in Britain was particularly odd since many economists had expected it to perform better than most other countries. As an oil producer, Britain was not made poorer by rising oil prices in 1979. They merely redistributed income within Britain from oil consumers to oil producers – or rather to the Government which took some 90 per cent of any oil price increase in additional tax. The

Chancellor could have used the oil revenues to reduce VAT and hence counteract the effect on inflation of higher oil prices. That would also have handed back to consumers the spending power they lost in the oil price hike and would have supported demand and output.

This potential benefit was, it is true, offset by a disadvantage. The pound rose sharply because foreigners wanted to buy sterling rather than non-oil currencies like the German mark, which helped make our goods less competitive at home and abroad. But work at the Bank of England has suggested that this oil effect can only have been responsible for a small part of the rise in sterling.[3] After all, Norway's economy remained buoyant despite an even heavier dependence on North Sea oil. The Bank was too tactful to spell out the most likely culprit, which was excessively tight monetary policy.

Many people blamed the trade unions for the slump. Their restrictive practices and their attempts to raise living standards whether production was rising or not had certainly done much to damage Britain's economic performance over many years, but the trouble with explanations which relied on causes like the trade unions – or new technology or bad management – is that they failed to describe why these factors suddenly became sufficiently acute in 1979 to precipitate the worst recession for fifty years. All of them had been around for a long time.

So what did go wrong? The change in government policy in 1979 is still the most convincing culprit. An analysis by the National Institute for Economic and Social Research[4] concluded that by far the greatest part of the shortfall in national output between 1978 and 1980 was due to restrictive monetary and fiscal policies, either working directly to depress the domestic economy or working through an excessively strong pound. The NIESR was on the Keynesian side of the debate, but the analysis of the more monetarist economists at the London Business School was similar.

The monetarism of Mrs Thatcher and Sir Geoffrey Howe was qualitatively different from the policies of the previous Labour Chancellor, Mr Denis Healey. Certainly, Healey had set targets for the money supply, but he was essentially a sceptic who had been told to do so by the International Monetary Fund, and found it expedient to do so from the point of view of manipulating the financial markets and his own party's profligate tendencies. It was his incomes policy which did the counter-inflationary work by reducing business costs, and encouraging a slowing in prices. By contrast, the Conservatives believed that incomes policy was both harmful and unworkable – and they had the 1978/9 'winter of discontent' to back their case.

The Conservatives thought that strict control of the money supply (sterling M3 or notes, coin and bank accounts) would bring down inflation with only temporary losses of output and jobs. Tighter money would raise interest rates, and thereby make sterling more attractive to foreigners. The rise in the exchange rate would reduce the cost of imports, and inflation would come down as British companies tried to compete with cheaper foreign goods.

This squeeze on companies might, of course, prove to be a disaster. But an important part of the theory was that trade unions would rapidly see price rises slowing down, and would consequently slow down their wage demands. The temporary squeeze on profits would be alleviated quickly and the economy would once again enjoy growth with lower inflation. But if the Government's borrowing (or its own demand for savings) were to remain high while it was squeezing the money supply and attempting to control total spending in the economy, interest rates might rise excessively. Government borrowing would thus choke off or 'crowd out' private investment. So the Government was also pledged to cut its borrowing (the excess of spending over revenues, or the Public Sector Borrowing Requirement).

Monetarism was not the only part of the programme. To restore incentives, the Conservatives had also promised tax cuts, especially income tax cuts. And they had promised to honour the Clegg pay awards to public sector workers who had fallen behind during the Labour incomes policy. And they promised to increase defence spending. Tax cuts and more spending do not amount to less borrowing. It was a package that was just not going to add up.

The only way out was to make deep cuts in spending on areas other than defence or law and order, a task which the Cabinet found increasingly distasteful. So the Government tended to resort either to increased taxation or to 'spending cuts', which in fact involved increased prices – either nationalized industry prices, or health charges, or council rents and rates. It certainly helped to reduce the Government's borrowing but it was a funny way to fight inflation.

Sir Geoffrey Howe's first Budget was a case in point. To pay for his 3p cut in the basic income tax, he nearly doubled VAT. The inflation rate leapt in one month from 11.3 per cent to 15.8 per cent – and there was worse to come. OPEC's oil price rises were also feeding through. The private sector, which had been pent up in Labour's incomes policy, ignored the promises of lower inflation and tried to keep pace with prices. By the third quarter of 1980, earnings growth reached 22 per cent and inflation peaked at the same level.

Companies were caught between inexorably rising costs – which the monetarists had not predicted – and inexorably mounting financial pressures – which they had. Broadly, monetary policy becomes restrictive if the money supply is forced to grow more slowly than total spending in the economy (assuming in the short term that the link between the two remains stable). Over much of this period, the West German Bundesbank was aiming to get its money supply target no more than two percentage points below the growth of spending, so that its squeeze was never too tight. But the Chancellor had in 1979 already tightened his monetary target while rising inflation was pushing up money spending. With a nine-point gap between the two, his targets began to look draconian. Bank base rates went to the record level of 17 per cent in November 1979.

The pound should have fallen because Britain's costs were rising so much faster than those of our competitors. But record interest rates pushed sterling up. On the International Monetary Fund's measure of relative unit labour costs, Britain became 49 per cent less price competitive between 1978 and 1981 – a deterioration never before experienced by a developed country. With less sales revenue to pay rising debt charges, companies desperately cut orders to their suppliers and met their own orders from stocks rather than production. Output plummeted.

The 1980 Budget only accelerated the slump. The idea

behind the Medium Term Financial Strategy, which set monetary targets for four years ahead, was to reassure businesses and trade unions that inflation would abate, and help to change their behaviour. The Budget seems instead to have fostered the expectation that the recession would be long and deep. Investment was cut and companies did not follow their usual practice of hoarding labour while waiting for better times. By the end of 1980 unemployment was mounting by 100,000 a month.

Against this background, it is not hard to explain why the Government also began to miss its financial targets. There were unsightly bulges in credit and the money supply when the artificial 'corset' came off bank lending, but the ambitious nature of the targets was anyway a recipe for failure. The Government's chosen money supply measure (M3) wildly overshot the mark as loose cash poured into interest-paying accounts. There were also calls for a still tighter policy when the Chancellor exceeded his borrowing target for 1980/81 by nearly £5 billion. The Public Sector Borrowing Requirement (PSBR) – the gap between revenue and spending – is notoriously wayward, but this overshoot was anyway largely the consequence of recession rather than profligacy. Tax revenues were lower than expected while an extra 200,000 unemployed helped to push spending up. Indeed, the OECD has calculated that, after allowing for such tax and spending changes due to the cycle, the 1980 Budget raised taxes and cut spending by the equivalent of 2.8 per cent of potential output.[5]

The Chancellor was nevertheless determined to cut borrowing. His failure to persuade spending ministers of the need for more cuts meant that his only other option was to raise taxes. This he did in the famous 1981 Budget, which sparked a wave of protest, including a statement signed by 364 economists who predicted that present policies would 'deepen the depression'.[6] Taxes took a steadily higher proportion of national income. The taxes paid by a married couple with two children, earning three-quarters of average earnings, increased by more than a fifth between 1978/9 and 1981/2 after allowing for inflation. The economic effect was merely to compound what the monetary squeeze had begun. Tax increases take cash out of the economy and depress output. As the work of both the OECD and the NIESR has shown, the Chancellor's budgetary policy was deflationary in both 1980 and 1981. It postponed and damped down the natural upturn.

Nevertheless, the protestors underestimated the strength of three forces which were making for an upturn. First, the decline in inflation breathed some life into battered consumer confidence and spending. Secondly, companies had to meet more of their demand from output as their stock levels ran down. Thirdly, the Chancellor brought interest rates down by 2 percentage points to 12 per cent on the day of the Budget on 10 March. Fourthly, and most crucially, the pound was never to be as high again in trade-weighted terms. The pound averaged 99.7 on the effective index in March 1981 (1975 = 100). By the following March it had fallen to 90.8 and a year later it was 79.1. Without this easing in policy, the 364 economists may well have been vindicated. After all, bad slumps in the past had tended to lead to strong recoveries, while shallow recessions begat weak recoveries. We might therefore have expected a surge in output through 1981. But the recovery in industrial production a year after the May 1981 trough was only 1.6 per cent, compared with an average 6.9 per cent recovery in the year after the last five economic downturns.

In the face of the evidence of slow growth and an impending general election, pragmatism gathered pace. Sir Geoffrey Howe had promised never to change his monetary targets, but in March 1982 they were raised by no less than 3 percentage points. As the pound fell, the gain in price competitiveness in 1982 was 6 per cent, and in 1983 it was 8.5 per cent. The fiscal indicators suggested that budgetary policy relaxed in 1983. Unkindest cut of all, inflation fell despite the explosion of the money supply. The monetarist experiment was over, unmourned even by its adherents.

Notes

1 *The Times*, 3 August 1978.

2 For example, Professor Sir Terry Burns and Alan Budd argued in a paper to the House of Commons select committee in 1978 that a two-year strategy of reducing the growth of the money supply would involve relatively small costs in lost output. In evidence to the Commons Treasury committee

in 1980, Professor Milton Friedman said there would merely be a 'retardation of economic growth'.

3 'North Sea Oil and Gas: Costs and Benefits', *Bank of England Quarterly Bulletin*, vol. 22, no. 1 (March 1982).

4 *National Institute Economic Review*, November 1981.

5 Structural budget balances net of interest payments in Robert W.R. Price and Patrice Muller, 'Structural Budget Indicators and the Interpretation of Fiscal Policy Stance in OECD Economies', *OECD Economic Studies*, no. 3 (Autumn 1984), p. 56.

6 *The Guardian*, 30 March 1981.

A Budget for unemployment?

Assessing budgetary policy

- what computer models are
- why public spending boosts jobs more than tax cuts do
- the balanced budget multiplier
- limited potential of fiscal policy to cut unemployment
- targeted measures
- public investment as a counter-cyclical tool

You have money to 'give away' in the Budget. You have three million people who are unemployed, and the total is still rising. What is the best way of spending that money in order to bring the dole queues down? In other words, how powerful can fiscal policy be in reducing unemployment, and what type of fiscal measure would be most effective? This was the question that was at the heart of the policy debate in the mid-eighties, and which is still relevant at a time when unemployment remains relatively high by historical standards.

The only way of answering questions about the balance of macro-economic policy – interest rates, exchange rates, fiscal policy – is by looking at the results of a large econometric model of the whole economy. These encapsulate the research findings of the economic teams which build a representation or 'model' of the whole economy in the form of mathematical equations. The relationships between, say, rising incomes and rising spending, the level of the pound and exports, and the level of spare capacity and investment are all contained in the model, which can then be used to see how every aspect of the economy will react to a change. Models cannot provide definitive answers, but they can ensure that policy prescriptions are consistent, and they can give some indication of orders of magnitude and directions of change.

Britain's four leading computer models of the economy, including the Treasury's own, have in the past gone heavily against the Conservative view of the beneficence of tax cuts. All of them have traditionally come to the expected Keynesian result that a given increase in public spending is more effective in stimulating the economy than tax cuts costing the same amount. There are essentially two reasons for this result: first, none of the increase in public spending is saved, whereas some of the tax cut is saved by the people who benefit from it; secondly, very little of the increase in public spending goes on imports, whereas a sizeable proportion of the private spending stimulated by tax cuts flows out of the economy to foreign producers. Public spending thus has a higher 'multiplier' between the initial injection and the ultimate change in spending in the whole economy. This perception in turn leads to the so-called 'balanced budget multiplier', whereby a rise in taxes offset by an equivalent rise in public spending boosts economic activity despite broadly the same budget deficit or surplus.

A balanced budget increase in public spending would clearly boost the public sector more than the private. Carried to extremes, it would become a self-defeating exercise in which tax rates on the private sector were so high that it was choked off. Nevertheless, there is no evidence that Britain or any other major industrial economy is yet at the point where its public spending is so large and bloated that it has become a deadweight on the rest of the economy. Many types of public spending – on education and training, on roads and infrastructure, maybe even on health – are clearly complementary to private spending in the sense that they may encourage it. Research by Mancur Olson suggests that there is no relationship between overall growth and the size of public spending as we saw in the first essay.[1]

In any case, a decision on the relative merits of tax cuts or more public spending need not imply any overall change in the Government's strategy for holding down Government borrowing or for running a surplus. In 1984, for example, the Chancellor was predicting that he had £1.5 billion 'fiscal adjustment' to spend on higher public spending or lower taxes within his long-run targets for borrowing. In order to find out the effects of different courses of action at the time, the London Business School, the National Institute of Economics and Social Research and a modelling group called CISI-Wharton, which ran the Treasury model, participated in a comparison of the different effects. The Treasury model predicted that spending would create double the jobs of the same money spent on tax cuts; the National Institute said five times as many; the more monetarist London Business School said spending would create only 40 per cent more jobs.[2] Though the orders of magnitude were clearly different, the nature of the effects was unequivocal.

Ironically, though, the 1988 versions of both the London Business School and the National Institute models have changed in important respects. Table 15 sets out the results of the Warwick macro-economic modelling bureau's annual exercise comparing the properties of different models.[3] It shows, for example, the effect of income tax cuts costing £1 billion in the first year on inflation, unemployment, growth and the balance of payments in the second year. The table shows only the changes from what would otherwise happen: the method is to start off with a baseline forecast for the economy and then change policy in the direction given.

The latest comparison reveals two ironies, both of which underscore the fragility of using such model results. The first irony is that the NIESR, the most Keynesian of the groups, has become less Keynesian than the others: it finds that tax cuts are more stimulative than spending. This is a quirky result due to the very sharp boost which the private sector receives from the fall in the exchange rate which the NIESR model suggests is a result of tax cuts. The other three models very firmly suggest that public spending continues to be a more effective vehicle for reducing unemployment than tax cuts.

There is a second irony, for the comparison also shows that the traditionally monetarist London Business School model now points firmly to public spending as the best option for reducing

Table 15. Four views of Budget options: estimates of the effect on the economy after two years of £1bn worth of income tax cuts, public spending or cuts in employers' National Insurance contributions

	Tax cuts	*Public spending*	*NICs*
The Treasury view			
GDP	+0.22%	+0.48%	+0.27%
Inflation	+0.02%	+0.46%	−0.62%
Unemployment	−41,000	−98,000	−50,000
Current Account	−£658m	−£974m	−£458m
The Bank of England view			
GDP	+0.10%	+0.43%	+0.18%
Inflation	−0.28%	+0.18%	−0.52%
Unemployment	−8,000	−27,000	−12,000
Current Account	−£594m	−£499m	−£782m
The NIESR view			
GDP	+0.66%	+0.55%	+0.38%
Inflation	+0.55%	+0.49%	−0.50%
Unemployment	−59,000	−56,000	−53,000
Current Account	−£851m	−£752m	−£887m
The LBS view			
GDP	+0.40%	+0.80%	+0.13%
Inflation	+0.68%	+0.60%	+0.36%
Unemployment	−19,000	−130,000	−37,000
Current Account	−£941m	−£1,638m	−£19m

Source: Derived from *National Institute Economic Review*, August 1988

unemployment. Previously it had found that cuts in employer's National Insurance contributions were more effective because of a powerful influence whereby a fall in wage costs boosts demand for labour.

The results in table 15 must, of course, be interpreted with caution. No Government is in reality interested in only one economic objective: it tries to keep several balls in the air at the same time. And one of the most interesting features of the table is the way in which both the Treasury and the Bank of England models predict that tax cuts will have hardly any effect on inflation, in strong contrast to public spending. If this were actually true, it would be a strong argument for much larger tax cuts, providing that the resulting deterioration in the balance of payments could be staunched. However, this finding results from the belief that people reduce their wage demands (and hence business costs and prices) if they receive increases in take-home pay from tax cuts. The statistical evidence for this effect is very slim.[4]

Mr Nigel Lawson, when Chancellor, was always sceptical of economic forecasters, and of the results of economic models, even though he was a voracious consumer of their output. One of the conclusions that the Government drew from the computer model comparisons in the mid-eighties was the opposite of that being urged on them by their critics. Although the evidence of the models contested the Government's views about the relative merits of tax cuts or public spending, it also lowered expectations of what could be done. The model runs showed that, once Britain had arrived in the situation it found itself in after the 1979–81 recession, any likely shift in the traditional macro-economic levers was not going to lead to a substantial difference in the outcome for unemployment, and might endanger the prospect of stable inflation. It was simply not possible to run the history of the 1979–81 recession in reverse.

The model runs continue to suggest that any decisive improvement in economic performance cannot be achieved merely by twiddling the knobs better than the present incumbents. For example, an attempt to reduce unemployment by a million (which would not be far out of line with where it was in 1979) by means of increasing public spending would increase the balance of payments deficit by more than £12 billion even on the most favourable view of its effects. All this tells us is that it cannot be done: no Government would intentionally introduce a policy that would worsen the payments gap to such an extent, as it would almost certainly face a sterling crisis within eighteen months. Any real improvement in economic performance has to be bought by changes in the long-run relationships within the economy (such as the improvement of skill training) or by measures very specifically targeted at particular problems.

Professor Richard Layard, for example, has argued that the Chancellor could spend much more money directly on useful public works to absorb the long-term unemployed, and bring them back into the labour force.[5] The net cost per job created in this way is less than £4,000 after allowing for savings in benefits.

The sort of sums the Government has been prepared to spend on a 1p cut in the basic rate of income tax would have provided jobs for a quarter of a million people as a first impact effect alone. The inflationary effect of reducing the long-term unemployed is negligible because the economic evidence suggests that they have no effect on the labour market. It is the people who have been unemployed for only a short period of time who are attractive to employers, and who act as serious competition to those in work, and hence curb their pay aspirations.

The only remaining inflationary effect might arise from an increase in total spending power in an economy short of plant and equipment. The traditional answer to any such problem, in the short term, would be a rise in taxes. Since a rise in taxes of £24,000 a year causes only one extra person to become unemployed, it follows that around six jobs can be created for the long-term unemployed at the cost of each job lost elsewhere, without any increase in borrowing. Since the amounts of money involved are, by the Government's standards, relatively small, there is a strong case for including such targeted job measures in any overall package for the economy. The political snag is that the option involves tax increases, which have been off the agenda since Mr Walter Mondale lost to President Reagan by promising to be responsible in cutting the US deficit. And secondly it does not foster what the Prime Minister calls 'real jobs'.

If there is spare capacity and unemployment in an economy, there is a lot to be said for the old stand-by of public investment as a stabilization policy. There has anyway been a case for the better part of a decade for doing more about Britain's decaying capital infrastructure, as a National Economic Development Office report on this subject pointed out.[6] It estimated the maintenance backlog alone at £2 billion for hospitals and £5 billion for public housing. What this actually meant was that hospitals were not being painted as often as they should have been for hygiene reasons; lifts were not being replaced even when at the end of their normal life; the lintels and window frames of public buildings were rotting.

Spending on building and maintaining public assets is not a substitute for private output or spending; as the Confederation of British Industry has repeatedly pointed out, the extension of the road network helps to reduce their costs (which is perhaps one reason why the road programme received a fillip in the eighties). Public investment is often complementary to private output and spending. Public investment also leaves you with an asset which provides real economic and social returns for years to come. As a counter-cyclical device to relieve the depths of recession, public investment has two advantages. The first is that the spending is limited to the period of construction, so that you do not continue with a higher level of spending or a lower level of taxes beyond the period when it may be appropriate. Secondly, construction prices are relatively low in slumps – and extremely high in booms. The public sector gets much more for its money if it buys when the private sector does not want to.

In short, the Chancellor's reluctance to increase public borrowing during the years of recession looks curious – rather as if a business tried to steer itself merely by looking at its cash flow. Any sensible entrepreneur also takes a squint or two at his balance sheet from time to time. Certainly, there is debt on one side. But there are also assets on the other. Indeed the assets were increasing in value very sharply even in the early eighties, merely because of the rise in property prices. As long as there is something worthwhile to show for the Government's finance, it surely makes sense to undertake extra work at times of slack.

Notes

1 Mancur Olson, lecture at the London School of Economics, 25 October 1988 (mimeo). See also Olson, *The Rise and Decline of Nations* (New Haven: University of Yale Press, 1982).

2 *The Guardian*, 13 December 1984.

3 P.G. Fisher *et al.*,'Comparative Properties of Models of the UK Economy', *National Institute Economic Review*, no. 125 (August 1988).

4 D.S. Turner, K.F. Wallis and J.D. Whitley, *Explaining and Resolving Differences in the Properties of Large-scale Macro-econometric Models*, ESRC Macroeconomic Modelling Bureau discussion paper no. 15 (Warwick University, 1988).

5 Richard Layard, *How to Beat Unemployment* (Oxford, 1986), pp. 96–112.

6 *Investment in the Public Sector Built Infrastructure*, (London: National Economic Development Office, 1985).

The U-turns of Nigel Lawson

Lawsonian virtues, including inconsistency

- early Treasury days as a true believer
- father of the Tax and Price Index and the Medium Term Financial Strategy
- the easing of spending policy
- the gathering boom

At the time of his startling resignation in October 1989, Mr Nigel Lawson had just celebrated his sixth anniversary as Chancellor, the longest-serving incumbent of number 11 since Mr David Lloyd George. Rarely can a Chancellor have had such a ride on the switchback of public esteem. In the wake of his 1984 corporation tax reforms he was hailed as the great tax-reforming Chancellor whose ingenuity knew few bounds. At the beginning of 1985, Mr Lawson's stock was plummeting as sterling fell and interest rates rose by 3.5 percentage points in a fortnight. Saved by the fall in oil prices and a gathering boom, Mr Lawson entered 1987 as a miracle worker only to be garlanded by his party for the election victory in June of that year. A year later, beset by rising inflation and a soaring balance of payments deficit, Mr Lawson's reputation was taking another dive.

These wild swings were as much testament to the state of the economy as to Mr Lawson's private virtues, which were numerous. He was sharp, intelligent, funny, robust and, in the main, liked by his officials. He had two particular traits which made him eminently suitable to the Treasury. First, he was naturally at home with the workings of the economy, in a way that his predecessor Sir Geoffrey Howe never was. Secondly, he had a sceptical sense of holding the ring in the centre of Government, never kowtowing to special interest groups. Like Mr Denis Healey, his Labour predecessor from 1974 to 1979, Mr Lawson was an intellectual who was temperamentally independent of factions within his party. Neither man succeeded in building up a following on his back benches.

During the periodic bouts of popularity, Mr Lawson's hagiographers sought to portray him as the consistent architect of the 'economic transformation' – his words – or 'miracle' – theirs – of the Thatcher years. And it was true that Mr Lawson had been at the Treasury solidly since 1979, with the exception of a couple of years as Energy Minister between 1981 and 1983. Nevertheless, the accusation of consistency, never a political virtue, was grossly unfair. Mr Lawson's successes, such as they undoubtedly were, came from his ability to jettison old beliefs and pinch those of his rivals, rather than any dogged cussedness in defending the principles with which he first set out. His friends would call this the mark of the true intellectual.

Back in 1979, when Mr Lawson was the Financial Secretary to Sir Geoffrey Howe's Treasury, he was not just any old hanger-on of the monetarist group with which Mrs Thatcher and Sir Keith Joseph had surrounded themselves. He was one of the most intelligent and articulate of all the 'true believers'. Mr Lawson was the spur on the flank of Sir Geoffrey, egging him on, not merely to set monetary targets for the control of inflation one year ahead, but for four. After all, Mr Healey had set annual targets. The Conservatives had to establish that they really meant to control inflation. It was crucial to set the Government's intentions in concrete so that no one should be mistaken, and the inflationary expectations of wage bargainers would thereby be lowered.

In other words, Mr Lawson was at the 'rational expectations' end of the monetarist school which had captured the Treasury, which is to say that he was as far removed from being a world-weary pragmatist as it is decently possible for the democratically elected Conservative MP to be. It was the Financial Secretary who, in numerous private briefings with journalists in his dark office at the centre of the Treasury chambers, poured scorn on the Treasury forecasters' prediction of a deep recession. The adjustment to the free-market golden age would happen far more painlessly than that. The trade unions, like company managers, would recognize that the Government meant business and curb pay awards. As costs decelerated, the curb on total money spending would become less sharp and growth could resume.

In line with this somewhat optimistic view of the British labour market was Mr Lawson's belief that wage-bargainers could not be so foolish as to misunderstand that when VAT nearly doubled, they did not need to raise their pay demands, because the Government was providing an offsetting cut of 3p in the basic rate. Indeed, just to ensure that there could be no misperception, the Financial Secretary pushed a reluctant Central Statistical Office into producing a new statistical series called the Tax and Price Index, designed to measure the rise in gross pay needed to maintain living standards constant after price rises and tax changes. It performed as expected until the March 1980 Budget, when for several years it began to show faster rises than the generally accepted inflation rate. It was an early example of Mr Lawson being, in that uniquely English phrase which the French cannot understand, too clever by half.

In the first Medium Term Financial Strategy (MTFS), which Mr Lawson can claim above all other ministerial hands as his own, a declining path for the monetary aggregate of sterling M3 was clearly laid out. It was to fall from a rate of growth of 7–11 per cent in 1980/81 to 4–8 per cent by 1983/4 in four easy stages. Mr Lawson was clearly influenced in setting out these ranges by a repeated refrain of Milton Friedman that monetary rules were crucial, and that political discretion should be banished since it had led to all the inflationary stagnation of the seventies. Politicians were not to be trusted: monetary rules would serve to lash them to the helm so that they could avoid the sweet calls of the Sirens luring them on to the rocks.

True, there was the tiniest footnote in the 1980/81 Red Book, in type half the size of the main text, which said that the way in which the money supply is defined for target purposes may need to be adjusted from time to time as circumstances change. But the main thrust was up there in full-size type, pinning ministers to the mast: 'To maintain a progressive reduction in monetary growth in these circumstances, it may be necessary to change policy in ways not reflected in the above projections. The Government would face a number of options for policy changes to achieve this aim, including changes in interest rates, taxes and public expenditure. But there would be no question of departing from the money supply policy, which is essential to the success of any anti-inflationary strategy.'[1]

Defending that policy, Mr Lawson said in May 1980 that, unlike previous attempts at indicative planning, the MTFS was based not on targets for the economy, but on targets for the Government. 'Not on what we can't control, but on what we can,' he said.[2] He poured scorn on the idea that the exchange rate could be controlled: 'You cannot fine tune your exchange rate by this (exchange controls) or any other means.' In other words, Mr Lawson was a straightforward monetarist who believed in controlling the domestic monetary aggregates and leaving the exchange rate up to the market place. International co-operation was unnecessary since the market itself would send out the right signals through prices for each currency.

Through 1980 Mr Lawson's confidence in the ability of the Government to control the money supply took a battering. Sterling M3 grew by 20 per cent. But there were special factors, he said. We know this because, unusually for a junior Treasury minister, he put it into a long and thoughtful speech at Zurich in January 1981 which was meant to make his reputation, and did. It was typical of Mr Lawson that he did not show his lecture to the Chancellor before he gave it, and typical that when he became Chancellor he explicitly forbade junior ministers to give speeches without his prior approval. In Zurich Mr Lawson said that monetary conditions had not been inflationary so far (despite the sharp growth of sterling M3 in 1980) but that 'it is essential from now on to secure a lower rate of growth of broad money, and indeed, over the three remaining years of the MTFS it might well be prudent to claw back at least some of the excess growth that has already occurred.'

There could be no question of departing from the money supply target. 'The heart of our economic policy is the Government's published and indeed quantified Medium Term Financial Strategy, the core of which is a steady deceleration in the rate of monetary growth over a four year period, buttressed by a gradual reduction in the size of the underlying budget deficit, which in turn is to be achieved by a steady reduction in the real level of total government spending.' It was on this commitment to sterling M3 that the pound was driven up, and a fifth of manufacturing output sacrificed on the anvil of lost competitiveness and high interest rates.

By the end of 1982 it was evident to Treasury ministers that not all was going according to plan. The recession had been deeper than even the Treasury forecasters predicted. The Government's popularity had yet to be salvaged by the Falklands. Inflation was still higher than when Mrs Thatcher took office. First to go were the monetary targets. The ranges for sterling M3 were raised by 3 percentage points in the 1982 Budget, and suspended entirely in 1985. The original MTFS would have allowed a maximum 43 per cent growth in sterling M3 over the four-year period: the actual growth was nearly 70 per cent. Yet, oddly enough, inflation began to fall.

Next to go was the commitment to lower public spending in real terms. Initially, the Government simply became unpopular by cutting all the sensitive bits, like health and education, in order to make room for the growing bits, such as defence and unemployment benefit. Then it admitted that the aim was to hold the total constant. Then the aim was merely to reduce it as a share of (growing) national income. After the initial, sharp tightening of budgetary policy between 1979 and 1981, there was a marked loosening of policy.

The size of the Public Sector Borrowing Requirement is a poor indicator of tax and spending decisions and budgetary ease, because it is distorted by asset sales (which count as negative spending), and even more importantly it is affected by economic activity. The budget deficit naturally rises in recessions (as unemployment benefit rises, and tax revenues fall) and falls or even becomes a surplus in booms. If allowance is made for these cyclical effects, the OECD measures of fiscal stance show a sharp tightening of policy between 1978 and 1981 of 6.5 per cent of potential national income, followed by a loosening of 2.6 per cent between 1981 and 1984.[3] On the OECD's measures, half of Mr Lawson's six Budgets as Chancellor were expansionary.[4]

Mr Lawson, though, saved his major relaxation for monetary policy. In the years of his chancellorship, Mr Lawson smiled benignly on the lending boom which had been unleashed by the 1980 financial market liberalization and which was now given free rein by the abandonment of broad money targets. Mr Lawson also gradually shed his free-floating ideas for the exchange rate. When he became Chancellor, the pound was allowed to fall gently from its 1980 peaks, but the fall became too much of a good thing. As William Keegan has pointed out, the searing experience of the January 1985 sterling crisis was a major influence on the Chancellor, who henceforth displayed considerable interest in using the European Monetary System to fix the level of the exchange rate which he thought appropriate. This did not necessarily imply a strong exchange rate. Mr Lawson again allowed a sharp fall in the pound in 1986 in order to boost manufacturing industry in the wake of the oil price fall.

In reality, Mr Lawson ditched his rule-monetarism in favour of a pragmatic economic policy which looked much more like old-fashioned right-wing or neo-classical Keynesianism (with the exception, perhaps, of a blind spot about tax increases). His attempts to target the exchange rate were the cause of many of his ructions with the free-floating Prime Minister. Indeed, he had the temerity to propose at the International Monetary Fund annual meetings in the autumn of 1987 that the world should move to a system of 'more managed exchange rates'. Far from being uncontrollable, he kept the pound within European Monetary System bands of 2.25 per cent from February 1987 to March 1988. Indeed, in the 1987 Budget Mr Lawson stopped even pretending to target broad money. The only target that remained was for M0, nicknamed 'little M0' by the financial analysts who disparaged its disciplinary qualities.

Please, please, hagiographers, praise Mr Lawson for his true virtues, and think with Emerson: 'A foolish consistency is the hobgoblin of little minds, adored by little statesman and philosophers and divines. ... speak what you think to-day in words as hard as cannon balls, and to-morrow speak what to-morrow thinks in hard words again, though it contradict every thing you said to-day.'

Notes

1 Financial Statement and Budget Report, March 1980.

2 See David Smith, *The Rise and Fall of Monetarism* (Harmondsworth: Penguin, 1987).

3 *OECD Economic Studies*, no. 3 (Autumn 1984), p. 58. Inflation adjusted trend structural budget balances.

4 *OECD Economic Outlook*, nos. 40, 43.

5 William Keegan, *Mr Lawson's Gamble* (London: John Curtis and Hodder & Stoughton, 1989), pp. 156–7.

6 Explaining the Boom

Britain's productivity improvement

The importance of productivity growth

- the particular benefit of manufacturing productivity growth
- the key sector in enabling others to grow
- Britain's productivity record has improved since the seventies
- international comparisons
- the role of trade unions
- the influence of recession

One of the best leading indicators of good output performance in an economy is the sustained growth of output per person – productivity. Higher productivity growth means that businesses can afford to pay more (or earn more in profit) without raising the prices of their products. In other words, higher productivity growth means a lower growth of wage costs per unit of output (or unit wage costs), which is a reasonable approximation of domestically generated inflation. It thus enables the whole economy to grow more rapidly for any given inflation rate. However, there is an additional bonus from the improvement in Britain's productivity performance, because it appears, ironically, to be concentrated in the manufacturing sector which was for so long the Cinderella of the Thatcherite revolution.

Manufacturing is a reasonable proxy for those sectors of the economy that are more open to foreign trade, and a higher long-term rate of manufacturing productivity growth means a lower annual growth of unit wage costs and greater price competitiveness. It helps to alleviate the 'balance of payments constraint' whereby the growing domestic demand which is needed to boost jobs in services is stalled because it also boosts imports and widens the trade deficit. The tradable sectors of

Figure 23

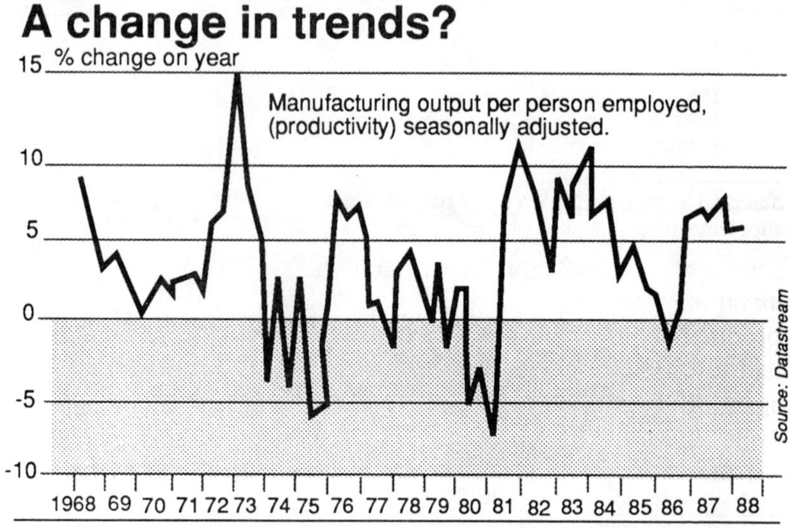

the economy are the key to growth and falling unemployment. They may not create many net jobs themselves. Manufacturing employment merely stabilized, even when manufacturing output was growing at an annual rate of more than 6 per cent. When the growth rate subsided a little in 1989, manufacturing employment began dropping again. Nevertheless, the tradable sectors set the conditions for the demand growth which allows jobs elsewhere.

A study by Professor David Metcalf, who has advised the Labour front bench and has no Thatcherite axes to grind, concludes that 'in the last seven years labour productivity growth in manufacturing has averaged almost 6 per cent a year, more than double the rate achieved in the previous 20 years. The reformation in industrial relations is paramount in explaining this transformation in economic performance. The climate of industrial relations has been altered by fear, competition and decentralization of collective bargaining.'[1]

The figures are telling (table 16). Output per person in manufacturing grew by 3.6 per cent a year between 1961 and 1973; by 0.7 per cent a year between 1973 and 1979; and by 4.2 per cent a year between 1979 and 1988.[2] This comparison may overstate the contrast between the 1970s and 1980s because the

Table 16. UK productivity growth, 1961–88 (annual percentage change in output per person employed)

	Manufacturing	*Whole economy*
1961–73	3.6	2.6
1973–79	0.7	1.1
1979–88	4.3	2.1

Source: Derived from Metcalf until 1979, and *Economic Trends*, 1988 annual supplement and September 1989

annus mirabilis of the Barber boom in 1973 – with 8.7 per cent productivity growth – is not included. It is arguable that industry had to catch its breath thereafter before it could move forward again. But even if the Barber boom is counted in the 1970s cycle, the productivity growth rate only goes up to an average 2.1 per cent. There is a clear improvement between the seventies and the eighties, and a small improvement compared with the sixties. Moreover, these comparisons are fair: they take the whole cycle from peak to peak rather than an arbitrary decade. The reason the Conservative Party propaganda uses decades as a basis of comparison is because output hit rock bottom in 1980. Comparisons which start in that year unfairly calculate growth rates from a trough to a peak.

The performance of manufacturing productivity has not only improved compared with our past history, but also compared with other countries. A National Economic Development Office paper pointed out that manufacturing productivity growth in Britain between 1979 and 1985 was 20.4 per cent, compared with 18 per cent in Japan, 12 per cent in West Germany, 7.8 per cent in the United States, and 3–4 per cent in France and Italy.[3] That relative productivity gain meant that Britain gained price competitiveness against West Germany in 1986 and 1987, despite an increase in annual earnings 3 per cent higher than in Germany.

A fully fledged international comparison from the OECD also shows that Britain's relative performance has improved markedly (table 17).[4] It looks at the whole business sector – the whole economy except general government – and finds that Britain's output per person grew by 0.5 per cent a year more than

Table 17. UK and OECD business productivity growth, 1960–86 (average percentage changes of labour productivity in business sector)

	UK	*OECD*
1960–73	3.3	4.1
1973–79	1.3	1.6
1979–86	1.9	1.4

Source: OECD Economic Studies

the developed country average between 1979 and 1986, compared with a shortfall of 0.8 per cent a year between 1960 and 1973 and of 0.3 per cent a year between 1973 and 1979.

However, in absolute terms the OECD study finds Britain's performance less impressive. Annual productivity growth still slowed from an average 3.3 per cent between 1960 and 1973 to 1.9 per cent between 1979 and 1986, reflecting a particularly sharp slowdown in services productivity growth. (This is in line with the Government figures for output per employed person in the whole economy, which show 2.6 per cent annual growth between 1961 and 1973, 1.1 per cent over the cycle to 1979, and 2.1 per cent since.)

The facts, therefore, suggest that Britain's absolute and relative performance has improved in manufacturing. However, slower productivity growth in the rest of the economy – private services like restaurants, retailing and so forth – means that productivity in the business sector or the whole economy has only improved relatively to other countries. It is still slower than it was during the long post-war boom. Nevertheless, this is an important achievement, not least because of the key rôle of tradable manufacturing.

Finding cast-iron explanations for why the improvement has come about is more difficult, but it is crucial in determining whether it is likely to last and therefore what the longer-term effects on output and living standards are likely to be. Early sceptics of the shake-out in manufacturing pointed to the so-called 'batting average' effect, whereby you improve the team's batting average by dropping the tail-end, low-scoring batsmen. The theory was that the plant closures of 1979–81 eliminated the low-scoring factories and hence raised the average level of output per person. It also raised the average growth from year to year, because the factories with higher productivity were also the factories with faster-growing productivity. Since you were really trying to maximize the score, there was little point in concentrating on the batting average.

However, some evidence suggests that many of the plants that were closed were larger ones, with relatively high productivity. The high interest rate, high pound regime culled companies which traded a lot and were highly geared. It did not necessarily cull the least efficient. Nor does the 'microchip' theory help to explain Britain's relative improvement, since microchips are available to our competitors too. Cyclical effects may explain part: output per person varies even more rapidly than output because some element of employment is fixed as an overhead. Subcontracting from manufacturing may also have boosted output per head. It is a freak of the figures that if a manufacturing company employs canteen staff, they are counted as manufacturing employees. If the canteen is then hived off to a contractor who does nothing else, they will be reclassified as services staff and will almost certainly boost the apparent output per person of the manufacturing company since canteens are labour-intensive, relatively unmechanized and have low labour productivity. The same applies to cleaning services.

The most popular explanation, and the one which implies that the trend may have shifted permanently, is the undoubted change in the climate of industrial relations as unemployment has soared. There is some evidence that people are working harder. The OECD study also implies that Britain has become relatively more efficient in using capital equipment. Demarcation lines and restrictive practices may be breaking down. The influence of the Government's trade union legislation is more difficult to pin down. The reforms have probably been important in undermining union resistance to change, and the fact that productivity growth has been higher in unionized sectors supports this. However, the union legislation may have been much less influential in shifting the balance of power to employers than high unemployment. Certainly, pay rises did not slow down as much as might have been expected, and the excess of trade union over non-union wages has grown a little in the Thatcher years. This 'union mark-up' rose from an average 26 per cent between 1974 and 1979 to an average 28 per cent between 1980 and 1987.[5] Only in 1986 and 1987, when skill shortages were beginning to bite and employers had to bid up wages to get the people they wanted, did the union mark-up diminish.

The facts are thus still in search of conclusive explanations, but it seems plausible that the shock of the 1979–81 recession galvanized many British companies into making changes that had been postponed for years. This was true of union and non-union companies, and it was particularly true in manufacturing, because the recession hit that sector hardest due to the overvaluation of sterling. Indeed, the recession became almost the perfect example of the sort of shock that Mancur Olson believes acts as an antidote to the steady encroachment of organized interests in a politically stable society.

Professor Olson argues that twentieth-century Britain has been a prime example of a society grown institutionally arthritic through the gradual accretion of power by coalitions of organized producer interests, whether trade unions or big business.[6] 'Most distributional coalitions, whether cartelistic or oriented to the lobbies of power, are harmful on balance to efficiency and growth,' he says. 'One reason is that organizations that try to raise prices or wages through collective action can only do this by restricting entry into the industry or occupation they control, and these barriers to the mobility of resources greatly reduce the speed at which an economy can adapt to changing demands and new technologies. Another is that the special interest legislation sought by lobbies encourages resources to move into areas in which (though privately profitable) the resources produce less value to society.'

The advantage of Olson's theory of sclerosis in politically stable societies is that it explains why Japan, West Germany and Italy succeeded after the war had shaken their institutions and why the victorious United States and Britain did not. Olson himself will not be drawn on whether the 1979–81 recession in Britain was a similarly cathartic event, but it is quite possible that history will show that it was. At the time, with unemployment rising at one point by 100,000 a month, there was little doubt how grave the crisis seemed. Whole managements and work-forces were made redundant.

Having a periodic crisis or having institutional arrangements which guard against interest group power may be a necessary condition of a dynamic economy, but they are certainly not a sufficient condition. A competing theory of why there was an improvement in Britain's performance in the eighties is being developed in a forthcoming book by Professor Leslie Hannah, and it is that Mrs Thatcher began to reap the rewards of the investment in higher education made in the sixties, together with other long-run changes in business structure. Indeed, it is the quality and even more importantly the quantity of Britain's inadequate education, training and research and development that induce the most scepticism about whether Britain can sustain the relative improvement achieved in the eighties.

Notes

1 David Metcalf, *Water Notes Dry Up*, Centre for Labour Economics, discussion paper no. 314 (London School of Economics, 1988).

2 Since these figures are subject to revision, it is worth noting the date of the estimates: index numbers for 1984 to 1988 are from *Economic Trends*, no. 425 (March 1989) and for 1980 to 1984 from *Economic Trends*, 1988 annual supplement.

3 *Pay and Productivity in the UK* (London: National Economic Development Council, 1988).

4 A. Steven Englander and Axel Mittelstadt, 'Total Factor Productivity: Macroeconomic and Structural Aspects of the Slowdown', *OECD Economic Studies*, no. 10 (Spring 1988).

5 These figures are calculated from table 29b of Richard Layard and Stephen Nickell, *The Thatcher Miracle?*, Centre for Labour Economics, discussion paper no. 343, (London School of Economics, March 1989).

6 Public lecture at the London School of Economics, 25 October 1988 (mimeo), but more substantially see *The Rise and Decline of Nations* (New Haven: University of Yale Press, 1982).

Dealing with the credit boom

The scale of the credit boom

- the beginnings of liberalization of credit
- some long run factors behind the demand for borrowing
- the proportion of younger people rising
- higher growth of incomes made it rational to borrow
- primary cause: the housing market
- reasons for house price rise
- interest rates a weak weapon against a price bubble
- case for credit guidance

The key to understanding the Lawson boom is understanding debt. The economy was lifted by a balloon of personal credit which expanded from a mere £90.5 billion at the end of 1980 to more than £328 billion in 1988.[1] This extraordinary explosion of lending became, after the growth of personal incomes, the greatest single motor behind the buoyant growth of consumers' spending, which in turn was the driving force behind the five years of high economic growth from 1984 to 1989. The credit boom ushered in a society built on the values which the leader of the Opposition criticized as those of the 'me and now'. It rescued the Government from the consequences of sharply reducing its own budget deficit by ensuring that the personal sector took up the slack by spending more. It floated the Conservatives to re-election in 1987. Britain came a long way from the Victorian values of scrimp, thrift and save.

Most people have contractual savings arrangements which are difficult to vary, such as contributions to their pension fund. They exercise control over the net amount they save by borrowing. Individuals' liabilities – their mortgages, personal bank loans, credit card debts and so on – rose from 45 per cent of pre-tax incomes at the beginning of the decade to more than 85 per cent in 1988.[2] Never before have so many borrowed so much so quickly. Savings amounted to 14 per cent of disposable income in 1980, when confidence was battered by the recession. If the savings ratio had stayed at that level instead of falling to 4 per cent in 1988, consumers would have spent £30 billion

Figure 24

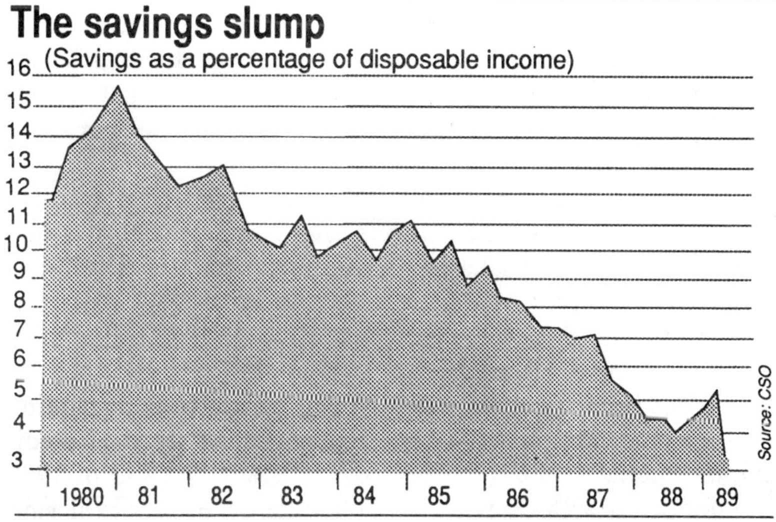

less in that year alone, before allowing for multiplier effects which would have occurred because other people's incomes would have been lower. Without the sharp decline in savings since 1980, consumers' spending would be 10 per cent lower and gross domestic product 6.6 per cent lower. The spending boom has in turn allowed the Government to reap unforeseen bounty in extra taxes, and turn its own finances into surplus, thus effectively privatizing the national (Government) debt.

Why did it happen? The essential precondition of the credit boom was financial market liberalization, notably the ending of the 'corset' restrictions on bank lending in 1980. The result was the unleashing of new and vigorous competition on the part of the banks in the mortgage market. Bank loans for house purchase rose by 79 per cent in 1981 and by 109 per cent in 1982.[3] The banks' share of total outstanding loans for house purchase (mortgages) went from a modest 5.5 per cent in 1980 to 14.1 per cent two years later. Not surprisingly, this intense new competition for business had a dramatic effect on the traditionally sleepy building societies. They struggled to compete, sharply relaxing their long-standing limits on lending and risk assessment. Suddenly, the mortgage queues vanished as lenders competed to make it easy to borrow money. Building societies took to the new environment like naturals, with their lending accelerating from a growth rate of 14.7 per cent in 1981 to 21.6 per cent in 1984. Mortgage lending zoomed. Other forms of credit – credit cards and hire purchase agreements – grew rapidly over this period, but it was loans for house purchase that led the pack.[4]

The liberalization of bank and building society lending removed constraints on borrowers which had previously been imposed by the financial system, causing a once-and-for-all rise in credit as many people were able to borrow what they had always wanted. However, several other factors at the same time increased borrowers' willingness to take out loans and thereby gave a double boost to the boom. The first two factors are relatively benign; the third has been a good old-fashioned financial market bubble.

A lot of research overseas has gone into the economic effects of the post-war Baby Boom, but relatively little in Britain.[5] The shifting age structure which the Baby Boom caused does, though, help to explain some of the increase in debt (and, perhaps, some of the improvements in the supply-side of the UK economy). Dr Norbert Walter, a former Kiel economist now at Deutsche Bank, argues that the younger working age groups from 15 to 30 give a double stimulus to the economy because they save little and because they are more flexible and responsive than their elders. In Britain, both effects may be apparent. There has been a steady net increase in the number of small businesses registering to pay VAT since the end of the seventies, after a couple of years of declines.

Walter argues that the coming German boom will follow the American and British booms because the post-war rise in the birth rate was postponed to the mid-fifties by the exceptional poverty in the wake of defeat, whereas both the American and British birth rates started rising in 1946 immediately after the war. However, calculations for the UK on the same basis as Walter's (shown in the heavy line in figure 25) suggest that the rise and fall of the under-30s in both countries is in fact surprisingly close despite Germany's slower start after the war (and hence the steeper rise in the proportion of 15–30s recently).

Figure 25

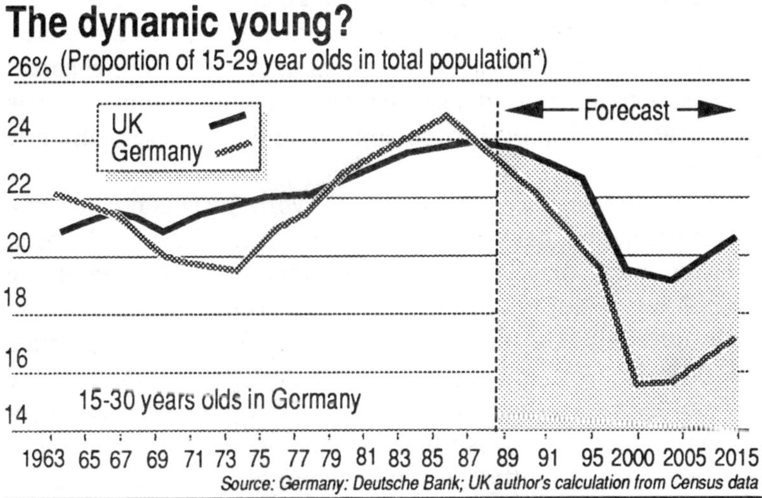

The age group's relative size in Britain peaked in 1987 at its highest share of the population since 1945. No wonder people love to hate yuppies.

The change in age structure may thus help to explain some of the fall in the savings ratio in both countries, but the far sharper fall in Britain must either have been because the liberalization of the financial system allowed it or because of quite separate factors encouraging borrowing. For example, the Treasury's favourite explanation at the time was that people felt more confident about the future. At the beginning of the eighties, a common view had been that the British economy might only grow by around 1 per cent a year. (Look at the Treasury's own ridiculously gloomy spending projections of the time.) Instead, even the cautious Bank of England was reckoning in 1988 that Britain could grow at 3 per cent a year. The higher one's future expectations of income, the greater is the incentive to borrow today in order to enjoy some of its fruit.

Probably the most important factor behind the credit boom was the behaviour of the housing market. The cost of constructing a house has risen more than inflation, but not by much. The reason why house prices have rocketed is the rise in the price of land (see the fourth essay in chapter 3) whose supply is essentially fixed, especially in those areas where planning restrictions bite hardest. The result was a confrontation between a fixed supply and a sharp increase in demand fuelled by financial market liberalization. Not surprisingly, prices rose sharply. Before long, the expectation that prices would continue to rise encouraged further borrowing and demand – and a bubble had begun.

There were some real factors at work increasing housing demand too: the baby-boomers meant more first-time buyers. The imminent abolition of the rates and their replacement by the poll tax removed an impost on land which was almost certainly reflected in a price rise. A greater degree of inheritance has probably led to higher demand for better homes. The favourable tax treatment of owner-occupied housing – the relief against income tax on the interest due on the first 30,000 and even more importantly the total exemption from capital gains tax – is particularly attractive in an upturn of prices, and gives it further encouragement. Nevertheless, the very steepness and scale of the increase, together with its regional concentration in the South East, reeked of a speculative bubble (figure 15). After all, the average price in London for a normal inter-war semi-detached home leapt by 135 per cent in the four years to 1988. Any Londoner who bought an average house in 1984, even with a 100 per cent mortgage, was sitting on roughly £60,000 in tax-free capital gains by 1989, which was probably just about what he or she earned before tax over the same period.

Moreover, the downside looked minimal because house prices had hardly ever fallen (although the real prices of houses fell sharply during the great 1973–4 inflation). And it is nominal prices which people compare with their mortgage debt, which is also denominated in current prices. This no-lose situation may change, because the Government is now paying less of an unemployed person's mortgage payments. The growth of the rental market will also mean that people can sell their home and live outside the owner-occupied sector, which was not a realistic option for most of the eighties. In Belgium and the Netherlands, the existence of a thriving rented market means that house prices can fall sharply. Nevertheless, the circumstances of the eighties in Britain encouraged home owners to believe they were onto a one-way bet. In the South East especially, house prices rose to a far higher proportion of earnings than had been the case in the past.

The land bubble encouraged people who made windfall gains to take part of them in the only way they could without moving into a tent or the rented sector: they borrowed. On one calculation, about half of all the loans for house purchase between 1983 and 1986 found their way out of the housing market altogether.[6] Elderly people traded down, and took some of the equity out of their homes for their retirement. People borrowed on mortgages and bought cars and stereos instead. Some people bought a second home on mortgage, while others sold it and spent the money. Initially, the pretence was maintained that mortgages were for homes or home improvements and borrowers had to testify as much to their lenders. By 1987 the Bank of England had even given up pretending.

In retrospect, some of the Prime Minister's friends accused the Chancellor of running an excessively lax monetary policy, with low interest rates designed to keep the pound down rather than keep the lid on the domestic credit boom. However, this analysis is one-sided. Real interest rates, after allowing for inflation, were historically high throughout the period. A central problem with the effectiveness of interest rates as a control on borrowing is that expectations about the future are crucial, and there was an extraordinary amount of optimism about in the late eighties, consciously fuelled by the electoral aspirations of the Prime Minister and Chancellor. If you believe that house prices are going to rise by 20 per cent this year and 15 per cent next year the small matter of 12 per cent or even 14 per cent mortgage rates is unlikely to deter you from borrowing and spending a part of your gains. However, if you think that prices are grinding to a halt, those interest rates may look rather high. Professor Paish used to say that monetary policy was like pulling a brick towards you across a table with a piece of elastic: nothing happened and then it hit you in the eye.

The persistence of a bubble in the housing market was a very sound argument for using other policy instruments to cool down the expansion of credit. Certainly, financial institutions would eventually find ways around old-fashioned 'administrative guidance' by the Bank of England. However, it might have had the desired effect of pricking the house price and lending bubble, which would then have settled down of its own accord. Alternatively, the Bank of England could have raised the amount of cash which lending institutions have to deposit with the bank for each extra pound they lend which would in effect reduce the profitability of their lending or cause a rise in their lending rates, for that type of lending.

The notion that any form of direct control on the financial system, other than interest rates, would be ineffective is simply not borne out either by British or overseas experience. After all, the explosion of bank lending after the abolition of the 'corset' in 1980 itself proves that it was far from being the cosmetic device which its detractors supposed. Moreover, a leakage in any system does not necessarily invalidate it. Hydro-electric engineers still build working dams despite the enormous loss of water through the lake bed. The notion that off-shore lenders need make substantial inroads into the British mortgage market, where a legal charge needs to be completed and upheld in British courts and stamp duty paid, is somewhat far-fetched.

Throughout the housing bubble, the Chancellor took the loftier liberal view that the Government ought not to be intervening to decide who or what should be able to borrow (although, to his credit, he would personally have preferred to abolish mortgage interest relief entirely, but was vetoed by Mrs Thatcher). His was, though, a rather selective economic liberalism. The Chancellor accepts the argument for intervening to stop bubbles in the foreign exchange market. Markets do make mistakes. The willing overseas investor may become unwilling and cause a run on the currency. The case for other policy instruments to provide some credit guidance remains strong.

Notes

1 Total personal sector financial liabilities to third quarter of 1988: *Financial Statistics*, May 1989, table 14.4.

2 Total personal sector financial liabilities (as above) as a percentage of total personal income before tax in 1988, *Economic Trends*, March 1989, table 4.

3 *Financial Statistics*, May 1989, table 14.4.

4 Mortgages totalled £52.6 billion at the end of 1980, a share of 58 per cent of total personal sector liabilities. By the third quarter of 1989, the total was £215.2 billion and 66 per cent.

5 See for example 'Demographic Factors and Economic Momentum', *Deutsche Bank Bulletin*, October 1988; Louise Russell, *The Baby Boom Generation and the Economy*, Brookings Studies in Social Economics (Washington DC: Brookings Institution, 1982).

6 Calculation of Dr Gerard Lyons of SBCI-Savory Milln.

Why the balance of payments matters

Resolving a deficit through recession or inflation

- the period of adjustment
- the arithmetic of removing a deficit worth 3 per cent of GDP
- consumer spending growth needs to halve
- five episodes of turning around large deficits without devaluation
- the lessons for Britain

There is a lot in the old adage that a healthy balance of payments is the sign of a country paying its way in the world. By contrast, a deficit simply represents an excess of imports of goods and services over exports of goods and services. A deficit can occur for a number of reasons. A country's trading performance over time may be poor. It loses market share and gradually goes into deficit. This in turn may be due to structural causes or to mismanagement of the elements of the macro-economy which are most important to the tradable sectors, notably in allowing an excessively high exchange rate. Alternatively, if spending – demand – grows very much more rapidly than the capacity of the country to supply it, there will also be a deficit as imports rush in to fill the gap. The record deficit which Britain acquired in 1988 was essentially of the latter kind, which made it no less worrying.

The most important question about any current account deficit is what price has to be paid to turn it round. In the past, large economies which have run deficits as big as Britain's in 1988 and 1989 have suffered a period of very slow growth of

Figure 26

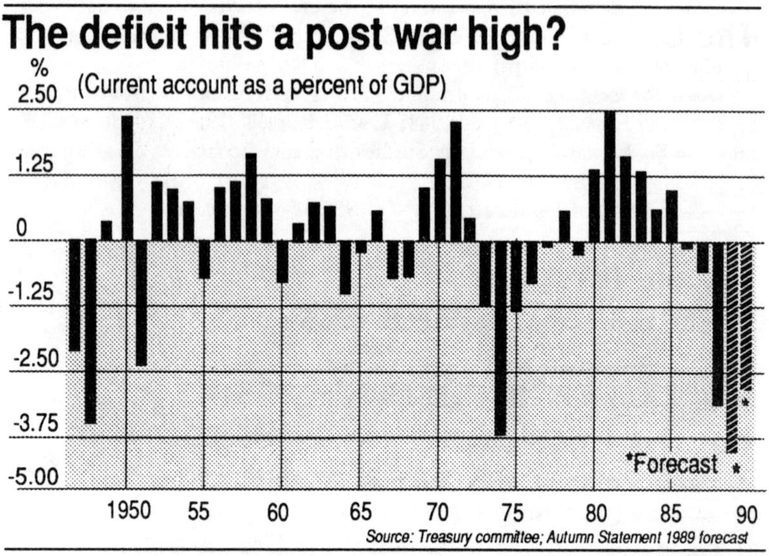

Figure 27

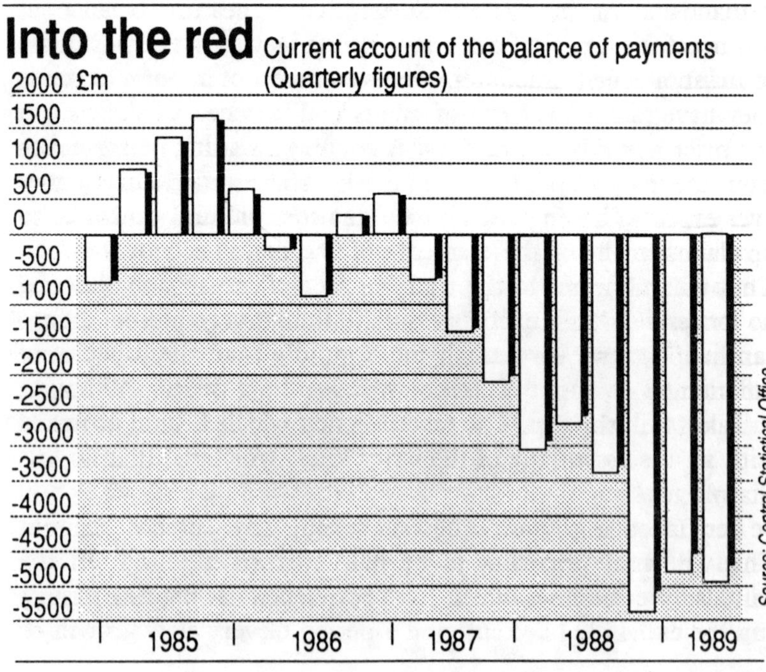

Figure 28

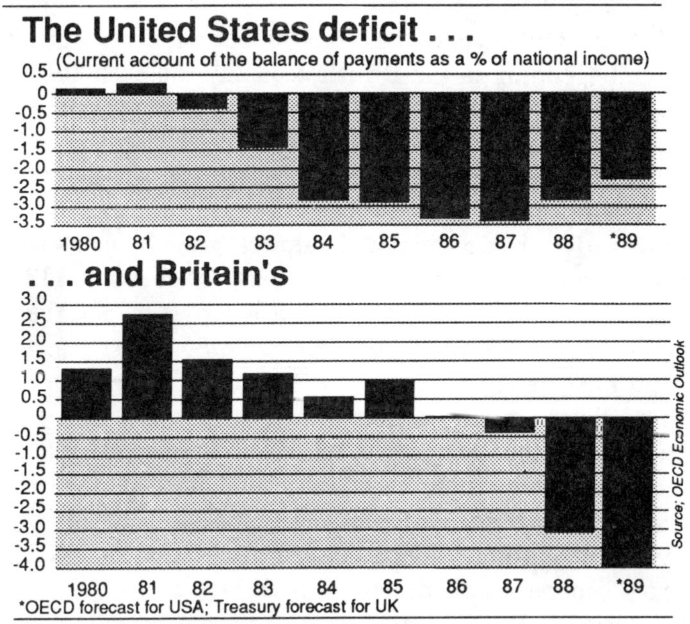

demand and living standards, coupled with recession. Output has not necessarily fallen, but it has grown so slowly that resources of manpower and machines become unemployed. Alternatively, they have had to accept a sharply higher inflation rate as part of the price of dealing with the problem. This brutal choice arises from the nature of the deficit. It represents an excess of imports over exports, which can only be financed by foreigners building up claims on the British economy – IOUs of one form or another. They will not go on doing so forever. When they decide that they no longer want to buy any more British assets, one of two things can happen (or a mixture of the two). The first option is more inflation. The second is recession.

Take inflation first. The foreigners have to be provided with an incentive to go on holding pounds. If the pound falls sharply to a level at which they believe it may go up, they will be persuaded to hold their pounds and they may even buy more. That will fund the deficit in the short term. In the long term, it will also reduce the price of our exports when priced in foreign currencies, and so increase the demand for them. At the same time it increases the price of our imports, which makes them less attractive to British consumers. Both mechanisms help to cut the deficit. The snag is that imports account for about a third of total spending in the British economy. So each 10 per cent fall in the pound directly adds 10 per cent to import prices, and 3 per cent to the average price level in the economy merely as an initial effect. If wages then rise in response, the inflation will become embedded.

The alternative to devaluation is slower growth or even a recession. In order to persuade foreigners to go on holding British assets, interest rates have to rise in order to pay them a risk premium. In effect, the gap between the interest rates in Britain and the interest rates overseas has to be larger than the expected decline in sterling against other currencies – or it will be worth while for the foreigners to sell. That interest differential also funds the deficit in the short term, and may help turn it around in the long term by depressing spending in the British economy – and cutting imports. As an alternative to interest rates, taxes can be raised or public spending cut, depressing domestic demand. But the message is the same: spending has to grow more slowly than production in order to export more and close the payments gap.

Needless to say, Mr Nigel Lawson, then Chancellor, argued in two key speeches during the course of 1988[1] that there was no longer such a thing as a balance of payments constraint which could force us into the sort of dilemma outlined above. Because the scale of international capital flows is much larger than it has been at any time since the twenties, he argued that we would be able to finance an excess of imports over exports for longer. Moreover, the deficit in reality represented a capital flow into Britain which was entirely due to the private sector, since the public sector was not borrowing money but was in surplus. However, Mr Lawson did not deny that it was the role of the Government to maintain sound policies, including a stable pound, bearing down on inflation. Since a large deficit undermines the pound, he was merely redefining the balance of payments constraint in new terms. He confirmed as much by conceding that at some point deficits on the scale of Britain's in 1988, if they continued, would prove unsustainable.

The key question is over what period the shortfall has to be made up. The shorter the period, the nastier the shock and the greater the risk that the depression of demand also induces a recession. If foreigners were to lose confidence, they would need a lot of compensation in higher interest to encourage them to take the risk of holding on to sterling. Interest rates might have to go to 15 or even 20 per cent. Suddenly there would be a collapse of demand. The housing boom would stop, and go into reverse. The disposable incomes of borrowers would contract sharply as mortgage payments soared, and they cut their spending. Businesses would find sales slowing. The cash would not be coming in, but the costs of output would continue. Profits would be squeezed mercilessly, as they always are whenever demand drops. Businesses would react by cutting costs and output. Since the stock market was expecting profits to go on growing, fund managers would react to the likely drop in profits and a fall in prospective yields on equities by selling shares and buying gilt-edged stock, or holding their assets in cash. Share prices would plummet, causing a loss of confidence among businesses, and a reconsideration of investment plans. The feel-good psychology of the boom would turn into the paranoia of a bust.

The risks of this nightmare scenario are high enough to be worrying, and should not be run. What the former Chancellor undoubtedly had in mind, however, was an altogether less alarming and more leisurely progress towards current account balance. Foreigners would go on lending Britain the money to finance its deficit. Indeed, they would be so enthusiastic that no decline in the value of the pound would be either necessary or desirable. They may be dazzled by Britain's overseas assets (although they are privately owned, and not available to bail the Chancellor out). More to the point, if the worst comes to the worst, the Chancellor can fund the deficit by drawing down $50 billion of reserves. Devaluation, the Chancellor said on the record, was most definitely out.

Nevertheless, even a lengthy process of adjustment will involve a sea-change in the swell of prosperity. In a world where we are constrained not to increase our current account deficit, the crucial determinant of our performance is exports. Let us generously assume that our exports grow in line with the OECD's forecast of developed world import growth of 8.5 per cent in 1989 (not allowing for price rises) and by 7 per cent for the two years thereafter. This will provide, after three years' growth, an extra £27 billion of foreign exchange in 1991 which can be used to cut the deficit or increase imports. Let us further assume that only £10 billion of this money has to go into improving the deficit. That would still leave a deficit of around £5 billion, or over 1 per cent of GDP, but it is clearly less worrying than now, and might be sustainable. We are then left with some £17 billion extra to spend on imports in 1991, or about 14 per cent more than in 1988. Since Mr Lawson ruled out devaluation and would not even think about import controls, the only way of ensuring that import growth is limited to 14 per cent between 1988 and 1991 is by limiting the growth of domestic spending to around the same amount.[2] If the prospect is really anything like this, it would represent a very marked shift in recent trends since it is less than half of the growth of domestic spending in either of the most recent comparable periods from 1984 to 1987 (+28 per cent) or 1981 to 1984 (+31 per cent). Even a soft landing does not look very attractive.

There is another twist. Spending growth, in the short term at least, also determines output growth in large parts of the economy which cannot export – like retailing, catering, hairdressers and so forth. The very act of belt-tightening is also likely to drive output growth lower than it would otherwise be. The economy is likely to be growing by less than its underlying real trend of about 2.75–3 per cent growth of output each year. Employment will stop rising, and unemployment may stabilize or increase again (depending on whether the Government is changing the toughness with which it administers dole benefits). Nor does this yet take account of the decline in oil output, which will also require us to pay for increased oil imports.

The prospect is deeply ungratifying, as the former Chancellor implicitly admitted. When, in April 1989, Mr Lawson was pressed by the Treasury select committee on whether a reduction in the deficit could come about without a fall in sterling, Mr Lawson had clearly come prepared. He cited five examples of countries – Japan, Germany, Austria, Britain and the Netherlands – which had achieved swings from deficit to surplus of between 2.5 per cent of national income and 4.1 per cent of national income without any appreciable fall in their currencies.

A closer examination of the episodes which he cites nevertheless highlights the general point that Britain cannot avoid retribution for his past errors in letting demand expand too rapidly. What Mr Lawson did not choose to highlight was that every single one of the cases which he cited suffered rising unemployment, and every country except one suffered at least one year of falling output. Here, case by case, are the five episodes adding some of the detail which Mr Lawson chose to omit.[3]

Germany 1980–83 The current account deficit, bloated by the second oil shock, was 1.7 per cent of GDP in 1980 and improved to a surplus of 0.8 per cent by 1983, a swing of 2.5 per cent. During this period, the IMF trade-weighted exchange rate of the German mark dropped only slightly from 100 (1980 = 100) to 98.8. What Mr Lawson did not point out was that domestic demand actually fell by an average 0.8 per cent a year over the period, which was instrumental in holding GDP (supply) growth down to only 0.3 per cent a year. This was well below the productivity trend of the German economy, so that unemployment rose sharply by 5 percentage points to 6.8 per cent of the labour force.

Netherlands 1978–81 The current account went from a deficit of 0.9 per cent of GDP to a surplus of 2.5 per cent, a swing of 3.4 per cent. The exchange rate fell only slightly from 95.7 (1980 = 100) to 93.2. However, domestic demand fell on average by 0.9 per cent a year, growth of output was constrained to 0.9 per cent a year, and unemployment rose by 3.2 percentage points to 8.5 per cent of the labour force.

Austria 1977–82 The current account improved from a deficit of 4.5 per cent of GDP to a surplus of 1.1 per cent, an astonishing swing of 5.6 per cent of GDP and by far the largest of Mr Lawson's examples. The exchange rate rose from 87.6 to

94. Domestic demand grew by 0.7 per cent a year and national output by 1.8 per cent a year. Unemployment rose by 1.7 percentage points to 3.1 per cent. This is a particularly unfortunate example for Mr Lawson to choose. The relatively favourable adjustment of Austria reflects its long-standing commitment to the sort of tripartite concertation between Government, employers and trade unions which is corporatist anathema to Mr Lawson.

Japan 1979–83 The current account improved over this period from a deficit of 0.9 per cent to a surplus of 1.8 per cent, a swing of 2.7 per cent of GDP. At the same time the yen rose spectacularly from 104 on the IMF index to 117.4 (1980 = 100). Domestic demand slowed down, but was nevertheless able to continue growing at an average rate of 1.9 per cent. And the growth of GDP (output) averaged 3.6 per cent a year. The result was that the unemployment rate edged up by only 0.5 percentage points to 2.6 per cent of the labour force. This is the most spectacular and impressive of all the adjustment examples, and is ample tribute to the extraordinary resilience and flexibility of the Japanese economy.

Britain 1973–81 Mr Lawson must have given this example as a joke, because it does not even fulfil his criterion of a stable or rising exchange rate. On the IMF index, the pound fell from 116.6 (1980 = 100) to 98.9. In addition, the period was far longer than the other examples, and contained not just one year of recession but four years of outright falls in output – two after each of the two oil price shocks. The current account turned around from a deficit of 1.4 per cent of GDP to a surplus of 2.7 per cent, a swing of 4.1 per cent. But domestic demand grew by an average of only 0.2 per cent and GDP grew by an average of only 0.7 per cent. Unemployment rose by 6.8 percentage points to 9.8 per cent of the labour force.

All of these episodes took place when many other countries also had balance of payments problems due to the rise in world oil prices. Britain had no such excuse in 1989. Moreover, the only one of these experiences which involved relatively little pain was the Japanese, and Japan was the most successful economy of the post-war period. The second was Austria, running policies to which the former Chancellor was wholly opposed. The most disastrous experience of all was in Britain.

The messages are hard to disguise. The first is to highlight the importance of tradable sectors like manufacturing, and to warn against the sort of policies pursued during 1979–81 which did such damage to much of their capacity. The second is that a devaluation is likely. The pain necessary to cure the deficit entirely by restricting the growth of domestic spending means that the Government is likely to accept the fall in the pound. (Indeed, it accepted a fall during 1989.) This does not, though, necessarily mean that living standards can grow faster: it simply means that businesses may be able to maintain a higher level of output by substituting for imports and by exporting. It is a further way of increasing the gap between domestic spending and output.

The reduction of Britain's high current account deficits is likely to prove a long, hard struggle – and a fulsome warning not to be so cavalier towards balance of payments problems again.

Notes

1 Speech to the Institute of Economic Affairs and to the annual meeting of the International Monetary Fund and World Bank in Berlin.

2 This implicitly assumes, for the *cognoscenti*, that the income elasticity of demand for imports is one, i.e. that imports rise broadly in line with incomes. In fact, past experience suggests that over time it is a good deal higher than this. The only exception which might justify this figure is the disproportionate squeeze on imports when spending is squeezed at the top of a cycle.

3 All the figures come from successive issues of the Organisation for Economic Co-operation and Development *Economic Outlook* or the International Monetary Fund *International Financial Statistics Yearbook*.

Dealing with too much success

Accusations between the Prime Minister and the Chancellor

- the weakness of the Prime Minister's view
- the pound not set too low during shadow EMS membership
- the defensible policy of letting the pound fall in 1986
- the 1988 Budget was the key problem
- the Chancellor had been warned
- computer model estimates of policy results

In June 1989, after the eruption of a record balance of payments deficit, a rise in inflation to more than 8 per cent and ten rises in interest rates to 14 per cent, the Prime Minister said in a radio interview that Britain had picked up its inflationary tendency while trying to shadow the German mark. Since this had been her Chancellor's policy, Mrs Thatcher's remarks immediately reopened the long-running debate between the Downing Street neighbours over the correct monetary policy to pursue. They implicitly conceded to the Opposition that something had indeed gone badly wrong in Britain's economic management. And they injected into the foreign exchange market the corrosive thought that the Prime Minister and her Chancellor were again divided on economic policy, a perception which undermined the Government's efforts to stop the pound falling. The row was ultimately to lead to the Chancellor's resignation.

The Prime Minister's case, though, was far from strong. It was not obvious, even with the benefit of hindsight, that the central fault of economic management was the decision to shadow the German mark between February 1987 and March 1988 with a ceiling for the pound of DM3.00. Nor was the mistake, as some senior Government advisers argued, that the exchange rate was set too low, even if the decision in principle to act as if sterling were a full member of the European Monetary System were correct. Nor was it the case, despite the Chancellor's confessions on several occasions, that his error lay in reducing interest rates too much in the wake of the October 1987 stock market crash, in common with his colleagues in the other industrial countries. The fatal error, without which a serious crisis in economic management may well have been averted, was the excessively generous tax cuts in the 1988 Budget.

First take the Prime Minister's view (or rather that of her personal economic adviser, Sir Alan Walters). True, Britain acquired $21 billion of foreign exchange reserves during 1987 and early 1988 in an attempt to sell enough pounds to hold the rate below DM3.00. However, this injection of sterling into the financial markets did not have any direct effects in boosting the money supply because the Chancellor 'sterilized' the intervention by selling Government bonds, mopping up more cash from the British private sector. Secondly, there was only a handful of people who argued at the time that the acceleration in the money supply was significant, since there had been bulges in M0 and M4 before without any inflationary ill-effects. Moreover, the dollar was falling through much of this period, so that the pound's link with the German mark meant that the pound was rising in trade-weighted terms. Indeed, the pound rose in trade-weighted terms by 10 per cent between its low in October 1986 and the end of the shadow membership of the European Monetary System in March 1988.

Nor is it easy to argue that the pound was set too low at the beginning of the period. Certainly, the Chancellor made the key decision of his period of office when he decided to let sterling drop in the wake of the 1986 oil price falls. Other countries let the oil-price fall reduce their inflation rates at home, but Mr Lawson offset that gain with a drop in the pound which pushed up import prices by a corresponding amount. At root, Mr Lawson was happy with inflation at around 4–5 per cent. Table 18 shows how he maintained the fiction that he was conducting a battle against inflation, while in fact indulging in a rather leisurely skirmish. The Chancellor repeatedly missed the targets in his Budget documents. He preferred to devote his efforts to making the economy grow as quickly as possible without inflation rising again. The 19 per cent devaluation between July 1985 and October 1986 unleashed startling growth from our trading sectors, notably manufacturing.

There was nothing dishonourable in that choice, especially against a background of very high unemployment. Nor was there any reason why it should have resulted in rising inflation rather

Table 18. Trying to beat inflation? Treasury inflation predictions and outturn, 1982–9 (percentages)

Public spending plan	*Projected GDP deflator for year*										
	1982	*1983*	*1984*	*1985*	*1986*	*1987*	*1988*	*1989*	*1990*	*1991*	*1992*
1982	8.0	7.0	6.5								
1983		5.5	5.5	5.0							
1984			4.75	4.25	4.0	3.5	3.0				
1985				5.0	4.5	3.5	3.0				
1986					3.75	3.75	3.5	3.0			
1987						4.5	4.0	3.5	3.0		
1988							4.5	4.0	3.5	3.0	
1989								5.5	4.0	3.0	2.5
Outturn	7.25	4.5	5.0	5.5	3.25	5.25	7.25*				

*1989 Budget estimate

Source: Treasury Select Committee

than stable inflation, were it not for the fatal error of the March 1988 Budget. The growth of credit associated with the housing market and the new competition between banks and building societies was extremely rapid, precisely because it had been pent up by the conservative rules of thumb operated by the lending institutions. Such demand for credit would not have been very sensitive to interest rate rises. It merited some direct measures to prick the bubble of house price expectations, such as Bank of England requests to moderate lending, limits on borrowers, or penal cash deposits to dim lenders' enthusiasm. The setting of interest rates was not foolishly lax unless you were intending to relax policy on some other front. The reduction in interest rates after the October 1987 crash was a mere 1.5 percentage points. Inflationary pressures in the labour market were largely associated with some public sector pay catch-up, and were not out of line with the period since 1982. The Budget was the main problem.

Before the Budget Mr Lawson had ample warning that he should avoid tax cuts. Some said that overall demand was simply growing too rapidly. Others argued that the main problem was an imbalance in demand, with exports growing too slowly and domestic demand too rapidly. The trend into payments deficit should be corrected before it became excessive. In both cases, the argument was that the Chancellor should not give away tax cuts because they would merely stoke consumers' spending even further, encourage imports, and ultimately force corrective measures to slow down demand which would undermine the expansion and the drop in unemployment. Mr Lawson is now fairly accused of squandering the chance to sustain the recovery. He gambled it on an untested theory about the beneficent effects of top-rate tax cuts. Once he had decided to abolish top rates, he was forced by his own political logic into cutting the basic rate by 2p. He could not be seen merely to benefit the best-off. The full year revenue cost of his tax cuts (which came due in 1989/90) was equivalent to more than 3p off the basic rate.

It was clear at the time that this was a terrible risk. The Bank of England's February bulletin appeared four weeks before the Budget and said: 'The fears that accounted for the response (in cutting interest rates) to the events of mid-October have now receded: the latest economic and monetary indicators depict a still buoyant economy amply provided with credit, giving little sign so far that the pressures from domestic demand will abate soon ... It will also be important for the preservation of both internal and external balance that the anti-inflationary burden continues to be shared between monetary and fiscal policy.'[1] That was bankspeak for 'Don't cut taxes'.

A common feature of forecasts before the Budget was a widening current account deficit. The OECD had just forecast that the UK deficit would reach $5.75 billion in 1988 and $9.5 billion in 1989. The Keynesian National Institute also foresaw widening deficits, although Mr Lawson's friends would argue that it always had. The London Business School had no such past, yet in its February review it too warned that it 'is unlikely that we shall be able to finance a sustained balance of payments deficit'.[2]

The official statistics also showed that there had been a sharp worsening in the deficit through 1987. The January current account figures, released on 29 February, showed a monthly deficit of £905 million. The annualized three-month deficit was already running at more than £7 billion, though most people could not believe that it was that bad. There might be uncertainty about the absolute size of the deficit because of the poor quality of the figures, but there could be no doubt both that the trend was getting worse and that the sooner it was reversed, the less pain would be incurred. If the economic misjudgement was clear, the political misjudgement may ultimately prove the more important. To have a giveaway Budget in the year after a general election was curious political timing.

The Chancellor subsequently defended his Budget on the grounds that the trade deficit was widening anyway, so the tax cuts could not be blamed for it. This is looking-glass logic. It was precisely because the warning signs were there that he should not have aggravated the consumer boom. Having ruled out other policy measures like credit controls, Mr Lawson aggravated the problem with tax cuts. He was left with interest rate rises as his sole weapon to control domestic demand and the exchange rate, a classic and impossible situation in which he was attempting to hit two objectives with only one policy instrument. Moreover, the subsequent sharp rises in interest rates in order to control domestic demand and stop the pound falling probably had ambiguous effects on the current account deficit.

The Treasury's line was that we had an inflationary problem, and the deficit (or, more precisely, import growth) was merely a subsidiary indicator of the strength of domestic demand and hence inflationary pressures. However, even if you were naive enough to believe that the deficit *per se* is not a problem (and senior Treasury policy-makers were not) the policy mix of tax cuts and interest rate rises was far from ideal. Tax changes directly and quickly affect consumer spending. However, rate rises hit investment (which increases output and reduces inflation) as well as consumer spending (which increases demand and raises inflation). The dwindling band of the Chancellor's apologists argue that consumer spending will now prove more sensitive to interest rates because debt is twice as high relative to income as it was several years ago, while investment will prove less sensitive because long-term interest rates have risen relatively little.

However, the Big Four computer models showed that the effects of the rises in interest rates took time to offset the inflation-raising effects of the tax cuts. If inflation is the 'judge

Table 19. The effect of a 3p cut in income tax on consumer prices in second year (percentage points)

LBS	*NIESR*	*HMT*	*BE*
+2.13	+1.95	+0.06	−0.93
. . . and a 4 percentage point rise in interest rates ...			
−3.68	−2.8	−1.36	−0.84
. . . combine to leave prices ...			
−1.55	−0.85	−1.3	−1.77

Note: LBS = London Business School; NIESR = National Institute; HMT = Treasury; BE = Bank of England
Source: National Institute Economic Review, no. 125 (August 1988)

and jury' of policy, as the former Chancellor used to say, then the tax cuts were still a mistake. The net effect of the policy changes in 1988 compared with 1987 – the Budget tax cuts combined with a 4 percentage point rise in interest rates[3] – was to reduce next year's prices (compared with what would otherwise have happened) by a maximum of 1.8 per cent (table 19).

In reality, though, the most dangerous problem was the widening current account deficit. So long as the markets were preoccupied with speculating against the dollar, high British interest rates supported the pound. But sentiment can change very quickly, and did. The size of the current account deficit undeniably concerned the markets, as the sharp falls in the pound through the summer of 1989 showed. To the extent that the deficit weakened sterling, it clearly represented suppressed inflation. Moreover, any fall in sterling could become extremely inflationary in circumstances where there was precious little spare capacity in British manufacturing. Instead of increasing output, British firms could decide merely to take advantage of more demand to raise prices. The passthrough from a devaluation to the domestic price level could be even higher than merely the direct effects on import prices.

Table 20 shows only too clearly how ill-judged the Budget tax cuts were from the point of view of turning round the deficit. Even the direction of the effects of the policy changes in 1988 is uncertain. The Bank of England model suggests

Table 20. The effect of a 3p cut in income tax on the balance of payments in second year (£000m)

LBS	*NIESR*	*HMT*	*BE*
−2,064	−3,012	−2,073	−1,995
. . . and a 4 percentage point rise in interest rates . . .			
+5,480	+3,648	+4,608	−644
. . . combine to leave a +/− balance . . .			
+2,516	+636	+2,535	−2,639

Note: LBS = London Business School; NIESR = National Institute; HMT = Treasury; BE = Bank of England
Source: NIESR, August review

that the combined policy changes still worsened the deficit. The effect of higher interest rates in raising the pound and hitting exports is greater, according to the Bank model, than their effect in curbing domestic demand and imports. In short, whether you take either inflation or the current account deficit as the test, the policy mix in 1988 was woefully inappropriate. Most of the economics profession, and the Opposition parties, are fully entitled to argue, with the Irishman, that they would not start in 1988 to get to Tipperary. The ideal mix would clearly have been a tough Budget with no tax cuts or even a tax increase, lower interest rates and a lower exchange rate. Domestic demand would have been curbed, while export demand was encouraged.

As for the subsidiary issue as to whether it was the Chancellor or the Prime Minister who was to blame, the answer is that they both were. They both ruled out any direct influence on credit which might have pricked the house price bubble. They both backed the Budget tax changes which fed the euphoria. The disagreement between them on monetary policy was significant most of all because they disagreed, which in turn caused the markets to doubt the Government's credibility when the problem became holding the pound up rather than keeping it down. But neither Mrs Thatcher's nor Mr Lawson's policy, pursued as each would separately have liked, would have avoided the problems which emerged with a vengeance in 1988 and 1989.

Notes

1 Bank of England, *Quarterly Bulletin*, February 1988.

2 London Business School Centre for Economic Forecasting, *Economic Outlook*, February 1988.

3 The rise in interest rates was very marginally more than this on average. Sterling Treasury bills yielded 8.38 per cent in 1987 and 12.91 per cent in 1988.

An end to relative decline?

The concept of relative decline

- international comparisons of income are misleading
- allowing for price differences between economies
- Britain's decline slows in the seventies
- reasons for relative improvement
- dangers ahead in balance of payments deficit
- a period of slow growth and painful adjustment

Britain's relative economic decline – the phenomenon of Britain growing more slowly than the rest of the developed world – has been an intermittent subject of debate ever since the end of the nineteenth century. Relative decline was of little significance when Britain's living standards were far higher than continental ones, as it could be attributed to a catching-up by other countries. In the post-war period, though, Britain was passed by Germany, France, Japan and smaller countries. Relative decline became a central issue in national politics.

The Conservatives now claim that the Government's policies have finally ended the years of decline, pointing to more rapid rates of growth than other countries in the late eighties, combined with higher profitability and a sharp improvement in industrial relations and inward foreign investment. Opposition politicians remain unconvinced. They in turn can point to a poor trading performance, the fortuitous advent of North Sea oil, and the prospect of a formidable work-out of slow growth and even slower consumers' spending growth to eliminate the trade deficit.

Start with the best assessments we have of Britain's relative income per head. One very misleading basis of comparison is the use of gross domestic product (GDP) at market exchange rates, because currency swings can have dramatic effects on the comparison without having similar effects on living standards. The only sensible basis of comparison is by using purchasing power parities (PPPs) – special exchange rates which equalize the average price of goods and services in different countries. The actual value of a currency reflects capital flows and the country's ability to produce traded goods. PPPs take into account the majority of goods and services which are not traded, and which tend, in poorer countries, to be both proportionately more important and cheaper precisely because labour costs are lower.

This PPP comparison is a major exercise because prices for all the different categories of goods and services have to be surveyed, compared and weighted. It is, though, undertaken at five-yearly intervals by a co-operative venture of the EEC, OECD and United Nations.[1] The data are collected for a 'bench-mark year' – in the latest case for 1985 – and then other years are calculated by applying the changes in real growth shown by the countries' national statistics. The statisticians go to inordinate length in comparing prices for goods which do not normally enter into international trade, getting tenders for stretches of road, house building and so on.

The first results of the latest study created the usual stir, because they showed that Britain was less far behind other countries than the crude comparison at current exchange rates suggested. Instead of enjoying only 43 per cent of the United States' living standards (measured by GDP per head), the PPP study showed that in real terms we were at 66 per cent of the US level. Other gaps also closed, of course: the French moved from 56 per cent to 69 per cent of the US level; the Germans from 62 per cent to 74 per cent; the Japanese from 67 per cent to 71 per cent. A corollary was that we moved from 86 per cent of the French level to 96 per cent of it.

The OECD and the EEC have published figures going back to 1960 which are constructed by applying the changes found in national statistics to the bench-mark year. So we have a new historical series which allows us to see whether any trend has

Table 21. International living standards: GDP per head as a percentage of EEC-12 average, 1960–85 (using purchasing power parities)

	1960	*1965*	*1970*	*1975*	*1980*	*1985*
USA	188.0	182.0	162.8	153.6	150.8	157.0
Japan	56.5	71.3	93.3	94.9	101.7	112.3
France	101.6	103.6	106.0	110.4	111.6	108.9
West Germany	114.67	116.9	113.7	109.7	114.4	116.1
Italy	91.6	93.8	100.8	97.6	102.0	103.1
UK	128.5	119.1	107.9	105.6	100.7	103.9

Source: Derived from Eurostat (see note 1)

changed. The figures show at least one change in trend – and possibly two. First, Britain's relative decline over the fifties and sixties clearly slows down in the seventies, whether Britain is compared with the average EEC level (which is slightly more favourable to Britain, because the EEC has been relatively slow growing) or with the average of the developed countries in the OECD area. Table 21 shows that, between 1970 and 1975, Britain was slipping at only a fifth the rate of the sixties. Between 1980 and 1985, there was a recovery. A similar pattern appears in the figures expressing Britain's living standards as a percentage of the OECD average (though these figures do not go back beyond 1970). We begin the period at 94 per cent of the average, slip to 93 per cent in 1975, and then slip more rapidly to 89 per cent in 1980. We then stabilized at 89 per cent for 1985.

There is, though, an important caveat about taking arbitrary five-year intervals as a comparison: some of the years are boom years near the peak of a cycle, others are slump years. Thus the apparent recovery (by comparison with the EEC) or stabilization (by comparison with the OECD) since 1980 owes a lot to the depressed figure for that year. (For example, we dropped from 104.8 per cent of the EEC average in 1978 to 99.8 per cent by 1981.) A moving five-year average smooths out some of the cyclical fluctuations and shows a stabilization at 93 per cent of the OECD average from 1974 to 1977, a decline to 89 per cent by 1982 and a stabilization at around that level since. It is, though, too soon to conclude that these figures conclusively show that Britain's relative economic decline has ended, because the period since 1982 has been in the upswing part of the cycle.

Several other features of the figures stand out: the relative improvement of our performance has been particularly marked against other EEC countries, less so against the United States and Japan. That is partly, of course, because of 'Eurosclerosis' – the slow growth of the key European economies. Secondly, the turning point may be 1979–81, but the trend was clearly bending before that time and therefore antecedes Mrs Thatcher. Thirdly, the historical data showing the times at which our living standards were exceeded by other countries have undergone quite sharp revision: the path-breaking Kravis, Heston and Summers work published in 1982 calculated that West Germany passed us in 1959, France in 1965 and Japan in 1972.[2] Those dates are revised to 1969, 1972 and 1980, which may instil humility about such comparisons.

There are probably four reasons why Britain's relative economic performance improved over the seventies and eighties. The longest-run factor is probably the delayed impact of the expansion of higher education during the sixties. Secondly, there probably is some 'Thatcher effect' or at least a recession effect which has shaken up managements and work-forces. The evidence now clearly suggests that the underlying growth of manufacturing productivity has speeded up since the trauma of the 1979–81 downturn (as argued in the first essay of this chapter). The other two factors are less flattering. The third factor was the discovery of oil, whose direct contribution rose from 1.7 per cent of GDP in 1978 to a peak of 6.5 per cent in 1984.[3] This made an important contribution to output, tax revenue and the balance of payments. Fourthly, the British economy has an established tendency (noticeable in the thirties) to perform relatively well when the world economy performs relatively badly. Both Britain and the world economy are growing more slowly than during the fifties and sixties but the rest of the world has slowed down more. This may simply be that British companies are able to keep up with a certain pace of growth but begin to fall behind if the world grows too fast.

Nevertheless, it seems unfair to move the goalposts just as Britain appears to be winning: the focus of public debate for many years was on relative decline, and the news on that front is good. A more worrying objection to the picture of an improved Britain is the evidence of the leading indicators – the economic signals which tell us something about the future growth of incomes. Certainly, productivity growth is sound. But the enormous trade deficits at the end of the decade signalled a long period of painful adjustment which was bound to slow down growth throughout the economy, and hence make Britain's relative standing in the world look less favourable. It is also going to involve a major shift in prosperity towards parts of the economy which have been bypassed during the Thatcher years.

In many ways, the coming adjustment to the balance of payments deficit will be the mirror image of the recession between 1979 and 1981. The tradable sectors will get off lightly; the small service businesses and the self-employed will find the going far, far tougher. This pattern is likely to be the result merely of the need to correct the deficit. Manufacturers, who still account for some 56 per cent of all our exports[4] although less than a quarter of all our national output, will be better able than any other businesses to divert production from the slowing home market to exports. They may also, in time, benefit from any devaluation. The continuing renaissance of manufacturing will also help those regions where manufacturing is strong: most notably the West Midlands but to a lesser extent the North too. We will hear less of the North–South divide. Providers of consumer services – restaurateurs, publicans, cinema-owners – will be less able to switch their output to export markets, so they will feel the slowdown in domestic demand.

In most cases, these shifts in economic fortunes will merely be relative ones. Some people's incomes will simply grow more slowly. However, it is worth stressing that the calculation in the third essay of this chapter that domestic spending would have to slow down from some 28 per cent over the period from 1984 to 1988 to some 14 per cent between 1987 and 1991 probably understates the likely shift. It is based on a series of assumptions which are favourable to the Government's views of our recent economic performance. The risks almost all lie on the downside. For example, it assumes that the deficit is cut to some 1 per cent of national income by 1991 compared with more than 3 per cent in 1989. If the deficit has to come down more, the squeeze on consumption and on the non-tradable sectors of the economy will have to be greater. Secondly, our exports are assumed to grow in line with world imports. This would be a good performance, fully commensurate with the view that there has been a basic improvement in the trend of manufacturing productivity growth. After all, Britain's export volume has grown faster than world import volume in only one year between 1984 and 1987. Thirdly, the calculation assumes that imports would grow no faster than domestic spending. Again, this would reverse a post-war history of rising import penetration.

The essential message that the Lawson boom could not continue is simply not sensitive to much change in the assumptions. Even if industry performs miraculously, the sheer size of the deficit at the end of the decade ensures that belt-tightening has to be severe. For those who prefer more sophisticated calculations, however, a research exercise using Britain's two main independent computer models comes to even gloomier conclusions.[5] The view that a major slowdown is in prospect comes out clearly even from the model whose view of the world most resembles the Government's optimism about markets: that of the London Business School (LBS).

'On plausible assumptions,' writes the author, David Turner, 'principally concerning how fast world trade is likely to expand, and on the further critical assumption that there is no change in the competitiveness of exports or imports, the LBS and NIESR (National Institute) models both suggest that UK growth can average no more than 1 per cent per annum over the medium term if there is to be no further deterioration in the current account.

'The major reason why the LBS published forecast is more optimistic than might be expected on the basis of the properties of the LBS model is that the LBS make substantial residual adjustments to the model predictions of both exports and imports in generating their published forecast. We examine a possible explanation for such adjustments, namely that there has recently been an underlying improvement in UK trade performance, but find no statistical evidence to support the case.' Just to stop a deficit of £5 billion a year over the next five years from getting any worse, unless there were a fall in the pound, would require GDP growth of only 1 to 1.5 per cent, the models suggest.

If those calculations are remotely accurate, the chances of Britain resuming its relative economic decline in the nineties must be ranked alarmingly high despite the signs of some underlying improvement in productivity growth and a sharp recovery in company profitability which certainly makes the corporate sector better able to withstand a squeeze. From the longer-term point of view, there have been precious few improvements during the Thatcher years in education, training, research and development or investment. On relative economic decline, the jury is still out.

Notes

1 See the special supplement to the 1987 edition of *National Accounts*, vol. 1 (Paris: OECD, 1987) and *National Accounts ESA Aggregates, 1960–1985* (Luxembourg: Eurostat, 1987).

2 Irving B. Kravis, Alan Heston and Robert Summers, *World Product and Income: International Comparisons of Real Gross Product* (Baltimore: Johns Hopkins University Press, 1982).

3 Richard Layard and Stephen Nickell, *The Thatcher Miracle?*, Centre for Labour Economics, discussion paper no. 343 (London School of Economics, March 1989), p. 52, table 26.

4 In 1987, manufactured exports totalled £60.7 billion and total exports of goods and services excluding interest, profits, dividends and transfers totalled £107.5 billion. *The CSO Pink Book*, 1988, tables 1.3, 2.3.

5 David Turner, *Does the UK Face a Balance of Payments Constraint on Growth?*, ESRC Macro-economic Modelling Bureau, discussion paper no. 16 (Warwick University, 1988).

7 The Labour Market

Why are people still unemployed?

The arithmetic of unemployment and growth

- the fear of rising inflation
- possible capital shortage
- possible balance of payments constraint
- labour market pressures
- the NAIRU or natural rate
- new classical explanations of unemployment due to the trade unions and benefits
- 'insiders' and 'outsiders'
- the problem of the long-term unemployed

Why is there still unemployment? This simple question unfortunately does not admit of simple answers. In one sense, there is still unemployment because the economy has not been growing rapidly enough for long enough to absorb the unemployed. It is true by definition that unemployment will fall if the growth of output exceeds the sum of the growth of output per person and the growth of the labour force. To take some illustrative numbers, productivity growth has averaged just under 2 per cent a year between 1979 and 1988. The labour force tends to swell and contract depending in part on the buoyancy of the jobs market, but a trend rise in the labour force due to more married women wanting to work and to population factors may be of the order of 0.75 per cent a year. Growth of output has to exceed the sum of the two – namely about 2.75 per cent a year – just to hold unemployment steady.

This definition clarifies some of the arithmetic, but not much else. Why does the economy not grow more rapidly when there is high unemployment? It is not because there is any satiation of wants. The impact of any tax cut shows that people can increase their spending easily, and are very happy to do so. In that case,

Figure 29

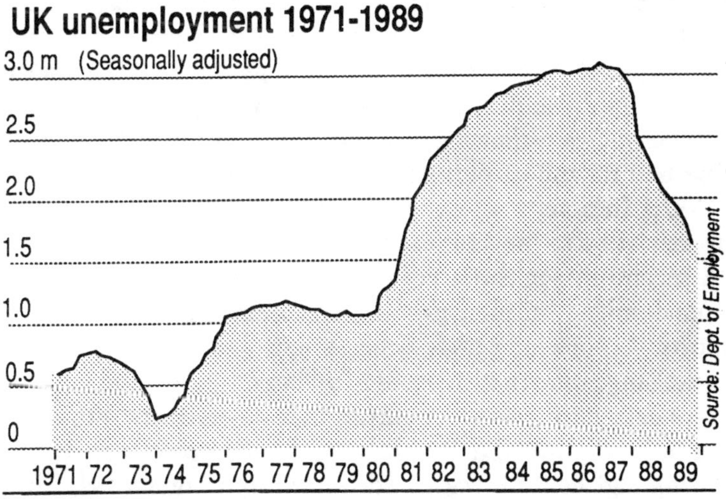

Table 22. British unemployment, 1851–1985 (unemployment rate = percentage of labour force)

Period	*Average*	*Maximum*	*Minimum*
1851–1920	4.4	11.9	0.4
1921–1940	14.0	22.5	10.9
1941–1970	1.5	2.4	0.4
1971–1980	4.0	5.8	2.3
1981–1985	11.2	13.1	9.1

Source: Oxford Review of Economic Policy, vol. 1, no. 2

why does the Government not ease monetary or fiscal policy in order to make the economy grow more quickly? The essential answer is that it is afraid of inflation. The argument is that an increase in demand might cause prices rather than output to rise, leaving unemployment unchanged.

There may be various reasons why this could arise. The first might be some shortage of capital, for which there is some evidence in all of the European economies. The long recession of the early eighties caused a lull in business investment and a concentration on labour-saving rather than capacity-broadening of goods which require plant and machinery could simply not be met by increased supply, which would lead businesses to take advantage of the situation by raising their prices and profit margins. Moreover, the fall in labour costs required to persuade employers to abandon particular types of technology could be very sharp. One estimate is that the capital 'gap' with what might be needed for full employment in Britain was nearly 13 per cent in 1987.[1] In time, such a capital shortage can be filled, although this may require the assurance of steady growth.

A second reason for inflationary pressures arising from faster demand might be increased imports unmatched by increased exports. A worsening trade deficit might then cause some fall in the exchange rate, in turn pushing up import prices and inflation. Such a balance of payments constraint in an economy with a lot of international trade, like Britain's, might effectively stop demand growing and hence block an adequate rate of output growth to maintain any fall in unemployment. In principle, this problem might be resolved by a change in the pattern of demand. The inflationary (and stimulative) impetus of devaluation could be offset by a tightening of budgetary policy through tax increases or spending cuts. However, the politics of such a package were tested in Walter Mondale's presidential campaign against Ronald Reagan in 1984, and found wanting.

A third reason why policy-makers may be reluctant to expand demand, and perhaps the most significant for most of the seventies and eighties, has been the effect such an expansion might have on the labour market. A fall in unemployment would reduce the pressure on those in work to accept pay settlements which can be afforded by the economy without pushing up price inflation, and hence lead to accelerating annual increases in consumer prices. On this view, unemployment is the key economic factor which resolves the conflicts within any economy about what the participants should be paid. If both employers and employees are trying to get more output in either profits or wages than there is to go round, the short-term result is rising inflation. And the Government's response is to curb spending power in the economy until demand subsides enough to persuade employers to accept lower profits and workers to accept a lower increase in wages.[2]

In other words, there is a level of unemployment at which inflation will not accelerate – the so-called Non-accelerating Inflation Rate of Unemployment (NAIRU) which is often called the natural rate. However, closer inspection of the NAIRU suggests that there is nothing very natural about it. It has clearly bobbed about in most economies with considerable alacrity. In Britain the level of unemployment at which earnings growth was stable in 1978/9 was only half the level of unemployment at which it was stable in 1984–6. Most economists would have expected the very sharp fall in British unemployment between 1987 and 1989 to have led to a considerable increase in pay pressures, but the upwards pressure was surprisingly modest. This variability of the NAIRU causes considerable difficulties. In principle, if unemployment is above the NAIRU, a Government can reduce the unemployment rate by relaxing policy. In practice, the uncertainties are so great that some economists even question the NAIRU's usefulness as a concept.

What sort of factors might have shifted the NAIRU? The new classical economists have tended to emphasize various supply-side factors such as a rise in benefit levels or a relaxation of the stringency with which they are administered, causing the unemployed to be less willing to take jobs. An alternative explanation is rising trade union power, causing wage levels to be driven above 'market-clearing' levels. Regulation of minimum wages helps set a floor to the whole pay structure which means that the effect of any shock to the system, such as the world recession or Mrs Thatcher's disinflationary policies, is to cause unemployment because pay cannot fall to provide an incentive to employers to hire more people.[3] In principle, all of these explanations can hold good but they cannot be pushed too far in the context of the eighties. Moreover, an unfortunate sub-theme of much of this work is that unemployment is in some sense the fault of the unemployed. In some cases, it is. But not in most.

In principle, one could abolish unemployment by abolishing any payment of benefit. That would force the unemployed to work for pitiful wages which someone would be prepared to pay. But that would merely substitute a poverty problem for

Figure 30

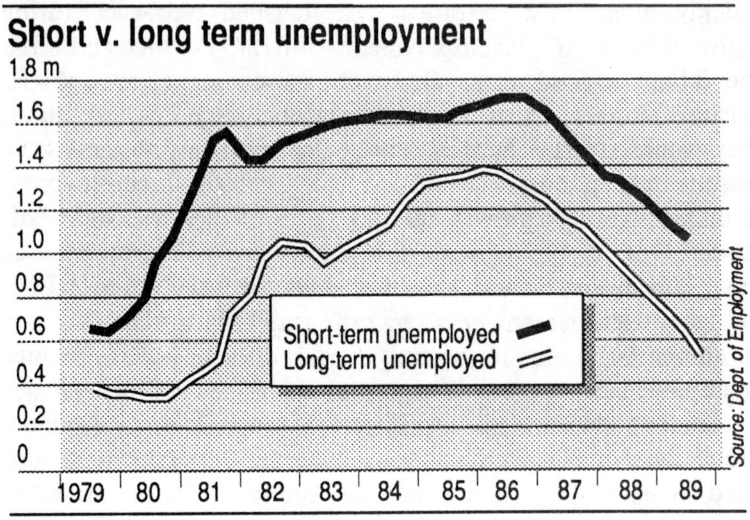

an unemployment problem. Moreover, it is simply inaccurate to highlight high benefits as the cause of the rise in unemployment over the seventies and eighties. The 'replacement ratio' – the level of benefit which someone who becomes unemployed can expect as a proportion of average earnings – fell throughout the period of high and rising unemployment. By the mid-eighties, the average benefit as a proportion of previous earnings for the short-term unemployed was as low as at any time since the late sixties, at 73 per cent, and was only 50 per cent for those unemployed for over a year.[4] Trade union power had been eroded by trade union legislation which limited the right to secondary strike action, insisted on strike ballots and made union officers subject to election. Wages councils were abolished. Yet all of these factors were in place while unemployment was still rising between 1979 and 1986. They should have been reducing the NAIRU, but in fact earnings growth remained remarkably stable despite the steady, gentle rise in unemployment until July 1987.

Explaining the rise in unemployment during the recession is not seriously at issue: it was a response to the reduction of demand caused by OPEC and by the Government policy tightening to control inflation. The real question is why unemployment (and the NAIRU) did not come down more quickly after these episodes, and why it continues to be high. Why does the market not adjust? One reason why the labour market may not work in the classical sense is because employers pay higher wages to their employees than they would strictly need in order to retain their services. The reasons for payment of these so-called 'efficiency' wages may be to make employees more motivated, and ensure that they work harder. Or perhaps to ensure their loyalty and commitment over time. The result is to create a fortunate group of 'insiders' in the labour market whose pay is divorced from what is going on amongst the 'outsiders' – the low-paid, casual workers and unemployed.

Another plausible cause of the slowness of the adjustment which falls into the category of 'hysteresis', after the Greek word *hysteron* meaning 'last', is the reluctance to hire people who have been unemployed for a long time. The people who were made unemployed during the recession were like flowers in the shop window. The first day they looked fresh and attractive to passers-by, and some of them were bought. When the others did not sell, they were moved further back in the shop. As more and more days passed, they were relegated ever further into the recesses of the florist's until no-one showed the slightest bit of interest. There is, unfortunately, a good deal of evidence that the long-term unemployed find it harder to get a job because employers clearly believe that their spell on the dole reflects badly on their motivation or productivity, while they in turn become discouraged and cease to look actively for work.[5]

This process of mutual discouragement by employers and the long-term unemployed means that a given total of unemployment becomes less and less effective in scaring wage earners into accepting the level of pay settlements which is compatible with what the economy can deliver without rising inflation. In other words, the NAIRU will tend to be higher, the larger is the proportion of the long-term unemployed. Since 1979 the proportion of the unemployed who have been out of work for more than a year has risen from around 20 per cent to around 40 per cent.[6] This phenomenon explains why unemployment has also gone up relative to vacancies, which used to be considered a sign either of 'voluntary' unemployment because workers are more choosey (say, if benefits have gone up) or as a sign that structural unemployment had increased because the jobs on offer were not suitable for the unemployed. However, if structural unemployment had increased, the unemployment/vacancy ratios would vary sharply from industrial sector to industrial sector. In fact there is less discrepancy than in the early seventies.[7] (This is not an argument against training. First, there is still some mismatch. Secondly, the evidence is that poor training traps Britain in low-technology types of production.)

The high levels of unemployment in many of the major western economies essentially arose because of the policies which they adopted to fight the inflationary climate of the seventies. Where they persist, it is due to the difficulty of reversing changes which take on characteristics of their own. The key is the relationship between pay pressure and unemployment. The seventies are not a movie which can simply be run backwards. The next two essays deal with old and new answers to the problem.

Notes

1 Charles Bean, 'Capital Shortages and Persistent Unemployment', *Economic Policy*, no. 8 (Cambridge, April 1989).

2 I am immensely indebted to Professor Richard Layard's thoughts on this subject over many years. His forthcoming book *Unemployment* with Richard Jackman, Stephen Nickell and Sushil Wadhwani is set to be the standard work.

3 The most prominent exponent of these views is Professor Patrick Minford. See his *Unemployment: Cause and Cure* (Oxford: Blackwell, 2nd edn, 1986).

4 N. Morris, comment in 'Unemployment and Labour Market Policies', *Joint Studies in Public Policy*, ed. P.E. Hart (National Institute of Economic and Social Research, Policy Studies Institute and Royal Institute of International Affairs, Gower, 1986).

5 See Jackman *et al.*, op cit., but also, for example, Pamela Meadows, Hilary Cooper and Richard Bartholomew, *The London Labour Market* (Department of Employment, 1988).

6 Jackman *et al.*, op cit.

7 See Richard Layard, *How to Beat Unemployment* (Oxford, 1986), p. 57.

Can workers price themselves out of jobs?

Pay rises as an economic problem

- the neo-classical view of real wages
- Treasury estimates of job gains
- real product wages
- no one sets real wages
- if they did, would real wage cuts boost jobs?
- the evidence of the Treasury model suggests policy relaxation is crucial
- jobs fall if real wages drop
- the people who push are not those who lose

It is fair to say that most economists see pay as one of the key factors, if not the key factor, in creating and sustaining unemployment. But it does not follow from that broad consensus that the differences of view are negligible. The previous essay argued that unemployment was the means by which the pressures from workers for more pay were reconciled with the pressures from companies for more profit. The worse the conflict, the higher the level of unemployment needed to stop inflation accelerating. One implication of this view is that no one can be held personally responsible for unemployment; it is a policy problem which has to be tackled by changing institutions and rules and ensuring that society reaches a collectively desirable outcome. However, many new classical economists still hold that unemployment is essentially a voluntary phenomenon due to the unemployed themselves. The market may be 'distorted' by high benefits or people may ask too much money for their labour. Workers can price themselves out of jobs – and back into them.[1] In essence, labour is just like any other product. A high price will encourage supply and discourage demand; a low price will discourage supply and encourage demand.

This view was implicitly accepted by the Government when it published a Treasury study called *Pay and Jobs* in 1985 as part of its campaign for pay moderation. The argument was that the high real value of wages priced workers out of jobs. Each percentage point change in the average level of real earnings – gross pay before tax but after inflation –

would in time change employment by 0.5 to 1 per cent, or by 150,000 to 200,000 jobs. The Treasury went on to point out that this need not imply pay cuts. The beneficial effects on jobs would happen if pay merely rose in line with prices. Gross pay would clearly be lower than it would otherwise be, but not lower in absolute terms. We would forego real wage increases. On this view, three successive years of such restraint would create a cumulative 1.5 million jobs. Moreover, tax cuts could mean rising living standards despite flat gross pay in real terms.[2]

There are, nevertheless, considerable problems with the simple way in which the Chancellor asserted that changes in real gross pay cause changes in jobs. Real earnings, after all, nearly doubled between 1946 and 1970, but the unemployment rate was exactly the same in both years. The reason why people did not 'price themselves out of jobs' in the post-war period was because output per person – productivity – rose broadly in line with earnings, thus keeping labour costs to employers for each unit of output fairly stable.

There is a definition of real wages which allows for the rise in productivity: i.e. it is the employers' cost of labour per unit of output. This is sometimes called 'real unit labour costs' and sometimes, rather misleadingly, the 'real product wage'. But the link between real unit labour costs and jobs is not strong. Between 1980 and 1984, for example, real unit labour costs fell in Britain, Germany and the United States but the only one of the three to create more jobs was the United States. In Japan real unit labour costs rose but employment remained stable. This, though, is not conclusive. New classical economists can point out that, in Britain, rising pay forced companies to boost productivity in part by investing in labour-saving equipment. This in turn lowered real unit labour costs but in the process caused a good deal of unemployment. It was a response, they argued, to the rise in wage costs in the first instance.

However, it seems simply incredible to argue that it was the rise in real gross pay between 1980 and 1981 which caused the rise in unemployment. The Government's anti-inflationary policies depressing demand were crucial. Indeed, the Government actually helped to drive up real unit labour costs by damping down demand, depressing output and initially cutting productivity. But that does not mean that the rise in real unit labour costs was to blame for the increase in unemployment: it was merely another simultaneous consequence of Mrs Thatcher's squeeze. Similarly, the Government's squeeze on demand meant that companies were not able to raise prices as quickly as before. So real wages, after allowing for price rises, were higher than they would otherwise have been if inflation had gone on unchecked. But again, the causal factor was the Government's squeeze, not the rise in a particular measure of real wages. In short, real wages may change for all sorts of reasons within the economy but they do not necessarily have any causal power themselves.

Indeed, the central question about the so-called 'real wage debate' is whether it can be meaningful to talk about real wages causing anything at all, since the level of real wages arises as a result of a whole series of other events in the economy. In the jargon, it is 'endogenous'. If, for example, employees all decide to accept a real pay cut in order to encourage employment, all they can do is cut their actual pay. What if employers then take advantage of the cut in costs to cut their prices in order to remain competitive with each other? Clearly, real wages will have risen again as prices fall, negating the employees' intention to cut the real cost of their services. Neither employers nor employees on their own can set a 'real wage' except for a very fleeting moment.

A second problem is the classic Keynesian one. Assume, for the sake of argument, that employees succeed in getting their real wage cut. They then decide that they will spend less because their incomes have fallen. This is the famous case of Chapter 19 of the *General Theory*.[3] It is not obvious that demand does stay stable if wages fall because it is quite likely that lower incomes will mean lower spending. A fall in the price of bananas boosts demand for them, because banana producers are an insignificant part of the whole economy. But people are not like bananas. There are too many of us to ignore knock-on effects from lower earnings on spending. When our earnings fall, our spending tends to be cut too. Nor is it obvious that some of the factors which might offset weaker consumption – such as increased competitiveness boosting exports – work for the world as a whole. Interplanetary trade is still in its infancy. So an increase in demand may be necessary on these grounds too.

The Treasury itself implicitly conceded these points in its paper, which contained various computer-model simulations of what might happen if pay pressures moderated. Its preferred simulation suggested that an initial 3 per cent wage cut (compared with what might otherwise happen) would encourage employers to reduce prices by 1 per cent. So real wage costs would fall by 2 per cent. After four years this was held to create about 300,000 jobs through various mechanisms: increased competitiveness, the encouragement of more labour intensive investment and so forth.

The main problem with this scenario is that it is not credible outside a formal incomes policy of the sort the Chancellor abhors. The Treasury had jumped from the 'what if?' school of economics to the 'if only' school. There is no sensible explanation of how such wage moderation might come about in the framework of essentially *laissez faire* policies. But the second objection is scarcely less damaging: even if such a real wage fall were to occur, it is clear that the Treasury had wilfully exaggerated the efficacy of real wage cuts in part by the nature of the policy framework it set out and in part because of some contentious elements of its model which lack supporting evidence.

Roughly a third of the extra jobs in the Treasury's preferred simulation resulted not from a real wage fall as such, but from what most economists would call a budgetary relaxation – a reflation. This happened because the Treasury assumed that Government borrowing – the gap between revenues and spending – remained a constant share of national output. However, the fall in the public sector wage bill allows more civil servants to be hired or it creates room for tax cuts within the new borrowing total. Rising output reduces public spending on the unemployed and also provides room for tax cuts. There was no good reason why the Treasury could not embark on this budgetary relaxation at the inflation rate which prevailed at the time, or even at a higher rate of inflation: all they were telling us was that if wage bargainers behaved themselves over pay rises, they would ensure that there were more output and jobs. If not, they wouldn't.

To be fair, the paper also contained a simulation of what would happen if there were a real wage cut of 2 per cent but interest rates, tax rates and real public spending were held constant – a more conventional view of unchanged policy. But this scenario was even more unrealistic, for wages had to fall by nearly 7 per cent to maintain the real pay cut, as the Treasury model said that employers would merely cut prices in line, reinstating the value of the real wage. If you can believe that this sort of actual pay cut could be accepted by employees, then the result would be to add about 200,000 jobs after four years as the long-term effects on the mix of labour and capital in the production process came through.

In the short term, though, the result was to make unemployment worse. The Treasury came up with the expected Keynesian result that real wage cuts would so reduce take-home pay that spending, output and national income would fall. Only later would it begin to recover as the country gained competitiveness and firms substituted labour for machines in producing more output. Even this result exaggerated the beneficial effects through what the uncharitably disposed might call model-rigging. One of the least powerful parts of the Treasury model in explaining the real world is the model of the corporate sector, but it has the happy property of showing that companies spend their extra income as the real wages of their employees fell. This is crucial in boosting the employment effect, as the published version of the paper concedes.

The original unpublished version of the paper which went to the Treasury's group of academic consultants contained a paragraph, subsequently excised, which admitted that the criticism of the corporate sector of the model carried some weight. 'The criticism is,' the uncensored paper said, 'that the simulation results depend critically on a system of adjustments which is entirely arbitrary and has no empirical basis. It has to be admitted that the empirical backing for this system of adjustments is not strong; after all, the main reason why such effects do not appear in the individual expenditure equations is that empirical research has been unable to establish their existence.' In other words, the Treasury was guessing. Needless to say, this was not a prominent feature of its public relations campaign.

There is a third fundamental problem with the simple Treasury view, which is simply that the people who create the pay pressure are not necessarily the same people who suffer the pain of unemployment. The typical unemployed person is low skilled and was low paid before losing their job. The typical source of wage pressure is highly skilled, lives in the South East, has never been unemployed, and is already at the top end of the income distribution, as we have already seen. If we are talking about pay moderation, who is it for? If the low-paid moderate their pay claims, will the well-paid merely intensify theirs? Who is pushing whom out of work?

Where does all this leave us? The implication of the Treasury model is that fiscal or monetary reflation – tax cuts or spending increases or interest rate cuts – can create jobs. However, a key caveat is that unemployment is already above the level at which pay settlements begin to accelerate. If it is not, then pay moderation is also needed if macro-economic policy is to be effective in creating employment. Real wage cuts on their own will not help in the short run: they are just as likely to lead to a fall in employment. It makes sense to see policy and pay moderation as the two blades of a pair of scissors needed to cut unemployment rather than to pretend that it is entirely up to employees to change their behaviour. Finally, policy-makers still face the thorniest problem of all – how to ensure that people do moderate their pay claims to what the economy can afford. It is rather easy to cut taxes or increase public spending to boost demand, but it is not at all easy to persuade people to take pay cuts – or even to forego pay increases.

Notes

1 See, for example, Patrick Minford, *Unemployment: Cause and Cure* (Oxford: Blackwell, 2nd edn, 1986).

2 *Pay and Jobs* (HM Treasury, January 1985).

3 J.M. Keynes, *The General Theory of Employment, Interest and Money* (London, 1935).

Policies for cutting unemployment

Cutting labour supply not good policy

- the lump of output fallacy
- the key is reducing pay pressures
- a source of collective failure in the labour market
- experience with incomes policy
- the need for sanctions
- tax-based incomes policy
- measures to combat long-term unemployment
- training and an active labour market policy

Many of the proposals put forward for dealing with unemployment would have no effect at all, or even make the situation worse. A popular, but counter-productive, solution is to persuade elderly workers to retire. What, then, would be the effect of persuading someone with particular skills in short supply to take early retirement? If the economy is in recession, then the early retirement will probably lead to a reduction in unemployment. But why is it better than taking measures to expand demand and increase output? If the economy is already operating at the level of unemployment needed to stop wage inflation from speeding up, then the early retirement will have no effect – or even an adverse one. The supply of a particular type of labour would fall, and the price would rise, worsening the amount of pay pressure for a given level of unemployment. The Government would then have to take restrictive measures in order to ensure that pay pressures subsided once again. The economy would settle back with a lower level of output and higher unemployment.

The example of someone with skills merely makes the conclusion easier to grasp, but in fact the conclusion holds more widely. In general, measures that reduce the supply of labour are either an inferior means of cutting unemployment (during a recession, when the alternative is to encourage demand and output) or a counter-productive one. Because this runs against common-sense intuition, it is worth spelling it out. If it were the case that falls in the labour force reduced unemployment, then surely increases in the labour force would lead to rising unemployment. But they do not. After all, Britain's population has soared from around 11 million at the time of the Napoleonic wars to 58 million today, but unemployment has not increased in line. There have even been sudden surges in the size of the labour force which have been accommodated in more jobs rather than higher unemployment.

After the Second World War, the number of civilian jobs increased by 2.31 million between 1945 and 1948.[1] There was another surge of more than a million new jobs between 1958 and 1962. And there was another sharp increase at the end of the eighties. Sharp increases in the labour force – through increased births, or through immigration, or through greater numbers of married women wanting to work – merely increase the capacity of the economy to provide goods and services, for which there is no fixed supply. Indeed, increases in labour supply can make an economy more dynamic, as appeared to be the case in Germany in the fifties and in the United States in the eighties. The central point is that there is no given 'lump of output' which stays the same: if the capacity to produce increases, spending power can rise to absorb the increased output.

The key to reducing unemployment is to find measures which reduce the amount of pay pressure for a given level of unemployment, which will in turn allow the Government to expand demand a little more rapidly and absorb some of the unemployment. This is easier said than done. The first snag is that the punishment – unemployment – does not necessarily hit the people taking the pay rises. The second snag is that no individual or group of workers can see that their own behaviour can make much difference. Self-interest rules. Everybody's first priority is to go for a high pay rise while everyone else takes a low one. This way you benefit from a big rise, but there is low inflation and high employment. The second preference might be to exercise mutual restraint so that everyone gets a low pay rise, and everyone benefits from low inflation and high employment. The third preference is for everyone to scramble for high pay for fear of being left behind. You ensure that you get the same as everyone else, but inflation is high and unemployment has to stay high to control it. Your fourth preference is the nightmare: you get a low pay rise and everyone else gets a high one.

The dilemma is that the pursuit of your first option – you get a high pay rise while everyone else gets a low one – automatically entails that we end up with the third. The only way we can end up with a second-best situation instead of the third preference is by some kind of mutual restraint. Imagine what happens if someone stands up in a football stand to get a better view of the match. The person behind has to stand up too, and before long the whole stand is on its feet. Everyone will have exactly the same view they would have had if they had remained seated, but they will all be less comfortable in the process. They would all gain from mutual restraint. Mutual restraint, though, requires mutual guarantees and collective sanctions of some kind to assure everyone that everybody else will play fair. What we need is multilateral disarmament in the labour market, because unilateralism does not work.

Most of the easy answers do not work. The offer of tax cuts if everybody settles for low pay increases – an offer made by both Mr Denis Healey and by Mr Nigel Lawson – is unlikely to have any effect on the labour market, because an incentive addressed to everybody is equally addressed to nobody. You will get your tax cut regardless of your individual behaviour, and you cannot affect anyone else's. Similarly, ministerial jawboning about wage rises is ineffective. Some sort of intervention which bears down directly on the sources of the pay pressure is also required.

One option is for the Trades Union Congress to run an incomes policy with teeth, so that trade unions which breach the agreed guidelines might be expelled from the TUC and suffer poaching of their members by other unions. This essentially corporatist incomes policy works in small, homogeneous countries like Sweden and Austria but it has a sorry record in Britain, as the winter of discontent in 1978/9 shows. Many groups of employees are not unionized, and trade union leaderships are anyway reluctant to turn themselves into instruments of restraint on their members. Ultimately, the political pressures on them to resume their normal role prove far too great. The experience of the Labour Government of 1964–70 suggests that the attempt to run union-based incomes policies merely led to the growth of rank-and-file agitation against union leaderships.

Partly as a result, incomes policy could prove effective only in the short term. Subsequently, pay caught up.[2]

Mr Denis Healey's experience of running incomes policy between 1974 and 1979 persuaded him of the need for specific sanctions. For example, he threatened the Ford Motor Company with the loss of Government contracts if they did not keep to the Government's pay guidelines. However, the arbitrary nature of the threat, which could not apply to any company which did not sell to the Government, caused a furore in parliament. The principle, though, was surely correct. If any type of incomes policy was to work, some penalties or incentives had to be devised which varied according to the wage behaviour of those involved. The only credible proposals are for some form of tax related to the size of the pay award. The original tax-based incomes policy was proposed in the United States in the early seventies, and would have varied a company's profit tax rate according to its wage bill.[3] The most persuasive British proposal is for a counter-inflation tax which employers of a certain size would pay if their pay bill per employee rose by more than a norm.[4]

The counter-inflation tax would allow firms to pay more to some people, and not to others. Or they can pay more, but also pay the tax. So it would not be as inflexible as the traditional incomes policy. Any money raised from the tax would be handed back to all employers equally in lower labour taxation, thus ensuring that companies did not merely pass on the cost of the tax in higher prices.

What are the problems? The tax would inevitably provide some handicap to fast-growing firms offering big increases in pay to attract staff, but on the other hand it might foster a more rapidly growing economy which would offset the disadvantage even to fast-growing firms. It would be administratively impractical to levy a counter-inflation tax on other than firms with more than 100 or so employees, which are currently a PAYE unit for income tax. However, that division would set up an incentive to avoid the tax by breaking up companies. Moreover, the proposal runs against the grain of a world where plant size is getting smaller, and more and more people are working in service businesses or are self-employed.

The biggest problems with such a tax, though, are political rather than economic. Neither employers nor employees want an effective incomes policy which they perceive would limit their freedom of action. This is not surprising, since the major beneficiaries are the 'outsiders' who are unemployed, but it does mean that it is difficult politically to introduce measures which cause some overt discomfort to those in work.

What other measures could be taken to reduce pay pressures for a given level of unemployment (or reduce unemployment for a given pay pressure)? If it is true that the long-term unemployed are effectively excluded from the labour market and exert no useful pressure on the pay of those in work, as was argued in the first essay of this chapter, then a high priority ought to be given to any measures which bring them back into contention. Unlike a reduction in short-term unemployment, a cut in long-term unemployment should actually be counter-inflationary. It will tend to increase the pressures on those in work to moderate their pay claims.

Indeed, this emphasis on the long-term unemployed has been a major thrust of Government policy since 1986, and helps to explain why it was possible to reduce unemployment by more than a million in two years without much sharper wage inflation. The Department of Employment began reinterviewing the long-term unemployed every six months in so-called 'Restart' interviews which put them under pressure to take a publicly supported training place or to start looking for work again. Tougher tests to ensure that benefit claimants really were available for work probably also led to a fall in the number of fraudulent claims.

Nevertheless, much more could be done positively to reduce unemployment, particularly in providing the long-term unemployed with a 'Job Guarantee'. Subsidies to additional employment of the long-term unemployed would help to overcome employers' resistance, and others could take a publicly provided training place if they could still not find work. But the essential commitment would be to ensure that anyone out of work for more than a year – about 3 per cent of the labour force in the summer of 1989 – would no longer be unemployed. Britain is still a long way from the kind of active labour market policies which have kept Sweden's unemployment rate at around 2 per cent of the labour force.[5] Through encouragement and subsidies for training and migration, Sweden makes a strong effort to match the unemployed to jobs. It also withdraws benefit after a period if the unemployed do not avail themselves of the offered opportunities.

An active labour market policy would also help to improve the link between unemployment and pay pressures in another way. By relieving shortages of key skills in the labour market, it would enable employers to increase overall employment without incurring sharply higher labour costs, bidding up wages, and disturbing traditional relativities which may cause a further leap-frogging amongst employees. The Training Commission, which has superseded the old Manpower Services Commission, still operates only the most rudimentary forms of labour market intelligence at local level – or, indeed, in monitoring how British skills levels compare with our competitors abroad. It should not be impossible to devise information systems which spot when pay pressures are rising sharply in a particular market, and that would in turn be the first step towards remedying the deficiency. The provision of training could be made much more responsive to price signals in a way which has a sound basis in economic theory. After all, it is a common finding of work on training that the social benefits far outweigh the private benefits of undergoing training to either an employer or an employee. A corollary is that the private market will tend not to respond quickly enough to shortages signalled by wage rises.

Intervention in the labour market does not have to be of the heavy-handed and traditional form via incomes policy, but intervention there still needs to be.

Notes

1 *The British Economy: Key Statistics, 1900–1966* (London: London and Cambridge Economic Service, 1966).

2 See, for example, the conclusions of a diverse group of economists in J.L. Fallick and R.F. Elliott, eds. *Incomes Policies, Inflation and Relative Pay* (London: George Allen & Unwin, 1981).

3 H.C. Wallich and S. Weintraub, 'A Tax-based Incomes Policy', *Journal of Economic Issues*, vol. 5, no. 2 (June 1971).

4 Richard Layard, *More Jobs, Less Inflation: the Case for a Counter-inflation Tax* (London: Grant McIntyre, 1982).

5 Richard Jackman *et al.*, *A Job Guarantee for Long Term Unemployed People* (Employment Institute, 1986).

What sort of jobs will there be in the future?

Productivity differences affect sectors

- the conventional view of declining factory jobs
- Leontief's input–output analysis
- advantages in looking at industrial structure
- a shifting pattern within a stable factory total
- the decline of clerical work
- the rise of the professionals
- the key is training

What sort of future will our children inherit? The most popular economic scenarios tend either to project a paradise in which an abundance of human ingenuity and technology provides for every want, or alternatively a society characterized by a growing gulf between ever richer haves and ever more deprived have-nots. Neither millenarian vision is likely. Economic phenomena tend to move more slowly than people expect. Moreover, the economics profession is at one in arguing that the saloon bar fears about new technology are simply wrong.

From the Luddites onwards, people have feared that machines will gradually displace workers, but economic history tends to suggest that it is more likely that there will not be enough workers to operate all the machines we shall want. Certainly, the structure of the labour force, when divided by industry or by occupation, will change. There will be job losses in declining sectors, and gains in others. Just as the Basingstoke ostler gave way to the Bath fireman when Isambard Kingdom Brunel built the Great Western Railway, so the new technologies of today will destroy some jobs. It will be hard for some people to adapt. However, the canals, the steam engine, the electric motor also created more products for people to buy and make. We are, today, more prosperous and less weighed down by drudgery than our forebears could have dreamed.

Amongst economists today, the orthodox view is that manufacturing industry will go on having a greater potential for the introduction of machinery than other sectors. We can see, for example, almost labour-free factories in Japan where robots have all but replaced human beings in assembling even sophisticated products like video recorders. The joke runs that you could fire a shotgun in a Japanese electronics factory and not hit anyone. The potential for labour-saving in other countries is thus clearly large. The Institute for Employment Research at Warwick University argues that manufacturing employment, which provided 30.6 per cent of British employment in 1975, will go on falling to only 19.2 per cent by 1995.[1] The biggest gainers are jobs in distribution and business services. As people are able to buy manufactured goods more and more cheaply (because high productivity gains allow prices to be held down) they will spend more and more of their extra income on labour-intensive services like restaurants, tourism and leisure services.

This sort of projection, like almost all forecasting, assumes that the future will continue to look much like the past. We have, in British economic history, several examples of sectors where the potential growth of output per person – productivity – was so great that it exceeded even the growing demand for its output. In those circumstances, employment can fall even though output is rising. The obvious example of this phenomenon in all the industrial countries has been the steady decline in agricultural employment, which engaged one in ten people in Britain at the time of the census in 1891 but which is now down to barely more than 2 per cent, despite steady increases in output.[2] On this view, manufacturing jobs will gently decline because output per employee rises even faster than output. As manufacturing continues to shed jobs, people will move into services like restaurants, hotels and leisure activities, the demand for which rises particularly steeply as income rises. How does this view square with the particularly sharp losses in manufacturing jobs in Britain over the last twenty years? The reason for the devastating fall in British manufacturing employment during the seventies and eighties – and particularly in 1979–81 – was simply that factory output did not rise over the period. This was a failure specific to the British situation, rather than to the nature of manufacturing or technology. Other countries' factories managed to increase output while also seeing factory jobs fall much more gently.

There is a different and intriguing scenario to the conventional economic wisdom. The distinguished and provocative Nobel prize-winner, Wassily Leontief, argues that the main shift in future employment will not be a decline in production (or factory) workers at all. If Leontief is right, they may even increase their share of total jobs. The category of workers which will be hit most dramatically will be office workers. And the category which will gain most will be the professionals.[3] Leontief's conclusions would have interesting implications for the economy, particularly for some of the most rapidly growing parts such as financial services, which now account for more than 15 per cent of total output. The squeeze on clerical work would particularly disadvantage women, who form a high proportion of office workers. The shift would revolutionize most city centres because the amount of floor space required by managerial operations would fall sharply. Moreover, as the structure of work shifted towards professionals, the opportunities for sub-contracting into smaller units would grow.

The Leontief research relies on input–output analysis, a method which the Russian economist pioneered and which is quite different from the more usual computer models of the economy which deal in highly aggregated totals such as consumers' spending, investment and so forth. Input–output analysis constructs a picture of each small sector of the economy and charts the inputs it buys from each other sector, and the outputs it sells to each other sector. This is a much more detailed approach than the conventional use of macro-economic aggregates like gross domestic product or investment, which are all that is necessary for short-term forecasting. Like all forecasting, it still relies on extrapolating past trends into the future. But by looking at each trend in a more detailed way, the input–output researchers hope to reach a more convincing picture of overall developments.

The input–output approach makes sense in the study of industrial and employment structure because it can monitor long–term trends at the level of the industry and occupation. Most of the impact of new technology comes through its gradual adoption as one old process is phased out, and the new one phased in. The structure of the economy is like the proverbial oil-tanker which takes 10 miles to change course. But in order to make their conclusions still more robust, the New York researchers project two different scenarios: one with a relatively rapid pace of change, and one rather slower. Leontief and his collaborator Dr Faye Duchin believe that the more rapid pace is the more realistic, so that is where our focus will be.

The research deals with the United States economy, which starts with a slightly different occupational structure to Britain's. (For example, the United States has more farmers than Britain.) However, the broad changes in the occupational structure will have their parallels in Britain and other developed economies even if the starting points look slightly different. Several important social implications stand out. Production workers – the blue-collar working class – do lose many of their existing jobs, but they are rehired in the booming industries required to produce new equipment for the technological revolution.

The people who lose out, in Leontief's view, are clerical workers whose share in the labour force declines from 17.8 per cent to 11.4 per cent as office automation gathers pace. There is simply enormous scope for improving office techniques by introducing word processors and other computer-aided equipment instead of paper. At present the average American office worker uses only $2,000 of capital equipment, compared with $25,000 for a factory worker. Dr Duchin, a woman, points out that this change could throw the trend towards more women in the labour force sharply into reverse, unless women can adapt themselves to the expanding occupations. In Britain and the United States a relatively high proportion of women work – and a high proportion of them work in clerical jobs.

Maybe more will, Russian style, become labourers. Others will move into the gently expanding crafts or services. But the best bet for anyone is going to be the most rapidly expanding series of occupations of all – the professionals. And within the

Figure 31

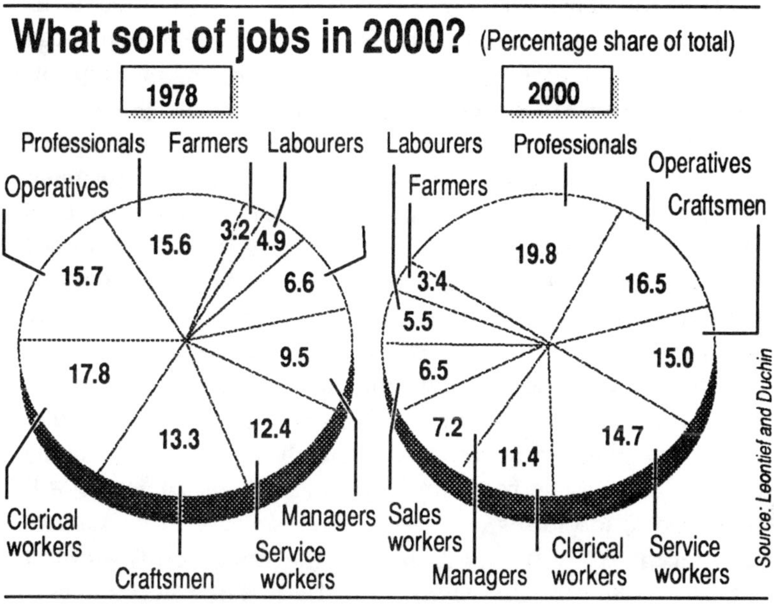

professional category, anybody with computer skills is going to be in great demand. These calculations about the changing occupational structure are the ones about which the Leontief team feel most confident, but they also shed some additional light on the saloon bar wisdom that new technology is going to destroy jobs.

When the researchers projected the growth of demand for various categories of goods and services as compiled by the US Bureau of Labour Statistics their favoured technological scenario simply generated too many jobs for what is likely to be the size of the American labour force in 2000 (figure 31). So they had to develop an alternative scenario which assumes a lower rate of technical change to create fewer jobs. In other words, the study strongly implies that the likely technological changes up to 2000 are going to increase the demand for labour rather than reduce it – exactly as past technological changes have done. If unemployment does stay high, it will be for other reasons, such as the deflationary response of governments to wage-bargainers' price-raising pay claims. It will not be due to new technology.

There is, though, a caveat to this conclusion. The job-creating effect of the new computer technology implies a lot of changing about within the overall total. But what if people do not, or cannot, train themselves up quickly enough to take the new job opportunities? Other evidence shows that such structural unemployment has not increased through the period of the seventies and eighties,[4] but it is clearly still a possibility. All the economists working in this field rightly stress the importance of training, not merely because it equips people for specific jobs but also because it tends to make them better able to learn new ones later. The faster a country adapts itself to the skills and the opportunities of technical change, the more likely it is to be able to enjoy lower unemployment and higher living standards. A failure to adapt is likely in the short run to lead to slower growing living standards, and then in the long run to a chronic inability to compete in world markets which would in turn lead to job losses.

A recent study by researchers at the Institute of Manpower Studies at Sussex University into the labour requirements of the City of London supports the argument that we may find ourselves short of key types of labour. The research found that it would be quite simply impossible to meet the demand of City institutions for university graduates even if there was a major expansion of higher education.[5] Nor was this demand coming from the securities businesses – the share- and bond-dealers – who tend to monopolize the public image of the City. Indeed, securities employment was the only area in decline. The demand for graduates was widely based across the growing City areas of insurance, banking, business services (like management consultancy) and fund management.

The growth of the professional salariat is essentially due to specialization. As many management functions become more specialized, it does not make sense even for very large companies to retain particular specialities on their staff. They go instead to consultancies which specialize in computer systems management, or accounting information systems, or business strategy and marketing work. This devolution of functions has important social and political implications because it begins to break down the Galbraithian world in which the classical multinational corporations hold sway. One of the features of professional work makes it rather like the medieval guilds: it need only take place in small groups, and there are relatively few economies of scale. This liberalization at the management end of the twentieth-century corporation is paralleled by a liberalization at the production end. Manufacturing is increasingly marked by 'just in time' production rather than long runs of identical products, and robots are doing the most repetitive tasks, leaving the work-force in a supervisory and maintenance role.

There is an additional reason why the Leontief–Duchin projections for manufacturing may prove correct in Britain, namely necessity. Britain's manufacturing output shrank from 26.6 per cent of national output in 1980 to 23.8 per cent in 1985; manufacturing employment collapsed by more than two million during the recession, to take its share from 27 per cent in 1979 to under 20 per cent in 1988.[6] However, it is precisely such a Leontief–Duchin reversal of deindustrialization which is probably also required to turn around the trade deficit, simply because manufacturing is so important to Britain's export performance.

Notes

1 See, for example, the Institute of Employment Research *Review of the Economy and Employment* (University of Warwick, 1987) and successive issues.

2 Peter Flora *et al.*, *State, Economy and Society in Western Europe, 1815–1975: a Data Handbook* (London, Frankfurt and Chicago, 1987), vol. 2, p. 525.

3 Wassily Leontief and Faye Duchin, *The Impacts of Automation on Employment, 1963–2000* (Institute of Economic Analysis at New York University (mimeo) and Oxford, 1985).

4 Richard Layard, *How to Beat Unemployment* (Oxford, 1986), p. 57.

5 Amin Rajan with Julie Fryatt, *Create or Abdicate*, a report for the London Human Resources Development Group by the Institute of Manpower Studies, Sussex (John Wiley, September 1988).

6 *Economic Trends*, 1988 annual supplement.

8 International Issues

The dollar, the twin deficits and the Reagan legacy

The Reagan legacy

- growth and jobs
- flat real incomes
- supply-side weaknesses
- the current account deficit
- the rundown in US net assets
- the dollar collapse scenario
- reasons for expecting a softer landing
- longer-term effects of dollar fall
- large capital flows
- official underpinning by G7
- two views on the dollar

Two books were on the *New York Times* bestseller list for more than six months as President Reagan's eight years in the White House drew to a close. Their titles said it all about the forebodings with which many Americans approached the future. The first was Ravi Batra's *The Great Depression of 1990: Why it's got to Happen*, and the second was Paul Kennedy's *The Rise and Fall of the Great Powers*. The country which patented self-confidence was rediscovering self-doubt – and with ample reason. President Reagan bequeathed an economic legacy which was in many respects more threatening than that of any of his post-war predecessors. The most ominous features of the inheritance, notably the twin deficits on the federal budget and the current account of the balance of payments, are set to dominate international economic policy for many years to come.

President Bush's task will prove all the more difficult politically because, so far, the performance of the American economy has been favourable. The economic indicators which refer to the present or the recent past – growth, inflation, unemployment – look respectable. It is an indicator which conditions the future development of the economy which still looks alarming, namely the balance of payments deficit. The parallel with Britain is close, except that in one respect the American problem is more serious. The Americans have been running large deficits for longer and have already temporarily sated the appetite of foreigners for the United States' IOUs, causing a run on the dollar. Though the dollar subsequently resumed its strength, it is no more possible to argue that the problem is over than it was during the phase of dollar strength until 1985.

The good news first. The growth of US national income (GDP) averaged 2.3 per cent a year between 1979 and 1988.[1] This was higher than growth in either Britain or the European Community, though not Japan. However, America's population has been growing at a rapid 1.1 per cent a year compared with negligible growth in Europe. Growth per head was still slower than elsewhere, although America's living standards are so high (on average) that this should be no surprise. Inflation has been subdued, and remained below 5 per cent (although prices began to accelerate in 1989). A flexible labour market made it much easier to pursue relatively high growth, which in turn ensured a steady fall in the unemployment rate to a little over 5 per cent of the labour force, comparable with most of the post-war period and which most American economists would define as 'full employment'. Further falls are likely to lead merely to accelerating wage pressures, inflation and policy action to brake growth.

The bad news comes in several parts, almost all of them with uncanny parallels in Britain. First, most Americans have scarcely participated in the prosperity of the Reagan years because the nature of the growth and the changes in the tax system benefited the top half of the income distribution. The bottom 20 per cent actually saw their tax burden rise despite the Reagan tax cuts, while the numbers in poverty have increased sharply. 'The purchasing power of the average weekly wage in 1987,' write Aho and Levinson,[2] 'was almost 15 per cent below the 1973 level. Family income, adjusted for inflation, has been flat since 1973, despite the increase in the number of two earner families. In 1986, median family income for those under 34 years old, adjusted for inflation, was below its level of 1980.'

The second piece of bad news is that many of the fundamentals which shape future performance have not improved in the Reagan years. Investment per worker in manufacturing – the key sector for international trade – is one-third the Japanese ratio. Civil research and development is still below Japanese or German levels (although a lot of Pentagon spending is an industrial policy under another name). There is concern about standards in US schools, with one study of seventeen countries suggesting that students trailed far behind those of other countries in biology, chemistry, physics and quantitative skills. A recent congressional commission noted that the lack of public infrastructure spending meant that every two days a bridge collapses.

The third piece of bad news is that the recent rise in consumption, as C. Fred Bergsten points out, has exceeded production by some $700 billion.[3] The history of Reaganomics has been of an enormous and enthusiastic consumer boom financed by borrowing from foreigners. One mechanism has been similar in Britain. Abetted by financial liberalization, individuals have borrowed far more. Net savings are the lowest proportion of disposable income for forty years. The ratio of private debt – personal and corporate – to gross national product has soared. Another mechanism behind the boom has been the sharp rise in the federal budget deficit (of spending over revenues) which peaked at more than $200 billion due to an excessively enthusiastic mixture of income tax cuts and defence spending increases. The third factor was the way in which the Federal Reserve counteracted the expansionary tax cuts by raising interest rates (see figure 32), thus attracting foreign capital into the dollar, and causing it to rise vertiginously from 1980 to 1985. This had the dual effect of raising American real incomes (because dollars could buy more imports in the short term) and of ensuring that a higher proportion of spending went on foreign goods. (This third factor is arguably merely a response to the first two. Even if the dollar had been fixed, the tax cuts would have fuelled extra

Figure 32

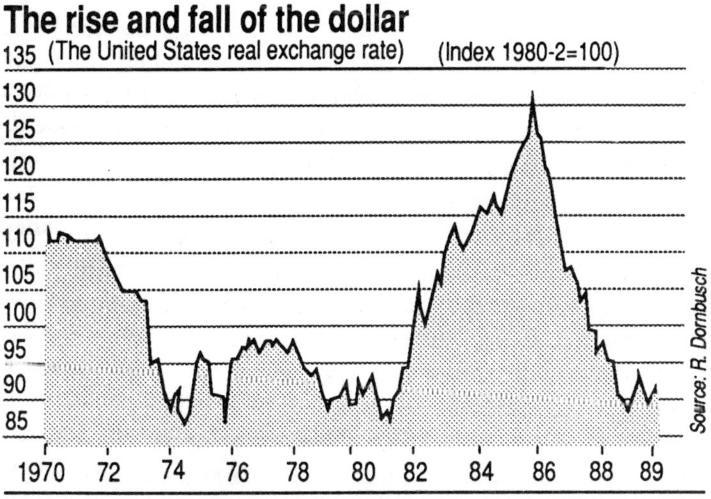

inflation within the United States, which would have led to lost competitiveness for US industry.)

The repeated payments deficits have devastated US net holdings of overseas assets, which had been worth some $140 billion in 1981, or just over 4 per cent of GNP. In the space of one short presidency, the US has gone from being the world's largest net creditor to being the world's largest net debtor. By the end of 1989 net overseas claims on the United States will amount to about 10 per cent of its GDP. The flow of dollars required each year solely to pay the interest and dividends on those overseas holdings of US assets is probably around $50 billion, which in turn means that if the US is to reach current account balance within the foreseeable future it cannot merely run a trade balance. It must have a trade surplus to meet its debt service.

The arithmetic of such deficits is simple. A prolonged period of living beyond your means, financed by foreigners' claims on you, eventually requires a subsequent period not just of living within your means, but well within them in order to generate a surplus to service the debt. Production must sharply exceed consumption. The issue which never surfaced in the presidential campaign is the unspoken theme of the Bush presidency: a period of slow growth in domestic demand and hence in output for those sectors which cannot trade or compete with imports. About this outlook there can be little disagreement since no economist is rash enough to suppose that the US external deficit does not have to come down. The disagreement is about the length of time over which it must come down, and what has to happen for the reduction to come about. The quicker and sharper, the more painful the adjustment.

The October 1987 stock market crash gave a foretaste of how the worst might happen, a situation in which the pressures for adjustment of the deficit are compressed into a short period and are correspondingly savage. Even on the most optimistic view of how quickly the deficit can be reduced, foreigners have to increase their holdings of dollars by some $200 billion. At any point, the dollar could come under downwards pressure; the value of fixed-interest Government bonds would fall as the markets expected inflation to rise; the rise in bond yields would be followed by a collapse of equities to bring their dividend yields into line, and this would in turn dim business and consumer confidence. The US would dive into recession, curbing imports and the deficit but at the cost of a wave of deflation throughout the world. Such scary scenarios are no longer the preserve merely of academics. The International Monetary Fund's *World Economic Outlook* has pointed out that market participants may 'eventually regard the prospective accumulation of US external debt as unsustainable and will reduce their demand for US assets'.[4] In short, there may be a run on the dollar. The Fund does not quantify the likely effects, but that is merely honest. Such crises besetting such large economies are fortunately rare.

There are some consoling thoughts which suggest that the United States and the world economy will muddle on through instead. The scary scenario may be more remote than it was, precisely because the dollar has already fallen so far from its peak in 1985. The downside must be smaller if only because the dollar is nearer the floor. The trade flows are clearly responding in real terms (although agonizingly slowly when measured in falling dollars). Moreover, the longer-term response is still coming through. There was $42 billion of inward direct investment in the US in 1987, much of it for import substitution. The Japanese companies are preserving a constant share of the US car market but are building up their output so that 400,000 more cars could displace imports between 1987 and 1989.[5] A comparison of absolute price levels and costs between the US and its developed country competitors shows that America is now a bargain. Even an advocate, in 1989, of a further 15 per cent dollar devaluation like Bergsten concedes that 'the main adjustment problem now seems to reside in the composition of US economic growth rather than in the exchange rate of the dollar'. US domestic spending has to slow down if net exports to improve, if only because the US is effectively at full employment. In these circumstances, a fall in the dollar without a slowdown in domestic spending would not help turn around the deficit.

Secondly, the United States (and Britain) may have longer to adjust than might have been conceivable only ten years ago. This is in part because of the enormous growth of world capital markets, and the freeing of controls on capital flows, which make finance much more readily available to creditworthy borrowers. Indeed, this change in capital markets has led to a fundamental conflict between two ways of looking at the world's large current account imbalances. The first is the traditional view that deficits are a sign of a weak trading performance due to mismanaged and excessive domestic demand, or poor trade competitiveness. The second is that current account imbalances are merely the counterpart – the obverse – of savings flows and investment opportunities. On this view, the Japanese and the Germans want to save a lot; the Americans have a lot of investment opportunities. The Japanese and Germans therefore run a capital account deficit (or outflow), while the Americans run a capital account surplus (or inflow). It is the capital flows which are causing the current account to go into deficit.

Does the current account lead the capital flows, or vice versa? The probable answer is that it is an unpredictable mixture of both, but no economist can yet give a conclusive reply, because our experience of a world of mobile international capital flows is relatively recent. Moreover, liberalization is still continuing, with the final capital controls in France and Italy only being removed in July 1990. The nearest parallels may be the period of the Gold

Standard before the First World War, when some countries (including the United States, Canada, Australia and Argentina) ran very substantial current account deficits (or capital inflows) for decades. Mr Tam Bayoumi has calculated the average size of capital flows each year in the major economies under the Gold Standard from 1880 to 1913, and has shown that they were much larger than during the post-war period from 1965 to 1986. Indeed, the average flow, as a percentage of GDP, for eight countries in the sample before 1914 was 3.25 per cent a year; the average flow for ten countries post-1965 was only 1 per cent.[6] However, it is extremely doubtful whether capital flows of this size would resume in the modern world unless there were a similar cast-iron commitment to fixing exchange rates and hence underwriting investors' currency losses.

No one argues that the United States, at its current high level of economic development, can justify running a current account deficit forever. There is no reason to believe that the United States has reversed the normal presumption that rates of return on investment are higher in less developed countries (because there are more unexploited opportunities and there is cheaper labour). Moreover, the Americans collectively do not like the extension of foreign ownership which the corollary of the deficit, even though they individually do not want to save. Finally, there remains the doubt about whether the deficit can go on being financed except at unacceptable cost. Even the larger scale of international capital flows failed to support the dollar in 1987, when on two separate occasions the private funds to finance the United States' appetite for imports were simply not available. However, this too leads to a consoling thought of a different nature. When the financial markets did lose confidence in the dollar, the Group of Seven (G7) leading industrial countries stepped in to underwrite it. Almost all the $154 billion deficit in 1987 was funded by official buying of dollars. That underwriting of the dollar revived private-sector confidence, and in 1988 the situation abruptly reversed. Net purchases of dollars by overseas Governments probably amounted to no more than $6 billion with the rest of the United States' $135 billion current account deficit being funded by private purchases.[7] Indeed, in 1989 the G7 countries were faced with precisely the opposite problem: the dollar's strength caused massive official purchases of non-dollar currencies.

It does not follow, of course, that private purchases will go on funding the US deficit. Nor does it follow that the United States can always rely on the other G7 countries, if push comes to shove, to bail it out. But the pressure on America's partners was there before, and may be again. From the United States' point of view, it is simply one advantage of its sheer size in the world economy, accounting for some 40 per cent of developed world output.

What does it all mean for the dollar? As the dollar rebounded in early 1989, most mainstream American economists, including notable thinkers like Martin Feldstein and Rudiger Dornbusch, argued that G7 should stop the rise and allow a further decline to promote trade adjustment. However, a rival view was also gaining ground. The United States current account deficit was set to be less than 2.5 per cent of national income in 1989, compared with nearly 3.5 per cent in 1987. Moreover, it was absorbing roughly 6 per cent of world savings, against 9 per cent in 1987.[8] It was not beyond the bounds of possibility that the deficit could be willingly financed, underpinned by relatively high United States interest rates and slow growing demand. If demand growth could stay buoyant outside the United States, sucking in American imports, the prospects for a 'soft landing' from the major world imbalances caused by United States policy during the eighties would be greatly enhanced.

Notes

1 US economic data from the *Economic Report of the President*, transmitted to Congress, January 1989, and from the International Monetary Fund, *International Financial Statistics*.

2 C. Michael Aho and Marc Levinson, eds., *After Reagan: Confronting the Changed World Economy* (New York: Council on Foreign Relations, 1988).

3 C. Fred Bergsten, *America in the World Economy: a Strategy for the 1990s* (Washington: Institute for International Economics, 1988).

4 International Monetary Fund, *World Economic Outlook*, April 1989.

5 See Lawrence A. Veit's contribution in Aho and Levinson, eds., op cit.

6 Tamim Bayoumi, *Saving–Investment Correlations: Immobile Capital, Government Policy or Endogenous Behaviour?*, International Monetary Fund working paper 89/66.

7 International Monetary Fund, *World Economic Outlook*, April 1989, p. 95.

8 David Morrison, *International Economics Analyst* (London: Goldman Sachs, July 1989).

The symmetry of German and Japanese surpluses

The counterpart of reducing the US payments deficit

- different reactions of surplus and deficit countries
- getting the pattern wrong means slower growth
- examples of deficit countries cutting back
- the interdependence of the European economies
- solutions to the German problem

If President Bush wants to keep making modest reductions in the United States balance of payments deficit without the pain of an American recession, he is going to have to worry about one of the oldest and most difficult problems in international economics – symmetry. It will be difficult enough for him to deliver the cuts in the budget deficit which will allow interest rates to fall, and help to close the trade gap without rising inflation. But he will also have to focus hard on an international dimension of cutting the deficit, particularly a European one. Just as important as cutting the United States trade deficit is ensuring that the right countries end up running down their surpluses. In the early years of the American deficit reduction, the parcel was getting passed to the wrong people. The result, in the medium term, was that the world was less able to absorb United States exports, which in turn implied that more of the burden of adjustment of the trade gap had to be borne internally by the United States through cutting its demand and its imports.

Every dollar reduction in the US deficit has in theory to be matched by an equal and opposite counterpart in another country's surplus or deficit, for exactly the same reason that any country's export is another country's import. But it matters whether a particular cut in the US deficit is followed by a cut in a surplus – or a rise in some other country's deficit. A surplus country will not necessarily react to an adverse shift in its trading position. Why should it? It still has a comfortable cushion of exports exceeding imports. The markets are unlikely to concentrate on any worsening in its surplus position, so confidence in its currency will not be undermined.

The position for a deficit country is very different. A further rise in its deficit will eventually force it to take action to curb domestic demand precisely because it fears a collapse of overseas confidence, a fall in its currency, and a fresh impetus to inflation. It will raise interest rates or run a tighter budgetary policy by raising taxes or trimming public expenditure, and will thus attempt to negate its rising deficit. This process curbs its domestic demand, and reduces its spending on imports. It will also, of course, put the brakes on US exports and bring to a halt the painless cutting of the American deficit.

Exactly this pattern occurred in the world economy between 1987 and 1989. The US deficit was coming down, albeit disappointingly slowly, from $154 billion in 1987 to some $123 billion in 1989.[1] The interesting feature of this decline of $31 billion was that the countries with the biggest surpluses accounted for less than half of the counterpart. Germany's surplus actually rose by $3 billion to $48 billion, offsetting a small $7 billion reduction in the Japanese surplus of $80 billion. The four Asian newly industrializing economies – Korea, Taiwan, Hong Kong and Singapore – cut their surpluses by $10 billion to $21 billion. The main counterpart to the US improvement is expected to be a widening in the deficits of countries which can least afford to see it happen, and whose policy responses in some cases have already been to dampen demand. This is particularly true in Europe.

The most enthusiastic increase in a deficit was in Britain, though it has to be said that this has less to do with a desire to help Anglo-Saxon cousins than to the excessive enthusiasms of the former Chancellor Nigel Lawson for financial liberalization and a relatively easy monetary policy (which caused savings to plummet) and personal tax cuts (which added a twist to the consumer and import boom). The result was a sharp tightening of monetary policy, with ten separate rises in bank base rates in little more than a year after March 1988, three of them in response to the announcement of record monthly trade deficits or downwards pressure on sterling. Thanks to the British deficit in 1988 and 1989 rivalling the United States' deficit at its worst, as a proportion of GDP, there was no doubt that Britain's domestic demand was slowing in 1989, whether naturally or under the duress of further policy tightening.

Spain, Portugal and Greece were sinking into deficits for similar reasons. Like Britain, they are European community countries without being full members of the fixed exchange rate European Monetary System (EMS) for most of the period (although Spain joined in the summer of 1989). Partly as a result of non-membership, they felt themselves able to allow domestic demand to grow at a most gratifying pace. These non-EMS countries saw real domestic demand growth of 21 per cent between 1984 and 1988, compared with only 13 per cent in the EMS block.[2] A part of these increases were due to sharp rises in investment associated with entry to the EC. Nevertheless, their policy-makers were beginning to show anguish as their deficits mounted. Spain's deficit in particular was widening sharply from balance in 1987 to more than 2 per cent of national income in 1989. Portugal and Greece were both struggling to control deficits of more than 3 per cent of gross domestic product.

Amongst the established full members of the EMS, there was also a sharp difference of experience between Germany and its surplus country satellites on one hand and France and Italy on the other. Germany's surplus with the rest of the world was rising not because it was increasing its surplus with the United States but because its trade surplus with the rest of the Community countries soared between 1985 and 1988. Italy and France, attempting to hold their currencies in line with the German mark, were constrained to relatively slow domestic demand growth in 1989. And that too was bad news for American export markets. Outside the Community, the counterparts to the reduction in the United States deficits were increased and sometimes embarrassing deficits for Austria, Finland, Sweden, Australia and Canada.

One solution to this problem of lop-sided deficit correction is an even more concerted attempt to bludgeon surplus countries into policy relaxation, particularly on budgetary policy since tax cuts feed directly into domestic demand and seep out into imports. By contrast, monetary policy relaxation tends to weaken their exchange rates, thus improving their price competitiveness with overseas producers, and counteracting some of the spillage of demand overseas. Within Europe it is very hard to see how much more of the United States deficit can be absorbed unless German domestic demand growth speeds up sharply, or unless the German mark is sharply revalued within the European Monetary System. Indeed, the only way many of the European countries with mounting deficits could avoid a sharp slowdown in demand is if the markets lift some of the heat from their payments deficits, and the only way they can do that is if Germany stops increasing its bilateral surpluses with the rest of the Continent.

Germany's sheer size makes it the crucial European economy, accounting for more than a quarter of EC output at market prices. Even in the case of large European economies like France and Britain, more than a third of exports go to Germany and its immediate and dependent neighbours like the Netherlands and Belgium. Germany is thus a very important key to the growth of the European Community as whole – and indirectly therefore to the solution of the world's major imbalance in the shape of the United States deficit. Germany's crucial trading links with the rest of Europe condition the room for policy manoeuvre of the whole Continent.

The interconnections between the relatively open European economies emerged very clearly from a European Parliament research study into the effectiveness of various policy measures in each member state.[3] The Parliament used the EC Commission's computer model to simulate the effect of each member state increasing its public investment by 1 per cent of gross domestic product while the other member states did nothing – and then it looked at what might happen if they all increased public investment together. The differences, shown in table 23, are dramatic and are testament to the power of the linkages between the European economies. On its own, each country's room for policy manoeuvre is extremely slight because so much of any increase in demand is spent on imports, which leads to

Table 23. Individual versus co-ordinated reflation in Europe: effects of an increase of public investment of 1 per cent of GDP after two years

	Germany	*France*	*Italy*	*UK*
Individual action				
GDP growth	1.0	0.4	0.5	0.9
Trade balance/GDP	−0.5	−1.0	−1.0	−0.6
Budget balance/GDP	−0.6	−0.1	−2.0	−0.9
Concerted action				
GDP growth	1.9	1.3	1.4	1.6
Trade balance/GDP	−0.4	−0.5	−0.4	−0.4
Budget balance/GDP	−0.2	−0.6	−1.7	−0.5

Note: Comet III simulations
Source: Albert and Ball, *Towards European Recovery in the 1980s* (1983)

a worsening deficit and pressure on the currency. Naturally, the benefits of co-ordinated policy relaxation are only useful if the balance of payments is the main constraint on increased growth. If inflationary pressures were to accelerate domestically, or commodity prices world-wide were to rise because of the co-ordinated demand expansion, it would ultimately prove counter-productive.

Nevertheless, there have been several occasions over the last decade when there clearly has been room for policy relaxation within Europe, and where the major obstacle has been the reluctance of German policy-makers to move either alone or in tandem with others. At the end of the eighties, though, German growth was particularly high, and was causing many industries to run historically high rates of capacity use (in part because of low rates of investment during the years of stagnation). Despite a persistent current account surplus and a modest inflation rate of 2 per cent, it was easier to sympathize with the German view that there was little if any room for faster growth. The real question was whether the growth could be better balanced, drawing more on domestic demand and less on foreign stimulus.

There are four half-way feasible solutions to the German 'black hole' in the heart of Europe. The first is a change in fiscal or monetary policy, but the conservatism of German policy-making is likely to ensure that any shift is marginal. The Bundesbank would clearly prefer to see the deficit reduced through a revaluation of the German mark, but this is politically difficult for the other EMS members, and in addition is unpopular amongst German industrialists, who are keen to maintain their profit margins in European markets. The second solution is financial liberalization, which should in time help to reduce Germany's savings rate (and increase its spending rate) just as it did in the United States and Britain. The German financial system is still conservative in its lending to the personal sector, and new competition in the run up to the single European marketplace in 1992 could well stimulate demand. The third solution is to press for services liberalization. Increasing services output is unlikely to add much to exports, because services are less tradable than manufactures. But increased service employment is likely to create spending power which will go on imports. The limits on shop opening hours is the best known example of state-imposed restrictions on service enterprise, but it is by no means the only one.

The fourth solution is to insist on cuts in German subsidies, which ran at about 2.1 per cent of GNP in 1986 compared with 0.6 per cent in the United States, 1.1 per cent in Japan and 1.7 per cent in Britain.[4] The amount of subsidy to industry is relatively small, although there were relatively large amounts to both coal-mining and iron and steel. Professor Hans Schneider, the chairman of the 'Five Wise Men', the official Council of Economic Experts, argues that reform can and should increase demand and imports. 'You can no longer make demand grow faster through the classical fiscal and monetary measures,' he says. 'The way is to remove barriers to imports, particularly in agriculture, mining, and telecommunications.' For example, Siemens has been able to rely on a monopoly of every appliance attached to the Bundespost phone network. When the monopoly goes, imports are bound to take a larger share of the market. However, the politics of farm reform and mining look none too easy. It is arguable that Germany's late-arriving baby-boomers may also help to stimulate the growth of demand and imports, though this should not be overestimated (see the second essay of chapter 5).

By contrast with the Germans, the Japanese have clearly

moved further and faster in both liberalization and in policy relaxation than many would have dared to expect at the end of the eighties. The short-term problem in Japan is slightly different: the surplus when measured in yen has fallen rapidly, but the rise of the yen against the dollar since 1985 has meant that it has taken much longer to turn around the dollar figure. In the medium term, though, there was still a question mark in the minds of many American policy-makers about whether free trade between the United States and Japan was sustainable while the Japanese performance in traded goods – particularly manufactures – was so impressive. The issue of Japanese investment in the United States – the counterpart on the capital account of the large US current account deficit – was becoming a politically sensitive issue. The only hope for defusing Japanese–American tensions lay in the fact that they had been defused before, in large part because of the political leverage which the United States has in a country which is still in geo-political and defence terms a client.

Notes

1 Organisation for Economic Co-operation and Development, *Economic Outlook*, no. 45 (June 1989), forecast for 1989.

2 European Commission, *Annual Economic Report*, November 1988.

3 Michel Albert and James Ball, *Towards European Recovery in the 1980s*, European Parliament working document (31 August 1983).

4 OECD, *Economic Surveys: Germany 1987/8*, p. 63.

Floating or managed exchange rates?

Two cases for floating exchange rates

- experience of overshooting
- effects of misalignment
- reasons for failure of the market
- lack of stabilizing speculators
- the Plaza and Louvre agreements
- intervention and other instruments
- target zones
- conflicts of analysis and interest

The tide of free-market ideas that swept through the western industrial democracies during the seventies and eighties was nowhere so strong as in the commitment to freely floating exchange rates. Once the old fixed exchange rate regime which had been designed at the Bretton Woods conference in 1944 had broken down, countries began to behave as if the constraints on good conduct of their economic policy had been suddenly removed. From the liberal and new classical end of the economic spectrum, economists argued that the control of the money supply would itself be enough to ensure low inflation, and the exchange rate should be allowed to find its own market level. From the left and post-Keynesian end of the spectrum, other economists argued that the ability to devalue would enable countries to pursue higher rates of economic growth without running into balance of payments deficits and having to choke off the expansion, as had frequently occurred during the fifties and sixties. Neither set of proponents of floating exchange rates proved to be correct. The decade after the breakdown in 1971 of the Bretton Woods system was characterized almost everywhere by stagflation, an unfortunate mixture of low growth and high inflation.

The collapse of fixed exchange rates was not so much a cause of the problems of that period as its symptom, but the new belief in autarky soon bred its own problems, most spectacularly in three separate instances of dramatic movements in the values of currencies. The first, hardly noticed at the time because it affected a small country, was the overvaluation of the Swiss franc when American investors used it as a bolt-hole out of the falling dollar during the second half of the seventies. The second was the extraordinary overvaluation of sterling, which rose slowly from 1977 to 1979, and then took off to peak in real terms 58 per cent above its 1977 level in 1981.[1] The third example was the run-up of the United States dollar, which appreciated in real terms by 40 per cent between 1980 and 1985. The problem was not day-to-day volatility, but a massive misalignment for prolonged periods. Each of these episodes involved 'exchange rate overshooting' as the financial markets pushed a currency way above what any economic view held to be their equilibrium (or sustainable) levels in relation to such fundamentals as relative price levels and the balance of payments. In each case, the currency subsequently dropped back almost as fast as it rose.

The failure of free foreign exchange markets to deliver stable exchange rates meant that world output, investment and employment were almost certainly lower than they would otherwise have been. Uncertainty is the most corrosive influence on business confidence, which is in turn crucial to future investment and output. The sudden swoops of major exchange rates may also have led to inflation ratcheting up. Devaluations tend to increase prices and hence wages more quickly than revaluations decrease them, because in every country earnings growth adjusts more slowly to falls in inflation than it does to rises. And the final and perhaps most important cost of currency misalignments of the eighties was mounting protectionism. As jobs were lost in tradable industries because of sharp appreciations in the dollar and sterling, the pressures for alternative means of combating foreign competition became intense. Throughout the period, there was a steady increase in non-tariff barriers to trade, especially in price-sensitive goods. The paradoxical cost of free foreign exchange markets was fewer free markets in goods and services.

Why was the theory of floating exchange rates so firmly confounded? At the beginning of the seventies, most proponents of floating would have said that exchange rates would stabilize because, as in most markets, someone will have an interest in speculation. And speculation ought to ensure that people buy when they think the price is too low, stopping a fall, and sell when the price is too high, stopping a rise. However, the reality of the foreign exchange markets is that speculators themselves can also put momentum behind an artificial trend. If financial markets see a price steadily rising and this creates the expectation of a further rise, they may continue to buy, thus aggravating the trend. It takes some shock, such as the announcement of official measures or some event such as an oil price rise in order to change expectations and reverse the trend. All the people who are buying may be very well aware that the price will eventually fall below even the point at which they purchase, but they will persuade themselves that they will be able to get out before the fall happens. If someone thinks he will have to pay more for a dollar later than now, even if the dollar will be lower in a year's time, he will buy and buy especially given the exceptionally short-term time horizons in the market. Even the most senior foreign exchange dealers in large financial institutions expect to square their book within the week.[2] There are no obvious private 'stabilizing speculators'. The notion that anyone save Governments has the financial resources to take the long view is simply fallacious. Private speculators are not able to sustain the short-term losses which are liable to arise from an investment strategy based on long-term fundamentals.

Real world factors also fed these speculative bubbles. Governments were often pursuing policies which were not neighbourly; high interest rates in the United States and in Britain were certainly part of the attraction of both currencies in their periods of rise. Ironically, though, once confidence in a currency's further rise began to evaporate, no realistic increase in interest rates was enough to stop it slipping. If a speculator expects the pound to fall against other currencies by 10 per cent over the next year, he will want to earn an extra 10 per cent in interest on pounds compared with other currencies in order to persuade him to hold on to them. Imagine the interest rate needed to persuade a speculator to hold pounds if he expects sterling to fall by 10 per cent not in a year but in a week.

There is a further factor which can lead to instability. The confidence of the markets may, for example, be conditioned by a country's trade balance. However, a depreciating currency which is needed in the long run to improve a trade deficit may in the short run paradoxically worsen it. This is the famous 'J-curve': because quantities of exports and imports react to a change in the exchange rate only with a time-lag, a devaluation in the short term has the effect of increasing the cost of imports and worsening the trade balance (when measured in domestic currency). It is only in time that foreigners are encouraged to buy exports and home consumers are discouraged from buying imports. The trade volumes thus turn round slowly to improve the balance. But in the interim the foreign exchange markets may be reacting to the worsening. The same effect in reverse may have encouraged the rise of the dollar and the pound in the early eighties.

The arguments for managed exchange rates made the quickest progress in Europe, in part because the European economies are small and hence do a lot of trade. The response, after a botched effort with the currency 'snake', was the European Monetary System in 1979. The more ambitious attempt to manage the dollar's exchange rate did not occur until the famous meeting at the Plaza Hotel in September 1985, when the United States and the other major industrial countries launched their effort to manage the swings in the three major currencies – yen, dollar and Deutschmark.[3] From that point onwards, some political responsibility for the major exchange rates was accepted as inevitable, though there were to be many periods when the markets sorely tested the apparent agreements of the Group of Seven (G7) – the United States, Germany, Japan, Britain, France, Italy and Canada – and even more so the inner group of the Big Three – Japan, Germany and the United States.

Essentially, there have been two broad phases in this new co-operation. The first was pushing the dollar down, which met with a good deal of success in part, the sceptics argued, because the depreciation had begun in the spring of 1985 and the G7 merely came along and gave it their imprimatur. The second phase began with the Louvre accord in February 1987 and was designed to stabilize the American currency, by then fully 25 per cent lower against the main currencies[4] and more than 40 per cent lower against the Japanese yen and the German mark. The exact undertakings given to each other by the G7 have never been published, but it is clear that at various times they have been operating covert bands within which commitments to intervene were given. That intervention was ultimately to be supplemented by changes in other policies which would also encourage currency stability: more expansion in the surplus countries and budget deficit cutting measures in the United States.

The first phase was a bumpy ride, with the financial markets constantly testing the finance ministers' resolve to defend the United States currency, and a corresponding huge intervention in the markets by the central banks of the Group of Seven countries which effectively funded the American current account deficit in 1987 (see the first essay in this chapter). The relative success of this operation gave ministers new confidence in their power to influence the markets. Much could be accomplished by concerted intervention, if only because together the leading countries control the supply of the goods – their currencies – whose price they were trying to influence. Though the gross flows into and out of currencies are enormous, it is the balance between demand and supply which moves the price. And that is much smaller.

In the longer run, however, intervention in the foreign exchanges would not be enough to alter the parities of particular currencies without serious side-effects. If, for example, the Americans had intervened heavily to hold the dollar down, they would have supplied dollars to the domestic markets, held interest rates down, and probably have caused a serious inflation. It has been argued that such a monetary expansion would have been preferable, since it would have put the pressure on the administration to cut the budget deficit.[5] However, that was never a serious option for the Federal Reserve.

For similar reasons, the German Bundesbank was a lukewarm participant in the intervention to hold the dollar up (and the German mark down) in 1987, for fear that excessive supplies of German marks to the market in order to buy dollars would feed back into the German money markets and ease domestic monetary conditions through lower interest rates. In short, it was held that intervention could prove inflationary in countries with strengthening currencies (a theme echoed in another context by Sir Alan Walters, the Prime Minister's former personal economic adviser). This was ultimately a corrosive influence on the currency agreement, since the Europeans and the Japanese felt that the Americans had not delivered their part of the Plaza and Louvre bargains, namely substantial cuts in the US budget deficit which would have enabled a reduction in both spending and inflationary pressure within the United States without high interest rates. Equally, the Americans believed that the Germans and the Japanese were not doing enough to close the US trade gap by expanding their domestic demand – and the demand for US exports.

A more decisive move towards managed exchange rates would imply the settlement of target ranges for currencies like those agreed within the European Monetary System, or within the old fixed exchange rate regime of Bretton Woods. The techniques involved in assessing an appropriate exchange rate for policy purposes have been developed by the Institute for International Economics in Washington[5] which calculates 'Fundamental Equilibrium Exchange Rates' or FEERs. These attempt to take account of the level of the currency needed to reach domestic equilibrium – namely some measure of full employment – and external equilibrium – in reducing trade gaps to a size which could plausibly be matched by long-term capital flows. Figure 33 shows the bands within which it might have been sensible to stabilize the major currencies, and what actually happened to them. The IIE argues for a 10 per cent margin around the central FEER – far wider than the EMS's 2.25 per cent margin – in recognition of the difficulty of reaching a certain assessment.

However, target zones would also imply a greater willingness on the part of the major industrial countries to change their domestic policies than they have so far demonstrated. Though the freedom to suffer the costs of floating exchange rates is no freedom at all, there is nevertheless a residual belief in the chimaera of monetary sovereignty which makes co-operation difficult. More fundamentally, there are also differences of view about the linkages between the major economies which make it hard to reach a consensus about policy measures even if there were not also real differences in interests to reconcile, a subject to which the next essay turns.

Notes

1 The measure of the real exchange rate – the movement in the currency allowing for differences in inflation between the country concerned and its trading partners – is relative unit labour costs given in the International Monetary Fund, *International Financial Statistics Yearbook*, 1986.

2 See for example Rudi Weiswiller, ed., *Managing a Foreign Exchange Department* (London: Woodhead-Faulkner, 1985).

3 For a valuable account of the process from the Plaza to the Louvre see Yoichi Funabashi, *Managing the Dollar: from the Plaza to the Louvre* (Washington DC: Institute for International Economics, 1988).

Figure 33

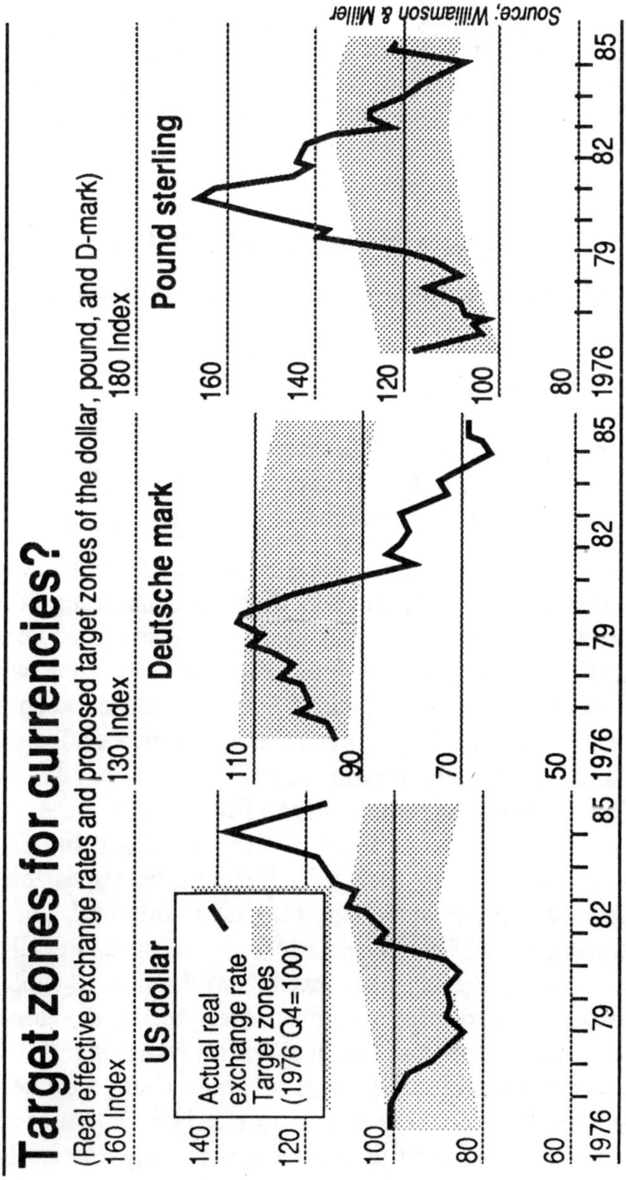
Target zones for currencies?
(Real effective exchange rates and proposed target zones of the dollar, pound, and D-mark)
160 Index
US dollar
Actual real exchange rate
Target zones (1976 Q4=100)
140
120
100
80
60
1976
79
82
85
130 Index
Deutsche mark
110
90
70
50
1976
79
82
85
180 Index
Pound sterling
160
140
120
100
80
1976
79
82
85
Source: Williamson & Miller

4 The end-month dollar rate in September 1987 compared with February 1985 against the Special Drawing Right.

5 See Peter B. Kenen, *Managing Exchange Rates*, Chatham House papers (London: Routledge, 1988).

6 See, for example, John Williamson, *The Exchange Rate System* (Washington DC: Institute for International Economics, revised June 1985), and John Williamson and Marcus H. Miller, *Targets and Indicators: a Blueprint for the International Co-ordination of Economic Policy* (Washington DC: Institute for International Economics, September 1987).

The foggy, foggy view of international economics

International management is more difficult than national

- the world current account discrepancy
- economic structures and interests
- differences over the way the world works
- ambiguous effects of fiscal policy
- ambiguous effects of monetary policy
- computer model estimates of policy changes

The business of managing national economies is like navigating in a Thames fog. It is not clear where you are going because the future is uncertain. It is not clear where you are, because the figures have not yet been published. It is not clear where you have been, because the Central Statistical Office keeps revising the data. Yet all these difficulties are compounded when the questions become international.

The statistics are even worse. For example, the world ran a balance of payments deficit with itself of $38 billion in 1987 and of $78 billion in 1988, which should be impossible since if somebody exports, somebody else has to import.[1] The problem is almost certainly under-recording of receipts of so-called 'invisible' earnings like interest, profits and dividends, which should probably be attributed proportionately to the developed countries. Nevertheless, the implications are worrying. The national figures are probably fairly truthful about changes in deficits and surpluses, because there is no reason to believe that the so-called world current account discrepancy is getting worse.[2] However, the level of individual deficits or surpluses must be wrong. Both markets and Governments may react to deficits whose absolute level is less worrying than the figures suggest. Economic policy may thus consistently be tighter than it would be otherwise.

The second problem in international economics is that the possibilities of conflicting and contradictory policies are even greater than they are at national level. In most cases national economic policy is set by one or at most two agencies: the finance ministry and the central bank. The chance of pursuing contradictory policies is not negligible – look at the United States since 1980 where, for much of the period, there has been a combination of loose fiscal policy set by the President and Congress and tight monetary policy set by the Federal Reserve Board – but it is much less than the likelihood of contradictory policies being pursued internationally.

The interests of different countries diverge because of their economic structures: the United States is a free-trader on agricultural policy but often wants to protect its industries; Germany and Japan are free-traders on industrial products but protectionist on farming. Interests also diverge because democratically elected Governments in the main industrial countries are rarely of one voice ideologically, and they may well themselves be pursuing sectional rather than national interests. And they may diverge because some countries have a much firmer grip on economic policy instruments than others. A unitary state like Britain, for example, is much better able to deliver the changes it promises in economic policy than a devolved and federal state like West Germany or the United States. Even where countries have common interests, they may find it hard to reach agreement on pursuing them because there is still plenty of room for argument about the distribution of costs and benefits from co-operative action.

However, there is a third and even more fundamental problem before finance ministers are able to argue about means. There is a disagreement among economists about the scale and sometimes even the direction of particular policy changes, which is far greater than it usually is at a national level. Indeed, Richard Cooper, a former economics official at the State Department under President Carter, has compared the state of international economic policy-making with the debates which used to take place about public health.[3]

In principle, everyone could see that it made sense to co-operate internationally to stop the spread of contagious diseases. But the existence of rival epidemiological theories made it impossible to agree on effective policy measures until a consensus had emerged.

The world has arrived at the first stage. Everyone sees that there are potential advantages in international economic co-operation, merely because of the growth of interdependence over the post-war period. As world trade has grown, domestic economies have inevitably become more subject to world trends and other countries' policy actions. Equally, interdependence has meant that economies are less subject to the influence of their own domestic policy. The growth of imports has meant, for example, that a given tax cut will boost domestic spending less than before, because a larger proportion will leak out of the circular flow of income to foreigners. The trend in all economies save that of Japan is unmistakable. Imports as a share of gross domestic product have risen sharply between 1961–70 and 1989: from 17.1 per cent to 24.8 per cent in Germany; from 12.8 per cent to 22.3 per cent in France; from 20.9 per cent to 28.5 per cent in Britain; and even from 4.7 per cent to 10.8 per cent in a continental, relatively self-sufficient economy like that of the United States. The only odd man out is Japan, whose import share has fallen from 9.5 per cent in 1961–70 to 8.4 per cent in 1989.[4]

Along with the growth of interdependence has come a gut understanding of how overseas policy affects each economy. The smaller European countries have realized this for years, which is why they have always been keen on formal institutions which require co-operation such as the European Monetary System. The bigger European countries increasingly recognize the influence of Germany in their midst, together with Japan and the United States. However, size is not the determining factor. Even the United States becomes keen on co-operation when the dollar is weak, because it faces domestic policy-makers with unpleasant choices between higher import prices, inflation and growth. It makes as much sense for interdependent economies to co-operate as it does for two people sharing a room, but with independent control of two heating and air-conditioning units. If one of them prefers a hotter room than the other, the odds are that they will both use a lot of energy cancelling each other out. One will have the radiator belting forth heat, while the other has the air-conditioning on full blast.

The economic problem is not only reaching agreement on sharing the costs and benefits of the policy, but agreeing on which policy instruments do what in a world which is much more complicated than adjusting the heating. Economic theory is not much help in telling us exactly what, say, a cut in interest rates will do for the balance of payments because it can identify contradictory effects. Take a couple of examples of ambiguous effects:

Tax and spending policy Will an increase in Government spending push the currency up or push it down? One effect of extra state spending will be to boost national income, and thereby increase private spending, and thereby increase imports, and worsen the current account deficit, and cause a greater supply of the domestic currency to foreigners, who may insist on a lower exchange rate in order to persuade them to hold it. However, another effect will be that the boost to national income will tend to increase the demand for credit, which will drive up interest rates unless monetary policy is relaxed, which will make that country's assets more attractive, which will stimulate an inflow of capital to offset the current account deficit. If capital is very mobile and confidence in the country's credit is good, the effect of the rise in interest rates in making the currency more attractive may be more significant than the effect of weakening the currency through higher imports: increases in Government spending may cause the currency to rise.

Indeed, the effect may be different from one country to another. Precisely because the United States can absorb foreign capital with ease, a fiscal expansion is likely to lead to a rise in the exchange rate. Smaller countries with less developed capital markets may find fiscal expansion driving their currency down.

Monetary expansion Will an easier monetary policy – an increase in the money supply – cut or increase a balance of payments deficit? It will reduce interest rates, push up national income, suck in imports, and worsen the deficit. However, it will also make US fixed-interest assets (Government bonds) less attractive, cause an outflow of capital, which will cut the value of the dollar, make US goods more competitive, and cut the balance of payments deficit. Which effect will dominate will depend on the sensitivity of domestic spending – on houses, consumer durables and so forth – to interest rates, and once again on the sensitivity of capital flows to interest rate changes.

These sorts of ambiguity can only be settled by looking at the evidence, which essentially means building computer models of the economy which track its past behaviour. Computer models should in theory offer the advantage of ensuring policy will be consistent, but also that any necessary changes in policy can be quantified. How much does the dollar need to fall ultimately to reduce the US current account deficit to sustainable levels? If the US budget deficit is cut in line with the Gramm–Rudman provisions, what offsetting interest rate cuts will be necessary to stop a recession? However, there is an important caveat about the usefulness of models. They are inevitably based on past relationships, which we know are changing very rapidly in a world where capital controls are being abolished and financial markets are being liberalized. Secondly, even those models which do exist come to different conclusions about the way the international economy works.

The Brookings Institution study provides enough ammunition to those sceptical about economics to keep them happy for a lifetime, or at least until the computer modellers succeed in producing rather more consensus about their results. Tables 24 and 25 show what each of the global computer models predicts will be the consequence either of a US monetary expansion or of an increase in US Government spending. (A cut in spending will have the reverse effect.) Four out of the eleven models say that a US monetary expansion will cut the current account deficit after one year. Seven of the eleven say the opposite, and their estimates of the effect varies from $1.4 billion to $9.5 billion for the same monetary expansion. The models are unanimous about the direction of the effect on the current account deficit

Table 24. Effect of an increase in US Government spending

	Effect in USA			*Effect overseas*	
Computer model	*Output* (%)	*Dollar value* (%)	*Current account* (*$bn*)	*Current account* (%)	*Output* (%)
DRI	2.1	3.2	−22.0	0.8	0.7
EEC	1.2	0.6	−11.6	6.6	0.3
EPA	1.7	1.9	−20.5	9.3	0.9
Link	1.2	−0.1	− 6.4	1.9	0.1
Liverpool	0.6	1.0	− 7.0	3.4	0.0
MCM	1.8	2.8	−16.5	8.9	0.7
Minimod	1.0	1.0	− 8.5	5.5	0.3
MSG	0.9	3.2	−21.6	22.7	0.3
Taylor	0.6	4.0	n/a	n/a	0.4
VAR	0.4	1.2	− 0.5	−0.2	0.0
OECD	1.1	0.4	−14.2	11.4	0.4
Wharton	1.4	−2.1	−15.4	5.3	0.2

Note: Increase is assumed to be worth 1 per cent of GNP; effects refer to second year after the increase.
Source: Brookings Institution

Table 25. Effects of US monetary expansion on the US current account balance ($bn)

Computer model	*Year 1*	*Year 4*
DRI	2.2	14.2
EEC	−1.5	−5.7
EPA	1.0	4.6
Link	−0.9	−17.8
Liverpool	−6.9	−8.6
MCM	−4.1	−1.8
Minimod	−9.5	12.2
MSG	58.7	1.1
VAR	1.4	9.6
OECD	−9.3	−0.1
Wharton	−2.9	−8.7

Note: M1 is assumed to increase by 4 per cent in year 1 compared with baseline forecast.

Source: Brookings Institution

from an increase in US Government spending, but this is less consoling that it might appear. Exactly the same size increase in spending – of exactly 1 per cent of GDP – is estimated to lead to a worsening of the deficit anywhere in the range of $0.5 billion to $22 billion. Given the difficulties of settling these matters, it goes without saying that the forecasting of exchange rate movements verges on the impossible.[6]

Pity the poor Group of Seven finance ministers. They have to do something, because someone has to decide interest rates, tax rates and spending. But they cannot be quite as certain about anything as they like to pretend to be about everything.

Notes

1 International Monetary Fund, *World Economic Outlook*, April 1989, table A30.

2 See International Monetary Fund, *Report on the World Current Account Discrepancy* (Washington DC, September 1987).

3 Ralph C. Bryant *et al.*, *Empirical Macroeconomics for Interdependent Economies* (Washington DC: Brookings Institution, 1988).

4 *European Economy, Annual Economic Report, 1988–89*, no. 38 (EC Commission, November 1988), table 38.

5 Bryant *et al.*, op cit.

6 However, the modellers have been making some small progress, according to P.G. Fisher *et al.*, *Econometric Evaluation of the Exchange Rate in Models of the UK Economy*, University of Warwick, ESRC Macro-economic Modelling Bureau, June 1989 (mimeo).

Elections make the world go round

Underestimate of 1988 growth

- policy relaxation due to bunching of elections and the US presidentials
- bunching of elections in 1972 and 1973
- effects on policy and inflation
- influences of America on other countries
- means of influencing real income growth

An under-rated but important influence on world economic activity is the pattern of elections in the major industrial countries. The remarkable bunching of elections in 1972 and 1973 was a key reason for the tightening of world commodity markets, the ability of the Organisation of Petroleum Exporting Countries to raise oil prices, and the inflationary excesses of 1974/5. The same thing very nearly happened again in 1988, when the coincidence of elections in the major industrial countries was the sharpest since the first oil crisis.

Take the example of 1988 first. The twin sisters of international official forecasting – the Organisation for Economic Co-operation and Development and the International Monetary Fund – both expressed themselves mystified about why growth proved to be so buoyant. Both of them were way out in their predictions. At the end of 1987 the OECD predicted a mere 2 per cent rise in spending (demand) in the industrial countries and a 2.25 per cent growth in output. The outturn in 1988 was 4.1 per cent and domestic demand grew even faster at 4.5 per cent, providing a substantial boost to non-OECD countries.[1]

The OECD explains its error by pointing to underestimates of productivity and profits growth, new competition in financial markets which made borrowing and spending easier, and some policy relaxation. Monetary growth was higher than expected (though so were interest rates) and budgets were looser too. These, though, are only proximate causes. What caused the policy relaxation? The answer should have been predictable – elections. Perhaps the institutions are just too coy to spell it out, but the evidence for a strong electoral-economic cycle in the world economy continues to accumulate.

1988 was a classic electoral peak year. There was an American presidential election, which is always a vital ingredient. There was thus a strong impetus from the world's main economy, which still accounts for 40 per cent of industrial world output. In addition, there was a cluster of elections in other developed democracies in both 1987 and 1988 which helped to power the upturn, and which also provided members of the Group of Seven industrial countries with an incentive not to let the world's current account imbalances foment exchange rate crises. Germany went to the polls in January 1987, Britain and Italy in June 1987, France in May and June 1988, and Canada and the United States in November 1988.

The implications of democratic electoral cycles for the world economy have enjoyed only desultory research interest, and not surprisingly are rarely highlighted by those in authority themselves. Nevertheless, it is at least arguable that the heaping of elections in six of the Big Seven economies during the eleven months from May 1972 to March 1973 was one of the most decisive economic events of the post-war years.[2] The election boom almost exactly matched the economic and commodity price boom which put paid to any renewed efforts to revive the Bretton Woods exchange rate system. Italy, Canada, Germany, Japan, France and the United States all held elections – a sum total of 78 per cent of the developed world, as measured by its output. The result of that particular bunching of the democratic process was two of the highest annual growth rates for the industrial world in the post-war period, 5.4 per cent in 1972 and 6 per cent in 1973. It was also the beginning of a lot of the subsequent problems in the world economy. The associated commodity price boom and the doubling of crude oil prices took industrial world inflation from 5.3 per cent in 1972 to 11.9 per cent in 1974.

If countries had still been attached to a fixed exchange rate regime, the cycle might not have been so pronounced. They might have been more concerned about expanding more rapidly than their partners (even though it was also the case that, under Bretton Woods, joint expansion led to no retribution except inflation). But policy-makers felt themselves liberated from the external constraint of maintaining balance of payments equilibrium, and there had also been a sharp build-up of official reserve assets which more than doubled between 1970 and 1974. The result was a substantial monetary and fiscal relaxation. According to the OECD's budget indicators, fiscal policy was eased in 1972 in Britain, Canada, France, Italy and Japan.[3] Real interest rates were relatively low in the United States in both 1971 and 1972, although when inflation subsequently rose they were to fall even further.[4]

Professor Tufte was among those who was concerned that the main democracies would increasingly try to synchronize their elections in line with those of the United States, but fortunately his worst fears have not been realized.[5] Nevertheless, the bunching in 1987 and 1988, although less dramatic than 1972 and 1973, has undoubtedly provided considerable stimulus. The Big Seven countries themselves account for 85 per cent of the output of the industrial world, and every single one of them bar Japan – accounting for 71 per cent of developed world output – had an election in 1987 or 1988.

Just in case all this sounds too cynical, it is worth updating Tufte's evidence to see whether the pattern of high growth in election years still holds. The answer is that the theory is still performing remarkably well, despite the strong ideology of the period that policy-makers were not able to influence economic activity. World GDP growth in 1988 of 4.1 per cent was the highest since 1984 – another American presidential election year when growth came in at 4.4 per cent. We have to draw a veil over 1980, because President Jimmy Carter appears to have been just about the only post-Second World War president who muffed his electoral cycle. But if one takes the whole period from 1957 to 1988, the average growth of the world economy in US presidential years was 3.9 per cent against 2.8 per cent the rest of the time.

Some figures for each of the Group of Seven are set out in table 26. Clearly, the comparisons are far from sophisticated. After all, the January 1987 election in Germany should mainly have affected growth in 1986. There were also the mistakes: Britain's last Labour Government fuelled a splendid election boom for 1978 but lost its nerve and postponed the election until 1979. Another mistake was the Volcker–Carter dip in 1980: excluding the botched Carter re-election bid, the average growth in a US election year is even higher at 4.5 per cent. Nevertheless, taking all the main countries together, the table suggests that all three categories of election year (years with only US elections, or with only national elections, or with US and national elections) outstrip non-election years on average.

The countries with the largest difference between growth rates in election and non-election years are the United States and West Germany, despite the latter's reputation for budget prudence. Ironically, both of these outstanding election boomers have relatively independent central banks setting monetary policy. Against that, though, both are less constrained by the

Table 26. Growth in election and non-election years, 1957–88 (average annual percentage increase in real GDP/GNP)

	Country's election and US election in same year	*Country's election only*	*US election only*	*No election in country or US*
Canada	4.4	3.7	5.1	3.8
France	3.9	4.2	4.6	3.8
West Germany	3.8	4.5	6.8	2.6
Italy	5.2	3.6	5.0	3.8
Japan	6.0	5.5	9.3	6.9
UK	5.2	2.5	2.7	2.2
USA			3.9	2.8
Overall	4.8	4.0	5.3	3.7

Source: Calculated from IMF and OECD data

sort of current account problems which have bedevilled other developed economies. The United States case has, over much of the period, been able to finance either current account deficits or long-term capital outflows by pumping out dollars, and ensuring that foreigners have held them because of the currency's reserve status. The West Germans have rarely had trouble with their trade performance.

Germany's trading success comes out again in the comparison of the countries which do best out of American elections. As one might expect, Japan is also extremely responsive to American elections. Of the more ordinary economies, Canada clearly benefits because of its proximity to the United States and the preponderance of the American economy in its export markets. Typically, Britain, France and Italy reap less benefit from increases in American demand. Taken individually, Canada, Italy and Japan do not appear to have an independent electoral economic cycle, although they all respond mightily to American stimulus.

For the sake of the ease of international comparisons, table 26 shows the IMF series of real gross domestic product, but this is almost certainly not what politicians who are seeking re-election are primarily interested in. They will be more concerned to boost real personal disposable incomes per head

– broadly what is left after paying taxes. Real GDP is a fair though not ideal proxy for real incomes, given the importance of incomes in determining consumption, and of consumption in determining growth. Nevertheless, the pattern of real income growth in Britain suggests that the connection with election years is even closer. The average growth rate of real personal disposable incomes in all the eight British election years from 1957 to 1988 was 2.9 per cent compared to an average growth of RPDI in years when an American election was being held of 3 per cent, and a growth rate of only 1.6 per cent in non-election years. In other words, real income growth in Britain has tended to be 75 per cent higher in election than non-election years.

Clearly, the main means by which Governments can influence their economies during election years is through the overall levers of demand management: interest rates, tax and spending policy and the exchange rate. However, the measures can be much more surreptitious than an overt tax cut. Tufte cites the examples of changed timing in social security payments in the United States. 'The blunt but sure instrument – putting larger checks in the mail during the months before an election – is naturally favoured in the short run,' he argues. In Mrs Thatcher's first parliament, her Government sharply increased the rates of grant payable to owner-occupiers who undertook improvements to their homes, but made them conditional on expenditure within a time deadline which ran out shortly after the election. Public money was used to prime additional private spending.

What of the future? The Japanese held a general election in 1990, but there is no real grouping of elections until 1991, and maybe not even then. Mrs Thatcher has a penchant for June elections after four years, which would take her to June 1991. But she may decide to make the most of the Bush re-election campaign instead, particularly given Britain's inflationary and deficit problems. She can go up to June 1992. The Germans are due at the end of 1990, and the French are to hold legislative elections in May 1993. But President Mitterrand, whose own term extends until 1995, could also decide to bring forward his parliamentary elections to 1992. Meanwhile, the world will trundle along with a nudge or two from the politicians' version of the invisible hand.

Notes

1 Comparison of *OECD Economic Outlook*, no. 42, December 1987 with no. 45, June 1989.

2 See Edward R. Tufte, *Political Control of the Economy* (Princeton, 1978) and Assar Lindbeck, 'Business Cycles, Politics, and International Economic Dependence', *Skandinaviska Enskilda Banken Quarterly*, no. 2 (1975), p. 60.

3 *OECD Economic Studies*, no. 3 (Autumn 1984), table 7, 'Structural Budget Balances'.

4 See chart 1 in Paul Atkinson and Jean-Claude Chouraqui, 'The Origins of High Real Interest Rates', *OECD Economic Studies*, no. 5 (Autumn 1985).

5 Tufte, op cit.

9 The Third World

The growth gap between the First and Third Worlds

The post-war catch-up of the Third World comes to an end

- the normal linkage between the growth of industrial and developing countries
- encouraging performance of China, India and the Asian tigers
- problems with the small low-income countries and the debtors
- the importance of commodity prices
- reasons for the fall in commodity prices
- high real interest rates
- the debt crisis
- protectionism

Over most of the post-war period, the developing countries' living standards gradually moved towards those in the industrial countries. Whether measured by gross domestic product per head, or by infant mortality, or by life expectancy, or by educational enrolment, the story was the same. There was a steady closing of the gap even though it remained huge. Over the eighties, however, the picture has become substantially more mixed. The slow relative improvement appears to have come to a halt in all of the main developing country groups except the newly industrializing countries (like Hong Kong and Korea) and the continental titans of the developing world, China and India.

The contrast has become particularly marked in the late eighties with the sharp revival of growth in the industrial countries, which grew much more rapidly than expected since the summer of 1987. This high growth would normally have sparked an even sharper upturn in the Third World, as its

Table 27. The growth gap: real annual percentage growth of GDP, 1971–88

	1971–80	*1985*	*1986*	*1987*	*1988*
Industrial countries	3.2	3.4	2.6	3.5	4.4
Developing countries median	4.9	3.2	3.6	2.6	3.8
15 most indebted countries	5.8	3.8	4.0	2.2	1.1
Small low-income countries	3.2	3.7	4.2	3.5	4.0

Source: IMF, *World Economic Outlook*, April 1989

economies responded to a rise in commodity prices and new opportunities for investment. But, the past linkage appears to have broken down. What is remarkable is the lack of response in the developing world, which bodes ill for its chances of future progress. The discrepancy has become so significant that the International Monetary Fund drew attention to the lack of the usual 'spillovers' in its *World Economic Outlook*.[1] The group of twenty-four developing country finance ministers began openly talking about a 'growth gap'.

The acceleration in industrial country growth began when oil prices fell in 1986. Initially, the fall caused the losers to cut their spending more quickly than the gainers increased theirs – so it dampened world activity. But from the middle of 1987, spending growth boomed. The October stock market crash only forced Governments to cut interest rates further, cancelling the jolt to confidence. The old rule of thumb used to be that every extra 1 per cent growth of output in the industrial world would lead to about an extra 1.5 per cent growth in the Third World. This time, as table 27 shows, overall growth in the industrial world has accelerated for two consecutive years but growth in the developing countries at first slowed down and then accelerated only sluggishly.

It is of course, dangerous to simplify a diversity of countries ranging from Taiwan to Mali into one group. In reality, there are large differences between four broad groups within the Third World. The first and most important group are what one might call the continental autarchs – the large self-reliant economies of China and India. The Chinese economic reforms have been spectacularly successful, with average annual real growth of gross domestic product running at 10.4 per cent

Table 28. Growth per head: real annual percentage growth of GDP per head, 1971–89

	1971–80	*1985*	*1986*	*1987*	*1988*	*1989*
Industrial countries	2.3	2.7	2.0	2.7	3.4	2.6
Developing countries	2.9	1.5	1.9	1.2	2.6	1.0
15 most indebted countries	3.1	1.6	1.9	0.1	−1.1	−1.4
Small low-income countries	0.9	1.3	1.4	0.7	1.4	1.4

Source: IMF, *World Economic Outlook*, April 1989

between 1980 and 1987 and growth rates of 16 per cent in 1988 – 14 per cent even after allowing for population growth. Not surprisingly, this has been too fast to avoid over-heating, rising inflation and the eruption of political strains. India too has been growing strongly, with their next five-year plan aiming at 6 to 7 per cent annual growth after attaining 4.6 per cent a year between 1980 and 1987 (and 1.8 per cent growth per head, after allowing for the rising population).

The other group of countries which are doing very well are the Asian newly industrialized economies – the 'tiger' economies of Korea, Taiwan, Hong Kong and Singapore. Thailand is also growing strongly. In all cases, their growth is being boosted by a highly competitive manufacturing sector. Their GDP growth rates are coming in well above the average for the developing world at nearly 11 per cent between 1986 and 1988. The scale of the benefits of recent industrial country growth to these countries is impressive: real export volumes from the four 'tigers' rose by an annual average of 19.5 per cent over the same three years.

There, though, the good news ends. The rest of the developing world is looking pretty sickly. Tables 27 and 28 show the two remaining key groups: the forty-five low-income countries excluding China and India (like Tanzania, Zambia, Bangladesh) and the fifteen highly indebted middle-income countries covered by the former US Treasury Secretary Baker's debt plan (such as Argentina and Brazil). There has been no speed-up in the low-income countries, while the debtors have actually slowed sharply despite the acceleration of industrial country growth. In the African (and to a lesser extent Latin American) case, the high looking GDP growth rates must be put in the context of almost equally rapid population growth. Table 28 gives the figures for GDP growth per head.

Real per capita GDP in sub-Saharan Africa fell in both 1987 and 1988. The pattern of overall GDP growth shows that there has been no pick-up along with the acceleration in industrial country growth. An important reason is the collapse of the traditional kicker mechanism of commodity prices. In the past, high industrial production growth at the top of the cycle in the developed world would force sharp rises in commodity prices and encourage increases in production: the commodity exporters benefited from higher prices and higher volumes. They could expand their domestic demand and not worry about higher imports forcing an exchange crisis.

This time they have been hit every which way. First, the growth of industrial country GDP has been slower than in previous cycles, and secondly more of that growth has been going into service industries rather than industrial production where the demand for raw materials is strongest. The recovery in commodity prices has thus been much weaker than the sort of spurt which occurred in previous cycles. Overall, non-oil primary commodity prices rose by about 18 per cent in 1988, but this was relatively little compensation for a sluggish cycle in which the trend has clearly been downwards. Most of the movement has been in metals rather than agricultural raw materials and food. Commodity prices were still about 7 per cent lower in 1989 than they were in 1980 in actual dollars, a catastrophic decline in real terms.[2]

The importance of commodity prices for the Third World can hardly be overestimated. For the low-income countries excluding China and India, primary commodities account for three-quarters of their total exports. Even for middle-income countries, commodities comprise 43 per cent of exports.[3] What makes the dampening of the commodity price cycle even more worrying is that it has certain structural features which are unlikely to disappear. Development may henceforth have to take account of a steady shift in the terms of trade by which commodity prices simply rise less rapidly than the price of manufactures.

This issue is nearly as old as development economics,[4]

but there are various reasons why it may be coming to a head. Improved techniques of stock control as computerization has spread has helped (temporarily) to reduce demand. More crucially, there has also been technological substitution of new materials for traditional commodities, and substantial savings in the amounts required. For example, the microcomputer on which this essay is written requires much less copper for its circuit boards than an electric typewriter, much to the disadvantage of producers like Zaire. The replacement of tin by plastics in packaging has cut demand for Bolivia's main exports. Recent research suggests that the commodity-intensity of northern (industrial country) production has been falling by some 2 per cent a year.[5]

Another feature of this cycle which has had important implications for all the developing countries has been high real interest rates. Interest rates are a way of expressing a preference between having money now or keeping it for later. The higher are interest rates, the larger the value of receiving money now rather than later, and the greater the temptation to sell finite resources like copper, bauxite or oil now rather than later.[6] In addition, high real interest rates encourage buyers of commodities to economize on holding stocks, because the money tied up in so doing could be earning a high return on the money markets.

Among the debtor countries, a further important factor in explaining the 'growth gap' has been the rise in the negative net transfer of resources made to their creditors – i.e. the amount by which interest and repayments on old debt (debt service) outstrips new lending. Negative net transfers have been running at around $30 billion a year since the debt crisis broke in 1982, and the banks refused to lend substantial new money. In theory, these flows can be generated by merely switching output from home consumption to exports, and even increasing growth. In reality, they generally involve tight demand policies which tend to contract output and imports too.[7]

The fourth reason why the linkages between industrial world and Third World growth appear to have broken down has been the steady increase in protectionism, the burden of which tends to fall disproportionately on the developing world because the industries which push hardest for protection tend to be declining sectors where a high input of relatively unskilled labour makes them particularly vulnerable to developing country competition.[8] The classic example is the Multi-Fibre Arrangement (MFA) whereby Third World exports of textiles, probably the most crucial single industry in the process of industrialization, are strictly limited by quota. The MFA is particularly pernicious because it also excludes poorer developing countries from competing with the traditional textile exporters, which secured quotas for particular product-lines when the deal was negotiated. Like all quota systems, it effectively freezes the pattern of trade, giving a price bonus to those who are in the system, and excluding the rest. For example, France and Britain strictly limited Bangladesh's exports of textiles from 1984, despite its poverty and the relatively small amounts involved. The World Bank also estimates that the share of developing country exports that face non-tariff barriers (such as bureaucratic inspections or other indirect means) is roughly 20 per cent, or about twice the share of industrial country exports. The proportion of Third World agricultural exports facing non-tariff barriers is even higher at 26 per cent.[9]

Many measures which are crucial to prosperity can only be provided by the Third World countries themselves. Peace and political stability, so often lacking in Africa, are essential. A passionate belief in education is a *sine qua non*. Land reform, spreading wealth and providing collateral for credit, was crucial in the case of Korea. Nevertheless, the developed world has a role too. Part of the solution to the problem of slow Third World growth has to be a resolution of the debt crisis, which concerns the next essay. A second part of the solution is to stop cutting aid, the subject of the third essay in this chapter. The World Bank reported to the annual meetings of the Fund and the Bank in Berlin in 1988 that aid had fallen in real terms by 5.4 per cent in 1987. Indeed, there are plenty of reasons for increasing it, including 950 million people in absolute poverty and a famine belt which scars Africa.

A third part of the solution is to do far more to encourage Third World exports, the route by which the newly industrializing countries reached success. With tariff protection after the Tokyo round of trade negotiations within the General Agreement on Tariffs and Trade (GATT) worth only some 5 per cent, the key to liberalization is increasingly the removal of non-tariff barriers. The World Bank cites estimates that the abolition of trade restrictions on Third World exports could add a recurring 5 per cent to national income.[10] Trade liberalization would also tend to reduce inflationary pressures in the developed world by making goods available at cheaper prices, and it might therefore improve the growth potential of the industrial countries. Without the opportunities which liberalization could open up, it is very hard to see how commodity-reliant exporters in the Third World can spring the trap of slow growth.

Notes

1 *IMF World Economic Outlook* (Washington DC, October 1988).

2 *IMF World Economic Outlook*, April 1989 (Washington DC), table A29.

3 *World Bank World Development Report* (Oxford, 1989), table 16.

4 See, for example, Raul Prebisch, 'The Spread of Technical Progress and the Terms of Trade', *United Nations Economic Survey of Latin America* (New York, 1949), and Hans Singer, 'The Distribution of Gains between Investing and Borrowing Countries', *American Economic Review*, no. 40 (1950).

5 A. Maizels, *Commodities in Crisis* (mimeo), forthcoming.

6 See Harold Hotelling, 'The Economics of Exhaustible Resources', *Journal of Political Economy*, no. 39 (1931).

7 For a discussion, see Harold Lever and Christopher Huhne, *Debt and Danger: the World Financial Crisis* (Harmondsworth: Penguin, 1985). Details of countries subjected to IMF programmes are to be found in Lance Taylor, 'Varieties of Stabilisation Experience: towards Sensible Macro-economics in the Third World', *WIDER Studies in Development Economics* (Oxford, 1988).

8 See, for example, Sheila Page, 'The Rise in Protection since 1974', *Oxford Review of Economic Policy*, vol. 3, no. 1 (Spring 1987).

9 *World Bank World Development Report 1989*, p. 15.

10 *World Bank World Development Report 1987*, p. 90.

Why the debt crisis matters

Middle- and low-income debtors

- bank lending dries up
- the need to run export surpluses
- the effect on domestic and world economy
- the fragility of the banks
- the Baker and Brady plans
- co-operative solutions
- unilateral defaults

The rise in world interest rates after 1980, in combination with high levels of debt in many developing countries, substantially aggravated development problems throughout the world. In the case of the poorest countries, however, lending had always been predominantly from the public sector, and had been seen as a type of aid. Debt has been a contributory factor in their economic difficulties, but not the essential one (see the following essay). The debt crisis *per se* properly refers to the problems of the middle-income countries like Mexico, Brazil, Argentina and Venezuela (the four biggest debtors). Their borrowing during the seventies, although encouraged by western Governments in the name of 'recycling' the oil producers' new profits as oil prices soared, was from the private sector western banks. It thus had the peculiar dynamic of private sector financial markets familiar in the booms and busts of share prices or floating exchange rates.

The present phase of the debt crisis began with the Mexican moratorium in the summer of 1982, when suddenly the private financial markets were no longer prepared to lend the major debtors more money. The banks were unable to suspend their disbelief in the commercial nature of the loans they had made, and were only prepared to lend more if the interest payments made by the debtors were even greater than the new lending – and then only if their arms were twisted.

The result has been an excess of interest payments and capital repayments to the banks over any new lending from them, which constitutes a substantial real outflow of resources from the debtor countries running at some $30 billion a year.[1] This outflow means that imports must be lower and exports greater than they would otherwise be in order to generate the required foreign currency. The need to depress imports has entailed slow-growing domestic demand and a prolonged period of outright recession followed by slow growth of output in most of the main debtor countries. The political difficulties which ensue mean that this type of debt service is unpredictable, which in turn means that banks are even more reluctant to lend. Yet such large transfers have still not been enough to meet the interest payments, so that the debt has gone on rising. These large negative transfers also impose costs on industry in the developed world's economies, ensuring slower-growing markets overseas and heightened competitiveness from Third World producers. Even the creditor banks have seen their share prices fall relative to the market, and rise when they bite the bullet and put aside ever larger provisions. In short, it is hard to see who is really benefiting from the prolonged work-out of the debt crisis.

The original presumption of the official debt strategy was that voluntary private sector lending would rapidly resume. As the debtors serviced their debt, so the banks would regain confidence in lending, and the debt service would in turn become easier. Debt service would increasingly be met by new lending, rather than widening trade surpluses. A virtuous circle would begin which would also encourage the return of much of the capital owned by rich individuals in the debtor countries. It is quite clear, though, that the world is as far, if not further, away from that situation than it was in 1982.

One measure of the distance from renewed voluntary lending is the value of debt on the secondary market. If there are substantial discounts on debt traded between banks, it is unlikely that fresh lending will be undertaken. After all, if a bank wanted to increase its exposure to a major debtor, it would make much more sense to buy its obligations on the secondary market than to lend afresh. Yet this indicator of how far we are from normal market relationships between banker and client shows a deepening of the crisis. The discounts on Third World sovereign debt traded between the western banks are volatile, but have clearly been widening over time. Over the period from June 1986 to September 1988, the price of bank loans in the secondary market (in cents per dollar of face value) fell from 64 cents to 22 cents for Argentina, from 75 cents to 46 cents for Brazil, from 60 cents to 47 cents for Mexico, from 76 cents to 51 cents for Venezuela.[2]

Another indication of the banks' attempt to withdraw from sovereign lending is the steady build-up of their reserves against loan losses, which has left them far stronger financially than in 1982, but is hardly consistent with a new willingness to lend. It has become increasingly difficult to extract even involuntary new lending, despite the return of all of that lending directly in interest payments. The smaller banks with low Third World exposures have been keen to wash their hands of sovereign lending for some time. As reserves gradually increase among the most exposed, larger banks, the same phenomenon has been spreading to them. The proportion of new lending from official institutions (the International Monetary Fund, the World Bank and other institutions) has risen sharply.[2]

The increasing difficulty of meeting debt service – principal and interest repayments – from new lending has meant an increased need to earn foreign currency from running surpluses of exports over imports. The trade accounts of most developing countries have shifted markedly from deficit to massive surplus, with a clear cusp for the heavily indebted countries in 1982 (figure 34). The dividing point is important, because it underlines the fact that we are not dealing with a crisis which affects different countries very differently (and which would help to justify the official 'case by case' approach) but a crisis which has overwhelming similarities. From a typical flow to the major debtors worth about 11 per cent of their exports before 1982, they have faced putting aside between 15 per cent and 26 per cent of their exports in real transfers since then.

This enormous shift, moreover, understates the genuine adjustment problems which these countries have faced, because the net resource transfer is the balance of exports and imports of goods and services (excluding interest, profits and dividends). It does not reveal the very substantial deterioration in the export prices of many of the commodities which these countries export, and hence the worsening in their terms of trade. Import volume collapsed by 16.3 per cent in 1982, and by a further 21 per cent in 1983.[3] Over the subsequent period to 1988, import volumes recovered only modestly by an annual average 1.3 per cent.

Figure 34

The transfer of funds from third world debtors

(New lending to the17 highly indebted developing countries minus their capital repayments and interest; transfer to them (+) and from them (-))

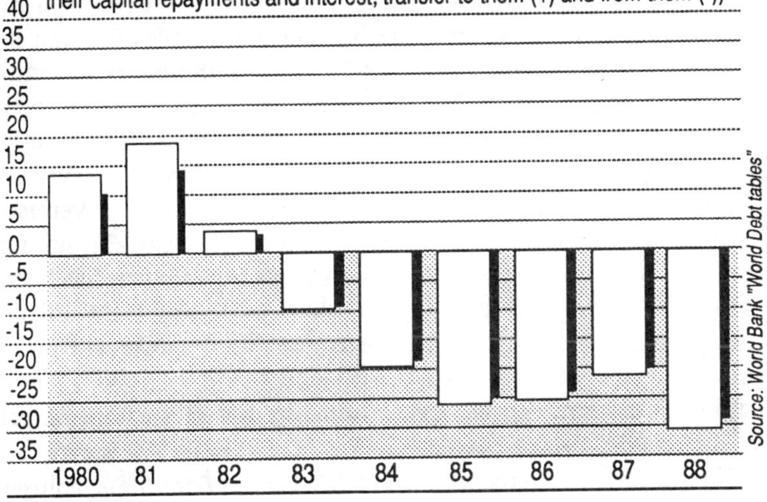

Domestic demand has been heavily deflated since the crisis broke. Per capita GDP in the fifteen heavily indebted countries is still more than 7 per cent below its 1980 level, having fallen ten per cent in the three years to 1983. The much lower growth path for GDP has in turn reduced investment and the potential for future growth. The average share of GDP going in gross capital formation between 1979 and 1981 in the fifteen heavily indebted countries was 24.8 per cent. In the three years from 1986 to 1988, the share had fallen to 17.2 per cent. This is hardly the best advertisement for the joys of 'adjustment' IMF-style.

The costs imposed upon the debtor countries are, however, only one element of the impact of the prolonged debt crisis. There are also major implications for the creditor banks, and for the trading partners of the debtors. The figures for end-1988 show that outstanding loans to the biggest four debtor countries (Brazil, Mexico, Argentina and Venezuela) outstripped the value of shareholders' equity in the case of five out of the nine leading US money centre banks.[4] Outstanding loans of the Big Nine money centre banks to the biggest twelve debtors were 89 per cent of their total capital, including loan loss reserves and borrowing. Moreover, the extensive Third World exposures come on top of other domestic exposures which have undermined the creditworthiness of many United States banks, which in many cases is rated lower than the industrial customers they are supposed to support. Nevertheless, the risks of a crisis affecting the whole financial system is declining in part because the banks have made enormous efforts over the past few years to increase their provisions against Third World debt. For example, Citicorp, America's biggest bank, has reduced its loans to Mexico, Brazil, Argentina and Venezuela from 112 per cent of its own capital at the end of 1984 to 34 per cent at the end of 1988.[5] Even more fundamentally, the risk of crisis has receded because it is clear that there is an implicit public sector guarantee for the major western financial institutions. The balance sheets, provisions, profits and even the dividend policies of the major banks are determined as never before by the guidelines set by their financial authorities.

The adjustment crisis of the debtors also has direct effects on the real economies of their trading partners in the developed world. The Federal Reserve Bank of New York estimated that the 40 per cent drop in US exports to Latin America between 1981 and 1983 cost some 250,000 American jobs in export industries.[6] UNCTAD estimates 2–3 million jobs had been lost in the developed world by the end of 1984.[7] Just as war reparations, on Keynes's argument, impoverished the victors after the First World War,[8] so it is clear that reverse flows from the debtor countries caused developed world markets to contract. In the long run, of course, there will be a gradual adjustment in western countries to the shift in purchasing power. But the structural changes can be prolonged, and leave substantial unemployment of both manpower and machines.

The belated recognition that there was no natural solution to the debt crisis began to dawn in 1985, when US Treasury Secretary James Baker proposed a plan to encourage new lending by the banks. However, he conspicuously failed to introduce any incentives which would change their behaviour, and the new lending did not materialize. By 1989 his successor, Nicholas Brady, proposed a change of direction which would put a new emphasis on debt reduction. Part of the money normally made available by the World Bank and the International Monetary Fund was to be put aside to redeem debt on the secondary market.

There were several problems with this proposal which suggested that it was unlikely to have more success than the Baker plan. First, the arrival in the market of a cash buyer for Third World debt might have the predictable effect of pushing up prices and making the relief less worthwhile unless some means of forcing the banks to sell could be arranged. Secondly, the discounts at which the countries bought back their debt would have to be even greater than those ruling on the secondary market if the constraints on their growth were to be relieved. After all, the redemption of $100 billion of debt with a 10 per cent interest rate saves only $10 billion a year of debt service – only a third of the negative net transfer. Thirdly, the only hint of a lever to force the banks to sell at high discounts was the promise that the IMF and World Bank could disburse loans even if countries were in arrears with their commercial creditors. Whether the leading industrial countries and the IMF would use that weapon aggressively enough, and whether it would be enough to persuade the banks to sell, was another matter.

One of the most promising co-operative approaches is the Lever plan proposed in 1983, and elaborated in Lever and Huhne.[9] The G7 or one of the institutions – either export credit agencies or possibly the World Bank – would support private flows to the debtors to the extent necessary to remove the negative transfers, and which would allow them to begin much more rapid growth. Such guaranteed lending would not count as direct public expenditure, because the guarantees would be contingent on a lack of service. But none of the debtors would have the incentive to default on the guaranteed lending because of the explicit objective of removing negative transfers, and providing some more normal positive flow of resources from the developed world to the developing one. A positive flow would also provide incentives to the debtors to pursue responsible macro-economic policies, without which the flow would cease. At the same time, the banks would accept the need not merely to forgive the existing stock of debt over a period of time in which such write-offs might be sustainable from their profits. This proposal has the merit of tackling the negative transfer, the stock of debt, and the fragility of the banking system. The resumption of confidence could also be expected to encourage a return of flight capital.[10] However, the details of any plan to alleviate the debt crisis are far less important than the mustering of the political will in the developed countries to tackle the problem.

The alternative to a co-operative solution is the inevitable growth of unilateral ones, exactly as occurred during the forties and fifties during the previous debt crisis which affected most of the present-day debtors a generation ago. Given the pains of generating large trade surpluses, combined with the steady increase in the debt totals for the major debtors despite their servicing efforts, it is perhaps hardly surprising that the number of debtors going into unilateral arrears has continued to mount. Though the Brazilian unilateral moratorium ended early in 1988, the Brazilian situation does not provide creditors with much cheer. The rescheduling agreement which it signed in June 1988 was relatively generous, suggesting at the very least that crime pays. The debt crisis is not over yet.

Notes

1 The World Bank estimates that the negative transfer was $43 billion in 1988, but this included a substantial flow in voluntary debt service by the successful Asian debtors. The negative transfer from the seventeen highly indebted countries was $31 billion. See World Bank debt tables, 1988–9 edition (Washington DC).

2 See Christopher Huhne, 'Some Lessons of the Debt Crisis: Never Again?', *International Economics and Financial Markets*, ed. Richard O'Brien and Tapan Datta (Oxford, 1989).

3 These figures refer to the fifteen heavily indebted countries and are from the International Monetary Fund, *World Economic Outlook*, April 1989.

4 Salomon Bros, *A Review of Bank Performance* (New York, 1989), figs. 31 and 76.

5 Harold Lever and Christopher Huhne, *Debt and Danger: the World Financial Crisis* (Harmondsworth: Penguin, 1985), p. 28, and equivalent figures from Salomon Bros, op cit.

6 Sanjay Dhar in Federal Reserve Bank of New York, *Quarterly Review*, vol. 8, no. 3 (Autumn 1983).

7 United Nations Conference on Trade and Development, *Trade and Development Report 1985* (Geneva), p. 5.

8 John Maynard Keynes, *The Economic Consequences of the Peace* (1919), *Collected Writings*, vol. 9 (London: Royal Economic Society and Macmillan).

9 Lever and Huhne, op cit.

10 An industrial country agreement to levy a witholding tax on interest and profits would also repel some flight capital. Until the industrial countries are prepared to ensure a more level playing field in the tax treatment of overseas residents' assets, they should at least stop delivering lectures about the need for sound policies. Untaxed returns will always be more attractive than taxed ones.

Does aid work?

Right and Left criticisms of aid

- the legacy of the withdrawal of public sector responsibility in the debt crisis
- the decline in the African economy
- the importance of aid in supporting living standards
- most aid is effective
- the South Korean case
- right and wrong conditionality
- the problem of falling raw materials prices and protectionism

One of the greatest victims of the sea-change in economic thinking which has occurred in the last two decades has been aid to the developing world. Ironically, aid first came under concerted attack from the Left, which argued either that it served merely to prop up unpalatable regimes which were an obstacle to development or that it was primarily a weapon wielded by the donors to pursue their own foreign policy and industrial goals. It was better for the Third World, the implication of this criticism suggested, to pull out of the aid business altogether.[1] The new Right subsequently needed little excuse to lay into the post-war consensus. The now-ennobled P.T. Bauer was one of the most forthright critics, accusing aid of fostering *dirigisme*, undermining market forces which were the only effective path to economic development, and thereby retarding growth and exacerbating poverty.[2]

Some of those fashionable views have now been around

long enough to create their own problems, most notably in the continuing crisis of Third World debt. Had it not been for the reflex insistence of finance ministers in the wake of the first oil shock that commercial banks would make sensible lending decisions in line with the wisdom of market forces, neither debtors nor creditors would be in the mess they are in today. Until 1974 it was well understood that the unregulated private sector financial institutions, with their short time horizons, were an unsuitable vehicle for development finance (see the preceding essay). The renaissance of *laissez faire* thinking, combined with budget stringency in the wake of sharp increases in social security spending in the seventies recession, also took its toll in the cuts in Third World aid budgets in most of the developed economies, but particularly in the United States and Britain, two major donors.

That in turn meant that the aid flows to Africa – indeed, to the low-income countries in general – actually fell back both in real terms and as a proportion of donor GDP during some years of the seventies and eighties (table 29). At the time, sub-Saharan Africa was experiencing a dramatic worsening of the conditions for its development. Part of these problems were political, in the form of civil and other wars. Part came in the shape of natural disasters, including the Sahel drought. But the cuts in aid compounded the injury. Total flows of finance – the net resource transfer – to sub-Saharan Africa collapsed sharply in the early eighties. In 1980 the sub-Saharan countries received a net $8.8 billion, enough to fund 14 per cent of their imports. After a small rise to 1982 the transfer collapsed to only $1.7 billion in 1985. Since exports were also falling, further reducing the availability of foreign exchange, imports fell by 30 per cent.[3]

The African debt relief agreed by the leading industrial countries in 1988 may have been some small sign of a turning tide in the antagonism to aid, but there are still enough horror stories of waste and corruption to ensure a ready band of critics. In that context it is refreshing to find that the most careful and reasoned recent analysis of aid comes to a broadly positive conclusion. In a major study funded by the donor members of an eighteen-government international task force and involving the outstanding development economists in the field, the conclusion

Table 29. Aid flows: aid flows as a percentage of donor GDP, 1965–87

	1965	1970	1975	1980	1985	1987
To all developing countries						
Total OECD area	0.48	0.34	0.35	0.37	0.35	0.35
of which						
USA	0.58	0.32	0.27	0.27	0.24	0.20
UK	0.48	0.40	0.42	0.39	0.31	0.28
Sweden	0.18	0.43	0.98	0.92	0.87	0.88
To low-income countries						
Total OECD area	0.19	0.11	0.10	0.08	0.08	0.12
of which						
USA	0.25	0.12	0.08	0.03	0.04	0.06
UK	0.23	0.16	0.12	0.16	0.09	0.09
Sweden	0.07	0.11	0.44	0.39	0.31	0.29

Source: World Bank, *World Development Report*, 1987, 1988

is that the majority of aid is successful in terms of its own objectives. Over a wide range of countries and sectors aid has made positive and valuable contributions. Moreover, the Cassen report rejects the accusation that aid fails to reach the poor or discourages the private sector.[4]

Aid is an important source of support for the living standards of the least developed countries, forming about 9 per cent of their gross national product, and about 3 per cent for other low-income countries. The low-income giants – China and India – receive relatively little at 0.2 per cent and 1 per cent of national income respectively. The disproportionate beneficiaries amongst the poorest are the sub-Saharan countries, for many of which aid flows (before deducting interest payments, as in the calculation of net transfers above) represent a fifth of GNP and up to 40 per cent of imports. Paradoxically, the report finds that aid in this region also tends to be less effective – measured in terms of rates of return or wider criteria – than aid in Asia.

It would thus be possible to improve the effectiveness of aid merely by targeting it more in line with population distribution amongst the poorest countries, but is that really what donors want? It is surely hardly surprising the aid is likely to be less effective in areas like the Sahel where development is most difficult. Indeed, there is bound to be a margin of allowable failure in aid projects which Cassen rightly suggests should be more openly discussed by the aid agencies, not least because they have not been good at learning from each others' mistakes. Certainly there are periodic examples of crass mismanagement and waste. But isolated examples among the many more successful programmes and projects do not make a case for running down aid in its entirety. The failure of the Ford Edsel does not undermine the case for a market-oriented or capitalist system, any more than the failure of Christians to live up to their own precepts discredits the Creed. The Cassen report's finding is that the vast majority of project aid – in the region of 65 per cent to 75 per cent – is effective.

Aid is a crucial part of the support for living standards in low-income countries, but the gap in output with the developed world is so great that it is still a tiny fraction of the national income of the donors (table 30). In the British case, real cuts in aid levels have reduced the proportion of national income to one-third of a per cent of gross domestic product (compared with the UN target, to which Britain still pays lip-service, of 0.7 per cent). In the United States, hitherto the world's largest aid donor, though proportionately one of its smallest, spending on domestic social programmes from the federal budget (pre-Reagan) was thirty-six times greater than the overseas aid programme. (In 1989, Japan was set to overtake the US as the world's largest donor.) Yet aid can clearly make a demonstrable difference to the lot of ordinary people in the least developed countries. On one simple rule of thumb, if aid adds 20 per cent to a country's level of investment (which would be typical in many of the least developed countries) then growth can be expected to be anything from 0.6 per cent to 1.5 per cent higher each year than it would otherwise be, given normal relationships between capital and output.

However, one qualification is that aid on its own is not enough. It may be a necessary but not a sufficient condition of development. Case studies show that policy changes have helped or hindered the development process in crucial respects. In South Korea, for example, the replacement of the Rhee regime in the military coup of 1961 marked a watershed in development efforts. President Park reversed the emphasis on building up import-substituting industries and an overvalued exchange rate

Table 30. Real income per head, 1977 (calculated at purchasing power parities, allowing for price differences)

	Income per head ($)
Africa	862
Asia	1,179
Europe	4,943
North America	7,795
Latin America and Caribbean	2,514
Oceania	1,134
Total	2,348

Source: Kravis, Heston and Summers, *World Product and Income* (1982), table 8-14

which made exporting unattractive. The export effort gradually attracted overseas investment. Aid was concentrated on training, education and technical assistance. Korean society is ethnically homogeneous, imbued with a strong commitment to education and meritocracy, and had the advantage of a land reform which left a fairly equal distribution of assets which spread both demand and capital. Regarded as a hopeless case thirty years ago, South Korea is now arguably the most successful of all the newly industrializing countries. Similar stories can be told for Taiwan, Singapore, Hong Kong. Both Thailand and Malaysia may be heading the same way.

The conditions attached to aid and lending by both bilateral donors and the multilateral agencies like the International Monetary Fund and the World Bank have been controversial for many years. One of the problems in the short term is that the size of the trade adjustments which economies have had to make during the years of the oil price rises have been out of line with the relatively small sums which the Fund and the Bank have had available to lend to cushion the transition. Stringent conditionality is a result of inadequate resources. Some conditionality, though, is crucial to a successful adjustment or long-term aid programme, if only because it is a fact of democratic politics that aid has to be seen to be effective if support for it is to be maintained in the donor countries. There are, however, clearly right and wrong conditions.

The wrong ones are old-fashioned 'tying' of aid, which limits the recipient to buying particular goods from the donor country. Though aid overall has gradually become less tied – with untied bilateral aid increasing from 37 per cent in 1976 to 46 per cent in 1982/3 for the developed countries as a whole – the proportion is still high. Moreover, governments are constantly inventing new ways of achieving the same effect, notably with mixed credits whereby an aid element (in Britain's case the Aid and Trade Provision) is used to subsidize an otherwise commercial package and win an order for the manufacturers of the country in question. Aid funnelled through the multilateral agencies is more likely to prove effective simply because project managers can buy what they need from the most competitive source.

The right sort of conditionality is to look for projects with a clear bias towards helping the 40 per cent of people in the least developed countries who are below any definition of absolute poverty, and indeed to concentrate more aid on those countries where most of them live. At present, more than a third of total official development assistance is still going to middle-income as opposed to low-income countries. Simple technologies, irrigation and extension services to promote better husbandry help to ensure a prosperous agriculture, which can in turn provide markets for urban production.

Aid is also bound to involve some conditionality about overall economic policies, simply because it is payable in foreign currency which is extremely fungible: i.e. though it is paid for one purpose, it can in fact be used for another. The aid may be tied to a particular project which would have gone ahead anyway, but the money effectively allows the Government to do something else further down its list of priorities. If only 10 per cent of the cost of a project is in fact in foreign currency, some 90 per cent of the funds will be sold to buy local currency – and will therefore be available for other uses. Much of the bank lending to Latin America in the seventies did not finance increased investment, but merely held up the exchange rate of the countries concerned while their richer residents bought overseas assets – a Miami apartment block or United States Treasury bills. The risk of misused foreign currency is less great in the poorest African countries, where aid is a high proportion of national income, but only because the conditionality tends if anything to be more severe.

For the rest, the donor countries should commit themselves to a more co-ordinated approach which provides a secure, long-term framework for development in the poorest countries. Education, agriculture, health and aid for land reform should be the priorities. There will also have to be a much greater commitment to protect them from changes in the world's economic environment (such as collapsing commodity prices) if aid efforts are not to be negated by far larger forces. The last ten years, far from being a period of swings and roundabouts, has left the poorest countries suffering lower export prices, higher debt service and lower outright aid flows in real terms. Moreover, there is an accumulation of evidence that raw materials prices will continue to fall compared with the price of manufactures, making it even more difficult for Third World countries reliant on exports of raw materials to earn hard currency and import the investment goods needed to grow. The essential problem is that western technology is either economizing on the use of raw materials or abandoning their use altogether.

The examples of the newly industrializing countries in Asia show that developing countries can escape the trap of falling commodity prices, but precious few have yet made the leap. Moreover, most developed countries have become increasingly protectionist in those industries like textiles, clothing and footwear in which it is easiest to take advantage of low labour costs. Open access to the developed world's markets, combined with increased aid flows concentrated on education, training and basic capital goods, are the twin tests of whether the First World means to encourage development, or pull the ladder up behind it.

Notes

1 See, for example, Teresa Hayter, *Aid as Imperialism* (Harmondsworth: Penguin, 1971).

2 P.T. Bauer, *Reality and Rhetoric* (London: Weidenfeld, 1984).

3 See Carol Lancaster and John Williamson, eds., *African Debt and Financing*, Institute for International Economics, special report no. 5 (Washington DC, May 1986), p. 202, table 7.1.

4 Robert Cassen and associates, *Does Aid Work? Report to an Intergovernmental Task Force* (Oxford: Clarendon Press, 1986).

Can economic sanctions work?

Four conditions for sanctions working

- defined and limited political objectives
- pain must exceed pain of concession
- success of South African sanctions against Lesotho
- success of the United States against Korea and Taiwan
- difficulty of assessing sanctions with large objectives
- review of sanctions against South Africa
- gold as the Achilles' heel of South Africa

Hardly a year goes by when some international outrage or another provokes a call in the western democracies for economic sanctions against the perpetrators. Recent candidates include the Chinese Government for its massacre of students in Tiananmen Square; President Noriega for his *coup d'état* in Panama; and that perpetual favourite, the South African Government, for its continued practice of apartheid and the often brutal measures required to support the system. The conventional wisdom amongst the worldly wise is that economic sanctions may purify the souls of the people imposing them, but they achieve little else. However, the evidence suggests that carefully designed sanctions can and do work even in hard cases like that of South Africa.

A monumental recent study examined 103 episodes of economic sanctions.[1] One in three could be accounted a 'success' and they all had similar characteristics which amount to little more than common sense would suggest. First, sanctions must not hurt your own side too much or the political pressures to turn a blind eye to their breach will be enormous. Secondly, sanctions work better against friends and allies than they do against enemies – take the United States' sanctions against Britain and France over their invasion of Suez in 1956. Thirdly, sanctions which hit a country's exports are generally more effective than ones which hit a country's imports: if it cannot sell, it equally cannot buy. But most important, sanctions have to hurt the receiving country harder than conceding whatever you want to wring out of them. Take the example of South Africa. If the objective of sanctions is a specific and limited concession, such as the release of Nelson Mandela and the unbanning of the African National Congress (ANC), then a package which might conceivably hurt the South African Government more could be designed.

If, though, the objective of sanctions is the ultimate destruction of the white regime, it is fairly predictable now that economic measures will be able to play only a part – and a minor one – in a political battle whose front line is in the townships and on the Republic's borders. On this view, sanctions are merely one element of the internal and external pressure which can be brought to bear on the regime, and which can ultimately destroy it. To take a Russian parallel, they are about turning the next 1905 uprising into the full-scale 1917 revolution where the *ancien régime* is weakened by fighting on at least two fronts. The success of such sanctions is barely measurable, since quite clearly other factors must be more important.

Nevertheless, specific measures introduced to achieve specific objectives work. Ironically, South Africa itself has been an enthusiast for a targeted use of sanctions. One of the most successful examples of economic sanctions was South Africa's threatened trade embargo against land-locked Lesotho, which quickly succeeded in depriving the South African freedom movement, the African National Congress, of a base for incursions into thc Republic. Other successes for sanctions include the United States' pressure on South Korea in 1974 and Taiwan in 1976 to stop them pursuing nuclear programmes which looked as if they could have military capability. The mere delay of a few export shipments of goods was enough. The Americans also succeeded in having an impact on Romanian and Hungarian restrictions on Jewish emigration by threatening to reduce tariff concessions on those countries' exports. In the main, however, these examples of successes have one thing in common: they pursued limited objectives which were not central to the concerns of the regimes affected.

The history of success in the pursuit of more thoroughgoing objectives has not been as marked. British sanctions may have undermined Amin's Uganda. The United States pressure on the

World Bank, Inter-American Development Bank and the New York commercial banks to cease lending to President Allende's Chile from November 1970 onwards weakened the regime, though a more direct 'destabilization' including instigation of a truckers' strike was widely reported at the time. President Carter probably did succeed in destabilizing the Somoza Government of Nicaragua in protest at its civil rights violations, and President Reagan certainly weakened its Sandinista successors. However, the limited sanctions against the Soviet Union imposed in the wake of its invasion of Afghanistan were notably ineffective, as was the long campaign of economic sanctions imposed by Britain and others against the white regime in Rhodesia.[2]

What, though, of sanctions against South Africa, the most perennial subject of international censure? The long-running and steadily mounting campaign against apartheid has already led to some effective measures, although the impact has seldom been precisely what was either intended or expected. Those already backed by Governments around the world include the sports boycott, the oil embargo, the ban on military sales and co-operation and the prohibition of collaboration in nuclear and other advanced technologies.

The long ban on sporting contact has had an effect out of all proportion to its apparent triviality. By forcing sports authorities in South Africa to think multi-racially for representative events, it produced the first U-turn in the history of apartheid – the partial abandonment of the principle of separate facilities. More specifically economic measures have had more mixed results. The oil embargo has been honoured as much in the breach as in the observance, but the threat of an effective embargo has certainly imposed serious costs. Billions of rands have been spent in building up reserves at high prices (on top of which had to be paid a black market premium) and on the Sasol coal from oil plants. However, pressure on the oil majors (notably BP and Shell) might make the embargo less leaky.

The military isolation of South Africa has also been circumvented, but again at considerable expense. Pretoria has had to build a large and costly home-grown arms industry which now exports. But the main effect of the embargo has

Figure 35

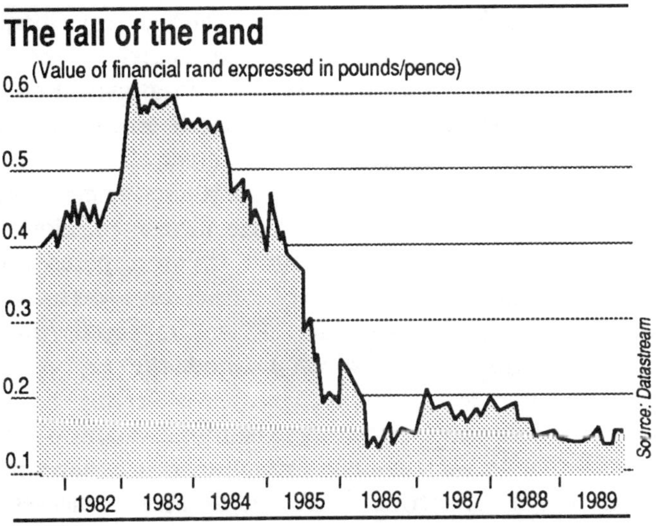

been to starve the defence force of modern warships, aircraft and tanks, for which there is no black market save in spares. The nuclear and technological embargo was too little and too late to stop Pretoria acquiring nuclear power or the ability to make the Bomb and enrich uranium. As with its efforts to get around the military embargo, South Africa was helped officially and unofficially by Israel, France, West Germany and others although any such embargo is vulnerable to the piracy of others' ideas. The easy availability of technical literature in the West and the portability of much high-tech equipment make evasion simple, if not cheap.

By far the most devastating measures so far have been applied by private enterprise – for hard-headed commercial reasons rather than moral ones. Chase Manhattan's decision to end private loans to South Africans in 1985 was quickly followed by other banks, which rapidly undermined the value of the currency. The financial rand – the exchange rate used by those who want to sell assets in South Africa – has collapsed from more than 60p in 1983 to under 15p in 1989. If the South Africans want to maintain the pretence that they are fully part of the international system and that there can be some return to 'normal' economic links, they will have to continue to negotiate with their creditors over the terms of reschedulings and interest payments. So far, the creditors have managed to extract capital repayments and interest substantially in excess of the new lending which South Africa has been able to attract. Like the Latin American debtors, South Africa has been making large net payments to its creditors.

For precisely this reason, any explicit Government sanctions which pushed the South Africans into a default on their international debt would, within a short period, give them more resources, because they would save both capital repayments and interest payments. True, the South Africans might lose the trade credit which finances the gap between having to pay on the nail for imports and receiving payment for exports, and this might force some painful short-term import cutbacks. But a lot of payment for imports is apparently in cash, and the South Africans' foreign exchange reserves are substantial.

If the international financiers ever changed their minds and decided after all that South Africa was worth investing in, then there might be some point to financial sanctions. At present, though, the market is being tougher than the most stringent anti-apartheid radical. Investors want out. Similarly, the bans on gold krugerrands and on loans merely formalized what had already happened in the marketplace. Investment overall has slumped, and foreign direct investors are already taking out more in interest profits and dividends than they are putting back in new money.

The slogan of 'disinvestment' is also too easy: there are no realistic ways in which western Governments could force companies to repatriate the physical assets they have in South Africa, even if Pretoria were to let them. If 'disinvestment' merely means selling the title to those assets, the odds are that some South African company will be acquiring something at a knock-down price – leaving the productive capacity of the economy unchanged. In the longer term, however, a freeze on new investment would cut away a large part of the impetus behind modernization and the growth of living standards. Like any small economy, South Africa is highly dependent on imported technology. However, any such embargo would be extremely difficult to police. One touted sanction – an end to the agreements which stop companies from being taxed twice on their profits – might discourage new investment, but it might also encourage foreign companies to retain more profits within South Africa. A prohibition on the reinvestment of foreign company profits would be easily countered by the South African imposition of stiffer exchange controls, new taxes or ultimately sequestration.

Other possible measures include ending the promotion of tourism, banning Government purchases from and contracts with South African firms, and stopping flights to and from South Africa. Of these, all except the last are already largely operative. Cutting air links, though, would have a useful psychological effect on the many white South Africans who have connections abroad by undermining their moralc, encouraging white emigration and the loss of skilled manpower, and sapping the will to hold out.

The realities of conservative Governments in Britain, the United States and West Germany mean that more radical sanctions are probably off the agenda for the moment, though some at least could be brutally effective. The most obvious target is South Africa's foreign trade, as successive UN resolutions vetoed by Britain and the United States have testified. A total embargo on trade could not be observed by South Africa's dependent neighbours, and would be evaded, though at some cost, by profiteers and Government agents. Nevertheless, South Africa would not have the advantage, unlike Rhodesia after 1965, of a relatively large, adjacent and industrialized ally. But only a complete naval blockade, of the kind once used against slavery, would make a trade embargo bite quickly.

At the end of the rainbow of possible new sanctions lies South Africa's great crock of gold. The ultimate selective economic measure would be aimed at gold sales. An embargo, as with diamonds, would be virtually impossible to enforce for such a high value, smuggle-prone product. But only a few Western countries need to decide to force down the gold price for South Africa's entire terms of trade – the amount of exports required to buy a given quantity of imports – to deteriorate dramatically. Nearly half of all South Africa's exports are gold. The advantage of, say, halving the gold price (and hence cutting total export earnings by a quarter) is that the South Africans would have to decide what not to buy, which would reduce the pressure against sanctions from western producers. Secondly, South Africa could not avoid the sanctions since it has to sell its gold somewhere. No one will pay a higher price than they need to. Measured against all the criteria needed for success, gold sales look most deadly.

The gold holdings of the International Monetary Fund alone, one of the smaller of the official holders, account for some 103 million ounces, or about four years' worth of South African production. Moreover, the IMF had already sold much of its stockpile between 1976 and 1980 as part of its policy to demonetize gold in favour of officially issued reserves like the Special Drawing Right. The Americans alone have a stockpile more than twice as large as the IMF's – followed by German, Swiss and French reserves of about the same size as the IMF's (and a more diminutive British one only a fifth the size). Even the announcement by these countries that they intended to hold the gold price to a certain level would probably be enough to make it collapse and put substantial pressure on the South African regime. Indeed, one study has argued that the Americans have already used sales of their enormous gold reserves to pressure the South Africans to squeeze the Beitbridge supply route to Rhodesia in 1976.[3] The gold price certainly fell over the year to January 1976 from $200 an ounce to $130, wiping nearly a fifth off the value of all South Africa's exports. The arithmetic of gold looks remarkably tempting for any group of Governments determined to put pressure on South Africa.

Notes

1 Gary Clyde Hufbauer and Jeffrey J Schott, *Economic Sanctions Reconsidered* (Washington DC: Institute for International Economics, 1985).

2 For a discussion, see Robin Renwick, *Economic Sanctions* (Centre for International Affairs, Harvard University, 1981), and M.S. Daoudi and M.S. Dajani, *Economic Sanctions: Ideals and Experience* (London: Routledge, 1983).

3 R.W. Johnson, *How Long will South Africa Survive?* (London: Macmillan, 1977).

The importance of OPEC

Macro-economic impact of oil price changes

- the history of the 1973 price rise
- reducing output to sustain the price
- demand stays up despite the price rise in the short term
- a second rise in 1979
- demand and supply begin to change
- strains on the cartel
- the Saudis' self-interest and the price collapse
- individual and collective interest
- the medium-term outlook

Oil is such an important commodity that its price affects inflation, growth and the balance of payments positions of all the world's major economies. The three sharp shifts in the oil price over the last two decades – upwards in 1973, 1979 and down in 1986 – have all had demonstrable effects not only on the distribution of world income between oil producers and consumers, but also on the amount of world activity. Some idea of the scale of the effects of oil can be gauged from the work of the Organisation for Economic Co-operation and Development, the intergovernmental body of the industrial nations which is best placed to assess the international impact of a major oil price change. Its Interlink model of the world economy suggested that the collapse in the oil price from an average of $27.45 in 1985 to $15.04 in 1986 would reduce prices, improve real incomes, boost spending and increase output. Its calculations suggested that the fall improved the developed world's trade balance by $12 billion in 1987; reduced inflation by 1.6 percentage points; and added 1.7 per cent to domestic demand in 1987, 1.2 per cent to output and 0.8 per cent to employment.[1]

These numbers are, of course, spuriously precise but they give an indication of the orders of magnitude which seem likely. In the longer term the effects can be even more profound. It seems clear that a major reason for the buoyancy of activity in the developed world from the summer of 1987, despite the October stock market crash, was a delayed effect of the sharp fall in oil prices. Although the effects on a country which is

Figure 36

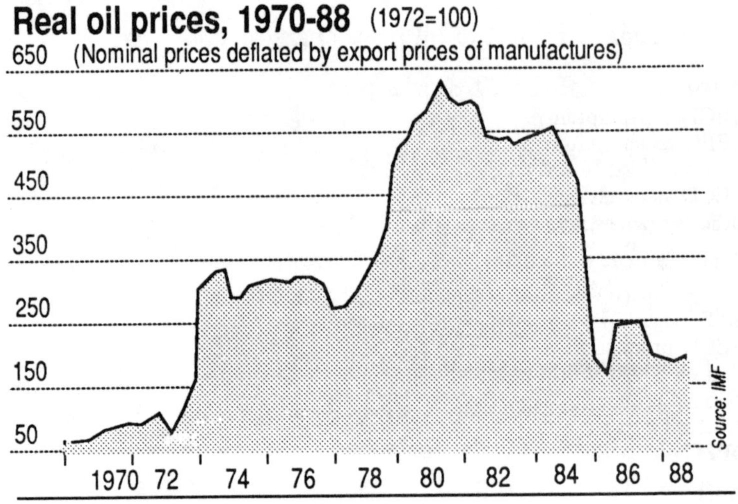

just about self-sufficient in oil like Britain are much less, the secondary impact of falling inflation and buoyant export markets is important.[2]

This is not to argue that all the problems which were visited on the industrial countries from 1973 were due to the oil price rise, though it had a significant effect. The fundamental reasons for the turbulence of the seventies lay in excessive demand in part due to the United States financing of the Vietnam War through budget deficits despite the lack of any spare capacity; and in part due to the breakdown of the disciplines of the fixed exchange rate system and the unfortunate coincidence of elections in the main democracies (which were in part the subject of an essay in chapter 8). The resulting excess demand led to a commodity price explosion across the board. Oil took advantage of the same trend, abetted by the Arab oil embargo imposed because of the 1973 Arab–Israeli war. The real question about the oil market was not why the price rose, but why it did not fall back along with other commodity prices when the developed world went into recession in 1975. The answer can only be that supply was effectively restrained by the main oil producers. The Organisation of Petroleum Exporting Countries (OPEC), which had been born as a mild trade union in 1960, became a militant cartel.

Table 31. Oil market conditions, 1986–9 (millions of barrels per day)

	1986	*1987*	*1988*	*1989**
Demand				
OECD consumption	35.4	36.0	36.9	37.5
OPEC consumption	3.7	3.9	4.0	4.0
Non-oil Third World consumption	9.1	9.4	9.9	10.5
OECD stock change	0.4	0.3	−0.1	0.0
Other stock change	−0.4	−1.1	0.0	0.0
Total	48.2	48.5	50.7	52.0
Supply				
OECD production	16.9	16.8	16.6	16.5
Non-oil Third World production	8.6	9.0	9.4	9.5
Planned economies' net exports	1.8	2.1	2.2	2.25
Processing gain	1.1	1.1	1.1	1.0
OPEC production	19.8	19.5	21.4	22.5
Total	48.2	48.5	50.7	52.0

*Forecast
Source: OECD Economic Outlook, June 1989, table 87

Venezuela and other long-standing oil producers, worried by the depletion of their reserves, had been pushing for an active price cartel throughout the sixties. But it was not until the oil embargo dramatically demonstrated the truth of its case that the rest of the organization accepted it. The demand for oil is relatively unresponsive – inelastic – to changes in its price, at least in the short run. Once people have invested in their cars or central heating equipment, they have to go on buying the petrol or the heating oil. If the supply of oil were largely determined by competing producers, all of whom had to accept the price in the market, the price would not be far removed from the cost of producing the final barrel required by consumers. At the end of the sixties, this marginal cost was arguably some 20 to 30 cents a barrel, a perception which formed the basis of a prediction in 1973 by one distinguished academic that oil prices were set to fall.[3] In this respect, oil should have been like any other product except that, as a finite resource, its price would tend to rise over time to match that of its substitutes when reserves run out.[4]

In reality, however, the oil market had never been characterized by a myriad of price-taking competitive producers. The seven sisters – the major oil companies – had managed the market through most of the fifties and sixties and from 1968 had co-operated explicitly in the London Oil Policy Group.[5] At its Caracas meeting in 1970, OPEC decided to try to wrest control of supply and prices from the oil companies, a trend which culminated between 1973 and 1979 in the effective nationalization of almost all OPEC production. From 1973 it was OPEC which set the world oil price. 'The issue for the producing countries – those which belong to the Third World – is how to transform their depletable resource, which is often their only source of economic wealth, into the reproducible assets of economic development,' wrote Ali M. Jaidah, a former OPEC general secretary.[6] Faced with relatively inelastic demand, OPEC discovered that relatively small shifts in supply were enough to ensure that the price stayed high. The surplus or 'rent' it was able to extract was phenomenal. OPEC cut its production between 1973 and 1975 by 12.5 per cent to 27 million barrels per day,[7] but that modest reduction was enough to support the price of Saudi light at $10.72 compared with $2.70 in 1973 (and only $1.90 in 1972).[8] Total OPEC revenues trebled to more than $100 billion.

There did not appear to be much cool calculation in OPEC's behaviour; it acted out of opportunism and a learning process by which it discovered its own power. OPEC took advantage of another cyclical peak in demand, and another shock to supply in the shape of the fall of the Shah of Iran, to raise prices again in 1979. Prices averaged $12.70 a barrel in 1978 and $28.67 in 1980. However, this time the cutback in OPEC supply was a good deal more painful and was to be the harbinger of even more substantial reductions. OPEC production fell from 32 million barrels a day in 1979 to 20.1 million barrels in 1982,[9] where it stayed until the price fall in 1986. Cartel power still made sense, but the trade-off was beginning to look less attractive. Prices were up a little more than double, but output was down by rather more than a third. What was happening, slowly but surely, was that demand and supply were at long last responding to the rise in price.

The long run began to arrive, and in the long run the rise in price encouraged consumers to cut their oil purchases, and provided incentives to producers to find alternative oil wells. On the demand side, the size of cars fell and their energy efficiency rose. Investment became less energy intensive. Insulation reduced energy waste. Before 1973, each 1 per cent rise in output in the developed countries entailed a 0.8 per cent rise in energy use. After 1983, each 1 per cent rise in output required a rise of only 0.34 per cent in energy use.[10] On the supply side, whole new oil fields outside the Middle East and other OPEC members were developed: in the North Sea, in Alaska, in Mexico. Such was the amount of exploration activity which the price rises provoked that proven oil reserves actually increased at a faster rate than production throughout the period.[11] Non-OPEC supply from developed, developing and Eastern Bloc countries rose from 20.8 million barrels a day in 1979 to 25.9 million barrels a day in 1985.

Until 1985, the cartel proved able to withstand the pressures put on it by the increase of non-OPEC oil supply and the steady progress of energy conservation in the industrial countries. In 1985, however, the strains began to tell. OPEC output was about 14 million barrels a day lower than it was in 1979. OPEC was meeting less than 40 per cent of world oil demand, compared with more than 60 per cent in 1979. Nor did the cartel's problems end there, for many of its poorer and most populated members – notably Nigeria, Venezuela, Libya, Indonesia and Ecuador – were thought to be exceeding their agreed production quotas, often by wide margins, a phenomenon made no easier to police by the proliferation of different sales arrangements, including barter, extended credit terms, processing deals and so forth. These 'high absorbers' – countries able to spend a high proportion of the extra revenue they acquired from oil price rises – evidently believed that they were able to enjoy high prices without production cutbacks. Increasingly, the result of the activities of the OPEC 'cheats' was to force Saudi Arabia to cut its production by even more than it had agreed in order to keep the price up, and the Saudis began to be riled. Not only were non-OPEC oil producers like Britain, Norway and Mexico pumping out all they could manage at the high cartel prices, without bearing any of the output sacrifice, but even their supposed fellow members were doing the same.

The Saudis' output in 1985 was estimated to be less than that of the North Sea, some 40 per cent below their OPEC quota, and less than a quarter of their full potential. The danger for OPEC – and other non-OPEC producers – was that Saudi Arabia was being pushed perilously close to the point at which it was indifferent between dramatically restraining its output to fetch a cartel price and unleashing its output to get a free-market price. To see why this was so, take a look at some simplified calculations of the options for the Saudis just before the oil price collapse. They were producing about 2.5 million barrels a day at some $26.70, or getting about $67 million a day (disregarding shipping costs). With a free market, they might believe that they could produce 11 million barrels a day at between $3 and $11 a barrel (the sort of price estimates then current of what would happen in a free oil market). Saudi revenue would be between $33 million and $121 million a day. In other words, the OPEC cheats were pushing the Saudis into the danger zone where participation in the cartel no longer had clear-cut advantages for revenue. The denouement was predictable, and predicted.[12]

The difficulties of sustaining the OPEC cartel when the sacrifices became bigger are a perfect illustration of the way in which the short-term individual interests of members of a group can triumph over collective and longer-term ones. There can be no doubt that all the OPEC members benefited from production restraint and the resulting high prices, because even in the medium term oil demand is relatively unresponsive to price. The higher price far more than compensated for the required production cuts, but the cartel was unable to ensure that members accepted those cuts fairly. This is, of course, the famous 'Prisoners' Dilemma' case from game theory. Imagine two people who are given the choice between receiving $10,000 whatever the other person does, and ensuring that the other person receives $50,000. The best option is for them both to agree to vote the other person $50,000, but if there is no way of enforcing their agreement it is rational for the individual to go for the $10,000. At best, he can hope for his own $10,000 plus the $50,000 voted by the other person. But if he votes $50,000 for the other person, he may end up with nothing at all. The point about this example is that people who refuse to act for their mutual benefit are not necessarily irrational or stupid; they may be perfectly rational.

None of this is to argue that cartels cannot work, or that oil prices will stay at relatively low levels for ever. Clearly OPEC did work well on behalf of its members for some time. But without some mechanism for enforcing agreements between members, cartels are doomed to be unstable. However, the outlook for oil prices is encouraging for OPEC. The oil import price for the developing countries averaged just under $14 a barrel in 1988, but it was edging up through most of 1989 despite some generally unsupportive OPEC politics. It was not at all clear that oil demand would stay as subdued as some of the optimistic international organizations of the developed world believed. Though OECD area consumption remained fairly stable, oil demand in the non-oil developing countries was increasing rapidly, not least because the types of industry which many were putting in place were much more energy-reliant than the new high-tech industries in the developed world. Equally, OECD oil production was tailing off.[13] The conditions were gradually being set for OPEC to reassert its dominance over the oil market without the sort of sacrifices which proved so contentious in the late eighties.

Notes

1 *OECD Economic Outlook*, no. 39 (Paris, May 1986); author's calculations from the Technical Note on p. 164, assuming government expenditure on goods unchanged in nominal terms, effects in the second year.

2 Two Treasury economists suggested that the effect of a falling oil price might worsen UK inflation because the exchange rate would have to fall and import prices rise. See Stephen Powell and Geoff Horton, *The Economic Effects of Lower Oil Prices* (HM Treasury, April 1985). However, it is not clear in retrospect that the pound was a petro-currency.

3 The academic in question was the unfortunate Professor Morris Adelman of MIT in his *The World Petroleum Market* (Baltimore: Johns Hopkins University Press, 1972). However, journalists were marvellously wrong too. Shortly after the first oil shock, *The Economist* in a leader entitled 'The Coming Oil Glut' announced that prices would fall sharply.

4 In theory, the price should be given by the cost of substitutes when

the non-renewable resource runs out discounted back to the present by the current interest rate. See Harold Hotelling, 'The Economics of Exhaustible Resources', *Journal of Political Economy*, no. 39 (1931).

5 For the history, see Peter R. Odell, *Oil and World Power* (Harmondsworth: Penguin, 8th edn, 1986).

6 Ali M. Jaidah, *An Appraisal of OPEC Oil Policies* (London: Longman, 1983).

7 Arnold Safer, *International Oil Policy* (Lexington Books, 1979), table 3-1.

8 *IMF International Financial Statistics Yearbook 1986* and subsequently.

9 *OECD Economic Outlook*, no. 36 (December 1984), p. 155, table 65.

10 Odell, op cit., p. 256.

11 Odell, op cit., p. 261.

12 See Christopher Huhne in *The Guardian*, 20 June 1985, but also Safer, op cit. for a longer-term expatiation on the effects of demand and supply responses.

13 For a persuasive bull case for oil prices, see Andrew MacKillop, *Price Outlook for the 1988–1993 Period* (mimeo) forthcoming in *Energy Economics*, August-October 1989.

10 The European Community

For and against the European Monetary System

Labour and Conservative objections to EMS membership

- the system is not biased towards inflation
- the credibility argument is unimpressive
- the real advantages in reducing volatility and misalignments
- encouragement to trade
- monetary sovereignty versus co-operation
- the degree of freedom within the system
- Mrs Thatcher's political objections
- Sir Alan Walters' objections

The debate on whether Britain should fully participate in the European Monetary System (EMS) of fixed but adjustable exchange rates is tiresomely circular. No sooner has one set of objections been dispatched but the opponents of sterling's participation in the exchange rate mechanism come up with precisely the opposite reason for not joining. In 1979 the objection of the then Labour Government was that the commitment to fix the pound at a given parity against the other Europcan currencies would force more restrictive interest rate and tax and spending policies than would otherwise be possible, and hence impair the battle to reduce unemployment. The objection of the Conservative Government, or more particularly of Mrs Thatcher, has always been precisely the reverse. The EMS would mean that Britain might have to pursue dangerously lax monetary and fiscal policies which resulted in higher inflation. Whatever the other arguments, both of these propositions cannot be right at the same time.

It is Mrs Thatcher who has clearly been wrong. In reality, the European Monetary System has had a bias towards fighting inflation which has been spectacularly successful in meeting the

Table 32. International inflation rates, 1971–88 (private consumption deflators, percentages)

	1971–80	*1978*	*1988*	*Change 1978–88*
Belgium	7.1	4.2	1.2	−3.0
Denmark	10.4	9.2	4.6	−4.6
West Germany	5.2	2.8	1.2	−1.6
France	9.4	9.1	2.7	−6.4
Ireland	14.3	7.9	2.1	−5.8
Italy	14.6	12.9	5.0	−7.9
Netherlands	7.5	4.5	0.7	−3.8
UK	13.3	9.2	4.9	−4.3
USA	7.2	7.0	4.1	−2.9
Japan	8.6	4.5	0.5	−4.0

Source: European Economy, November 1988, table 24; *OECD Economic Outlook*, June 1989, table R11

objectives of the participants. This may not be inherent in the system, of course. It may reflect merely the priorities of its members over the ten years since 1979, but it certainly cannot be argued that the system has been inflationary. There has been a substantial convergence around lower inflation rates which, as table 32 shows, now leaves Britain with a relatively high inflation rate by the standards of the Continent.

One possible advantage of membership is that it may have reduced the costs in slow growth and rising unemployment of cutting inflation. It is arguable, though impossible to prove, that adherence to the system made the member states' commitment to an anti-inflationary policy more credible to the financial markets and their own labour markets. The result may thus have been that interest rates did not need to stay as high to maintain a given exchange rate target, thus helping investment. Equally, the credibility of membership may have persuaded the work-forces in the EMS countries that the authorities really did intend to cut inflation, which in turn may have reduced the growth of earnings and made inflation easier to bring down without high unemployment. However, the same hopes were nurtured for the effects of monetary targets, and they were sorely disappointed. In the real world, trade union shop stewards do not regularly study a finance minister's exchange rate commitments or have

Table 33. International unemployment rates, 1978–88 (standardized OECD definition as percentage of total labour force)

	1978	*1988*	*Change 1978–88*
Belgium	7.9	10.2	+2.3
Denmark	7.3	8.6	+1.3
West Germany	3.5	6.2	+2.7
France	5.2	10.1	+4.9
Ireland	8.2	16.7	+8.5
Italy	7.1	11.8	+4.7
Netherlands	5.3	9.5	+4.2
UK	5.9	8.3	+2.4
USA	6.0	5.4	−0.6
Japan	2.2	2.5	+0.3

Note: Standardized unemployment rates are not available for national definitions for Denmark and Ireland. There is a break in the series for the UK and West Germany in 1983 which suggests that the rises in both cases are underestimated.

Source: OECD Economic Outlook, June 1989, tables R17, R18

any knowledge of the German Bundesbank's impressive anti-inflationary credentials. For what it is worth, some econometric evidence suggests that this 'credibility bonus' may only have applied in the case of France,[1] but even that seems dubious. The trade-off between falling inflation and rising unemployment has varied sharply both within the group of EMS members and outside it, and is much more likely to be dependent on national labour market practices.

There are, though, two advantages of EMS membership which are much less contentious. The first is that the system has clearly reduced day-to-day variability of exchange rates. Given the relatively small size of the EC economies, and hence their exceptional dependence on trade with each other, this is certainly an important advantage. Work by the EC Commission which looked at the first five years of operation of the system suggested that the variability of the EMS currencies was sharply reduced compared with their previous variability before 1979, and was less the half the variability of non-EMS currencies.[2] The argument that this nominal variability does not impede trade because of the existence of forward and futures markets which enable companies to know with certainty what their revenue in their home currency can be is simply mistaken. First, the forward markets only effectively operate over a year or so. It is extremely hard to guarantee overseas incomes streams with any longer time frame. Secondly, that insurance nevertheless requires the company to pay a premium which is just as much a cost of the transaction as, say, a tariff.

The second and perhaps even more fundamental advantage of the system is that it substantially reduces the risks of a serious misalignment of a member's exchange rate. One of the ironies about the Labour Government's objection to full EMS participation in 1979 is that the pound proceeded to soar, becoming the most important instrument in the collapse of manufacturing and the depth of the recession, as even former critics such as Lord Kaldor recognized. 'In the light of this record,' Lord Kaldor said, 'I regard it as more than doubtful whether we could do better, from the point of view of the UK economy, outside the exchange rate mechanism than inside it ... The probability is rather that the application of the rules and conventions of the EMS would prevent the adoption of foolish policies which on past occasions made the prospective situation of the economy a great deal worse.'[3] Over the period since the beginning of the EMS in 1979 both sterling and the dollar suffered historic over-valuations with devastating consequences for the tradable sectors of their economies. By contrast, the eleven realignments of nominal rates within the EMS served to ensure a remarkable stability of real exchange rates, after allowing for the differences in inflation between the EMS members. Clearly, the sharp rise in German trade surpluses with other EMS members suggested that either German demand should grow faster or the German mark should be revalued within the system, but the degree of imbalances were small by comparison with the problems created between Japan, Europe and the United States.

It is in this context that the debate about monetary sovereignty must be seen. In strictly theoretical terms, a country which joins the system clearly does relinquish freedom of action. For example, in one of the first realignments in February 1982 the Belgians were prevailed upon to accept an 8.5 per cent devaluation rather than the 12–15 per cent they had wanted. The Danes had asked for 7 per cent, but had to limit

Figure 37

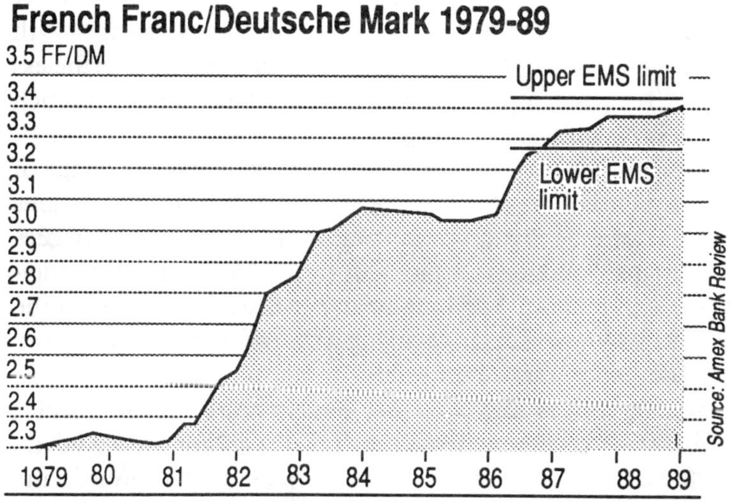

themselves to 3 per cent.[4] However, the country also acquires an influence over the decisions of others which it would not otherwise have. It is able to control its monetary environment in a way which avoids the competitive 'beggar my neighbour' devaluations of the inter-war years and recognizes that an interdependent trading bloc like the European Community has common interests which are best served by rules and a framework of co-operation. The EMS is one tentative mechanism by which countries' commitments to co-operation can be made more solemn and less prone to reversal.[5] Most participants would argue that their real sovereignty over their exchange rates is increased by membership, and that the freedoms of floating are an illusion. It is a set of arguments which has also persuaded most of the leading economic policy-makers in Britain.

Nor should the degree of constraint be over-estimated. Participating countries which can make a good case for a change in their parities generally get their way. If they have higher than expected inflation, and lose competitiveness more quickly than anticipated, they may want a devaluation to compensate. Denmark, in the early years of the system, effectively pursued a policy of fairly regular realignments in order to gain price competitiveness for its exports and stabilize a chronic foreign payments position. Between 1978 and 1982 Denmark's relative unit labour costs actually dropped by nearly a fifth.[6] By contrast, France has become wholly committed since 1983 to a policy of the *franc fort*, itself ruling out devaluations even when trade deficits and a relatively poor export performance might warrant it. It has used its EMS membership to remove doubts in the financial markets about its commitment to a strong exchange rate and counter-inflation policy. In both cases different policies were pursued more effectively within the EMS than they might have been outside it. EMS membership does not in itself imply the pursuit of a particular exchange rate policy; it is a means by which the policy can be pursued.

Why, then, does Mrs Thatcher remain so resolutely opposed to full British membership of the European Monetary System? She has had various reasons, one of the most important of which was the fear that a commitment to pegging the pound might rebound on the Government in the run-up to an election if the Labour Party looked as if it might win. Under floating rates, the pound could be allowed to fall, and Labour would get the blame. Under a fixed rate, the Government would have to tighten policy by raising interest rates – and mortgage rates – and the Prime Minister feared that the electorate would then blame the Government. When the pound was strong, Mrs Thatcher argued that it was unnecessary to join the system. And when the pound was weak, she has argued that it was not possible to join the EMS at a time of vulnerability. In short, she has been antipathetic to going cap in hand to other EMS members about changes in British monetary policy. In her gut, she does not like it.

Of course, she has been primed with more sophisticated arguments too. Her former adviser, Professor Sir Alan Walters, believes that the exchange rate mechanism is likely to crumble as the final element of controls on capital flows within Europe is removed. Britain will not only be able to avoid abolishing the pound, as the tabloids put the creation of a single European currency, but even to avoid joining the EMS. This was why, at the Madrid EC summit in June 1989, Mrs Thatcher felt able to move on from the Government's previous position that it would fully join the EMS when the time was right, the uncomfortable compromise which papered over the Cabinet's differences of view. She then defined the right time as when three conditions had been met. The first was that all remaining capital controls were removed within Europe, so that capital could flow freely in and out of every currency. This was scheduled for July 1990. The second condition was that Britain's inflation rate was reduced nearer to the European average. The third was that proper progress was made on creating the single internal market, a catch-all which at times has appeared to make EMS membership subject to a satisfactory agreement on such details as lorry cabotage (allowing trucks to pick up goods *en route* between two EC countries).

These were not weighty arguments. To all intents and purposes, capital controls had already been removed and the fixed parities of the EMS had survived without collapsing under the pressure of surging speculative flows. The only remaining controls were those which stop people from holding foreign currency bank accounts. The abolition of Britain's exchange controls in 1979 showed that people prefer to maintain the money they use for spending in their home currency. There were unlikely to be shocks when the restrictions came off.

Nor is it important to get inflation down before joining. This objection is based on the fear that putting the pound into the EMS would force Britain to run a lower level of interest rates than is required to control our inflation.

The argument is that the markets would flood London with hot money to take advantage of our high interest rates because they would see there was no risk of a fall in the pound. Either sterling interest rates would have to fall or the pound would have to be revalued within the system. This objection, though, is based on the assumption that markets can be sure that the system will guarantee a fixed parity as if the future were as predictable as the past. In practice, the future is always uncertain and that uncertainty allows different interest rates in different EMS member states. The difference in short-term interest rates in France and West Germany averaged 3.6 percentage points in 1988. A better parallel with Britain may be Italy, which operates the wider 6 per cent margin of fluctuation for the lira against other

European currencies, instead of the 2.25 per cent for everybody else. This wider band introduces a further element of uncertainty which in 1988 allowed a 6.9 per cent average difference in Italian and West German short-term interest rates.

At some point a British Government is going to put the pound into the EMS and discover the truth or otherwise of all the various arguments which have been put forward. The betting, on the basis of the experience of the system since 1979, is that the benefits are likely to prove less dramatic than its proponents suggest, but that the costs are less onerous too. After all the heat, it may well prove an anti-climax.

Notes

1 See Franceso Giavazzi and Alberto Giovannini, *Can the EMS be Exported? Lessons from Ten Years of Monetary Policy Co-ordination in Europe*, Centre for Economic Policy Research discussion paper no. 285 (London, 1989). This result has not stopped the London Business School economic forecasters arguing that EMS membership would help Britain get inflation down with less cost in slow growth.

2 Tommaso Padoa Schioppa, 'Policy Co-operation and the EMS Experience', *International Policy Co-ordination*, ed. Willem Buiter and Richard Marston (Cambridge, 1985).

3 Memorandum given in evidence to the Treasury and Civil Service select committee of the House of Commons, 10 June 1985 in *Memoranda on the European Monetary System*, session 1984–5.

4 Peter Ludlow, *The Making of the European Monetary System* (London: Butterworths, 1982), p. 288.

5 A very similar argument applies as in the case of individual versus collective failure in the case of the OPEC cartel (see essay 5 in chapter 8). The EMS is one way round the problem of the 'prisoners' dilemma' in international economic diplomacy.

6 *European Economy*, November 1988, table 33.

A single currency for Europe?

The effects of the single market

- eastern European liberalization
- the likelihood of British participation
- the interests of the City
- the Chancellor's arguments against EMU
- no threat to nationhood
- the theory of optimum currency areas
- hedging against uncertainty
- the importance of a fiscal safety net

The sceptics about the Delors report for a single European currency can point to the past commitment to exactly the same thing in 1972 and to the vain promise that monetary union would be established by 1980.[1] Yet there is just a chance that this time events will turn out differently. Two fundamental changes in European politics make the nineties quite different to the crisis-torn seventies. The process of achieving the single European market in 1992 has caught the imagination of European businessmen, and has already brought substantial benefits in encouraging an investment boom in most of the EC economies. The perceived success of 1992 has made it far easier to put more radical proposals on the table. In the mid-eighties, the Delors report would have been regarded as laughable. It is no longer. Secondly, and most fundamentally, there is the cracking of Yalta's ice floes in the east. Mr Mikhail Gorbachev's *perestroika*, and the rapid democratization of Poland and Hungary, open up horizons of a liberal, trading central Europe which offer untold political and economic opportunities, particularly to Germany.

It is the possibility of a new German *Ostpolitik* that has really put economic integration onto the front burner for other western European states, the most important of which is France. President Mitterrand is well aware of the geo-political implications if the reform process in eastern Europe continues. A prime objective of French policy within the European community has always been to anchor West Germany firmly to the West, a consideration which has its atavistic roots in the 1922 Treaty of Rapallo which was the harbinger of the Nazi–Soviet division of Poland and the *casus belli* of the Second World War. For a man of Mitterrand's generation, the prospect of a reunified Germany at the centre of a network of clients in central Europe is the prospect of a country which could dominate the Continent.

A reunified Germany *per se* is not as threatening as the wartime generations understandably suppose, in part because of the republic's successful experience of democracy (and East Germany's unpleasant experience of totalitarianism) but in part because of German demography. At present the population of West Germany is 61 million, and that of East Germany is 16.7 million. By contrast, the populations of Britain and France are respectively 57 million and 55 million. However, the exceptionally low German birth rate means that the population of West Germany is expected to fall by as much as 9 million by 2025, leaving even the combined populations of West and East Germany at 67 million people, a little more than a fifth of the European Community and not a quantum leap from the predicted 60 million Britons or 58 million French.[2] Moreover, any attempt to put obstacles in the way of reunification would almost certainly prove fatally counter-productive.

The only strategy which can protect western European interests is a continued and accelerated process of economic integration, whether motivated by old-fashioned fear of a German *Drang nach Osten* or by a fresher desire to provide a powerful western pole of attraction towards which the liberalizing eastern Europeans can be drawn. Only integration can ensure that conflicts are resolved within the new Europe by the rule of law, rather than between nation states by the rule of the powerful. There will no doubt be pitfalls and embarrassments, and the whole process will take a good deal longer than its proponents anticipate. But the bottom line is that the liberalization of eastern Europe makes the political pressures for European economic integration and for a single European currency all the greater and quite possibly irresistible.

What is more, the clever money will be on British participation, albeit with the kicking and screaming which is the peculiar hallmark of Her Majesty's Government in its attitude to Europe. There is a long list of cases where Mrs Thatcher and like-minded ministers have had to eat crow after the sort of intemperateness which they displayed in 1989 towards the Delors report.[3] The British spent much of 1985 objecting to an amendment to the Treaty of Rome which would limit national vetoes being wielded to obstruct the creation of the single European market – and then climbed down when the French and the Germans presented a *fait accompli*. The role of the City of London is likely to make this particular episode in Britain's pock-marked history of European integration only too similar. It is arguable, though it does not seem plausible, that the City's dominance as a financial centre in Europe might survive the creation of a single currency excluding sterling. It might even survive the institution of a European central bank in Frankfurt. After all, the Euro-dollar market was largely centred in London without Britain using dollars as a currency. However, other City areas – insurance, business services and consultancy, fund management – would find it much more difficult to compete if Britain were not part of the single currency area, not least because it would be unlikely that restrictions against non-national firms would come down quite as quickly.

But whatever the argument about actual interests may be, there is no doubt that the perception amongst leading City figures is that it would be a grave mistake to be left on the sidelines. That perception in turn means, for the first time in the succession of Britain's missed opportunities in Europe, that there is an exceptionally powerful interest group which is in favour of integration. The City is one of the handful of interest groups (the National Farmers' Union possibly being another) which is capable of turning Tory policy on a sixpence. Mrs Thatcher's gut nationalism may yet have to trim to a wider perception of the national interest or a narrower perception of the City's. Mr Gorbachev may not only give a European currency a push – but drag the British along too.

What, though, of the arguments? The Chancellor's main argument against EMU is that it is 'incompatible with independent sovereign states with control over their own fiscal and monetary policies ... The setting up of a European central bank or a new European institution to determine Community fiscal policies go to the very heart of nationhood. What organization would really be the Government?'[4] This is a surprising tack for any British

Chancellor, if only because none of the United Kingdom's four nations has submerged its identity despite many centuries of monetary union. Even the southern Irish maintained a fixed link with sterling until we drifted away by failing to join the European Monetary System in 1979. The Black and Tans, W.B. Yeats, the Easter Rising and the 1921 settlement had all managed to intercede without arousing serious questions about currency union. And what of that long period from 1876 to 1913 when the world's currencies were immutably linked to gold? No doubt there is a small band of people, of whom Mr Lawson may be one, who grow misty-eyed at the sight of Mr Somerset's signature on a fiver. But in reality the question of whether or not there should be a European currency is both more technical and more important than such symbols.

The argument boils down to whether or not Europe is an 'optimum currency area' in the theory pioneered by R.A. Mundell and R.I. MacKinnon.[5] This in turn hinges on whether the benefits of having an additional means of managing your economy – namely your exchange rate – outweigh the transaction costs, the extra costs of uncertainty, of gathering information, and of the fracturing of the market place which results from different currencies. One estimate suggests that the transaction costs of the present European currencies amount to some 1.5 per cent of their national income.[6] It is clearly not worth Liechtenstein or Andorra having its own currency, but at what point do the benefits outweigh the costs?

The reduction of uncertainty may be particularly important in encouraging investment. It is possible, of course, for any business to insure its export earnings against some rise in its own currency by using the forward markets for foreign exchange: it pays a premium now to guarantee or 'hedge' its future foreign earnings which represents a real cost to it, but which at least removes the currency uncertainty. However, it is not possible for that business to insure itself against its plant and work-force becoming uneconomic because of currency changes. Take Jaguar: it can hedge its future earnings of dollars, and thus ensure that it continues to receive the same number of pounds for a given number of dollars for a certain period. However, a rise in the pound would still make its British operations less profitable. It may pay to cut production and sell fewer cars – and to take the profit on its forward purchases of dollars. It cannot, in short, hedge its costs. A single currency area leap-frogs this problem entirely, and would therefore substantially encourage new investment which is currently deterred by exchange rate risk. The scale of the international capital flows might be about three times greater than they are today, a similar order of magnitude to those which existed before the First World War under the fixed exchange rate system of the Gold Standard.[7]

'Hard' money critics can also argue that ultimately all a separate currency allows a country to do is to choose its inflation rate, and there is no advantage in having a high inflation rate rather than a low one. It therefore makes sense to devise monetary authorities such as the US Federal Reserve or the Bundesbank whose independence can guarantee that the single currency area has low inflation.[8] Against that, there are clear costs of having a single currency for any area prone to economic shocks. It would surely have been an advantage for Texas to have had its own dollar in 1986, when the oil price fall devastated the state economy. A gentle fall in the exchange rate would have cushioned the blow of the oil price rise by encouraging the transition to other industries and services. In the short run there can be important choices to be made about the speed of adjustment and transition faced with a shock.

Take the hypothetical example of Britain in 1979: an incoming Tory Government doubles VAT, concedes large public-sector pay rises, and fuels a wage explosion. What would happen? In a single currency area, companies would gradually price themselves out of markets. Unemployment would rise until wages are back under control, and it might have to stay high for a prolonged period if the labour market adjusts only slowly. With a separate currency, however, the Government has the option of devaluing to offset partially or fully the increase in domestic costs. In doing so, it will ensure that prices can rise, and thereby stoke inflation. But it will have stopped unemployment rising.

The smaller the area involved, the less this mechanism will tend to work. Small countries trade a high proportion of their output with the outside world. And the more an economy relies on trade, and the higher its imports, the less benefit to output and jobs it will be likely to achieve from a devaluation. Devaluations will merely tend to stoke up import price rises and general inflation, rather than help boost output and jobs. Not surprisingly, it is small countries like Belgium and the Netherlands which are most keen on EMU.

Even within big countries, the balance of advantage of having your own currency may be crucially changed by what other arrangements are made to help adjustment to some economic shock. Countries which share a currency also erect an economic safety net for their worst-off regions. The MacDougall Committee which reported on this subject in 1977 found that in most western democracies one-half to two-thirds of the short-term loss of primary income in a region (due, say, to an industrial collapse) was made good through lower payments of taxes and national insurance contributions to the centre, and higher receipts of unemployment and other benefits.[9] Net flows of public finance worth 3 to 10 per cent of regional product were found to be common in Europe, with some relatively poor regions gaining up to 30 per cent of their income from public flows. If EMU is really on the cards, then there must be similar means of cushioning regions – countries or nations – from abrupt structural change.

This need not imply, as the former Chancellor Mr Lawson put it, 'grandiose attempts to reduce regional disparities by ever-greater resource transfers ... Subsidizing industries and subsidizing regions destroys their will to compete, and thus their ability to compete.' It does imply the existence of mechanisms at European level which would mimic the current fiscal transfers which take place ordinarily from rich to poor regions within a single currency country, merely through the operation of a flat-rate benefit system with progressive income tax. The MacDougall Report found that the average system reduced income inequalities by some 40 per cent, and carefully targeted schemes such as a budget equalization fund, a community fund for paying unemployment benefit, and a system of cyclical grants could have a similar effect for a quarter of the usual 20–25 per cent of GDP spent by federations such as the US and West Germany.

There would be a considerable advantage for Europe's economic efficiency in having a single currency, although there may be strong arguments for leaving the adjustment strains until after the completion of the single market, whose effects will be far-reaching enough. The real question, to which the Delors committee provided only a skeletal answer, is what measures must be put in place to compensate for the advantages of a flexible currency when it comes to adjusting to balance of payments and unemployment problems. To that extent, those who argue that economic integration must precede monetary union are surely right. True, the free movement of capital and people promised in 1992 makes that integration more likely, and there can be no doubt about the political impetus behind EMU. But the crucial question cannot be ducked: it is not whether there should be a single currency and a single central bank, but what else as well?

Notes

1 Committee for the Study of Economic and Monetary Union, *Report on Economic and Monetary Union in the European Community* (report to the European Council, 12 April 1989).

2 Central Statistical Office, *Social Trends,* 1989 and, for East Germany, United Nations.

3 See, for an example of the genre, the speech by Mr Nigel Lawson, then the Chancellor of the Exchequer, at Chatham House in London on Thursday 26 January.

4 Lawson, op cit.

5 R.A. Mundell, 'A Theory of Optimum Currency Areas', *Ammerican Economic Review,* no. 51 (September 1961); R.I. McKinnon, 'Optimum Currency Areas', *American Economic Review,* no. 53 (September 1963).

6 See Michael Artis in Samuel Brittan and Michael Artis, *Europe without Currency Barriers* (London: Social Market Foundation, 1989).

7 Tamim Bayoumi, *Saving–Investment Correlations: Immobile Capital, Government Policy or Endogenous Behaviour?*, International Monetary Fund working paper 89/66.

8 For an elegant statement of the case for a gradual monetary union and a move towards a Euro-bundesbank, see Samuel Brittan, 'Europe without Currency Barriers', *European Journal of International Affairs,* vol. 2, no. 4 (Spring 1989).

9 EC Commission, *Reports of the Study Group on the Role of Public Finance in European Integration* (Brussels, 1977).

The Common Agricultural Policy

Failure of budget discipline

- new commitments
- why the policy became expensive
- budget and consumer costs
- inequities among farmers and consumers
- the ineffectiveness of subsidy
- the rise in the price of land
- the long-term effects of the policy
- waste of machinery
- estimates of total economic loss

In all the annals of bureaucratic waste, there is something exceptional about the European Community's Common Agricultural Policy (CAP). There have been spendthrift Government programmes before. There have been policies which singularly fail to meet their declared objectives before. But rarely has any major item of public spending proved to be so systematically difficult to reform despite the widespread acknowledgement of its deficiencies. Instead of having to contend with the political difficulties of reform in one country, the CAP has had to contend with the peccadilloes of twelve. In each case the participants know that the costs of any particular benefits which they gain for their farming communities will be spread out amongst all twelve member states. These incentives naturally lead to profligacy. It is, as one shrewd observer of the Brussels scene once put it, as if twelve diners all ordered the most expensive items on the menu because each of them knew that the bill was going to be split equally.[1]

Mrs Thatcher thought that she had wrapped up a deal at the Fontainebleau summit in 1984 at which Britain conceded an increase in the revenues available to the European Community, on condition that strict 'budgetary discipline' was applied to the CAP. Rarely can a commitment have been confounded more completely. Nearly four years on, the Community was coming back for more 'own resources' to fill its coffers, but the main reason for its problems was once again soaring expenditure on the CAP. Indeed, the average annual real rise in CAP spending before Mrs Thatcher extracted her promise was under 1 per cent. In the four years after the commitment, the average annual rise was nearly 4 per cent.

Only time will tell whether the commitments reached by the twelve Community member states in February 1988 will prove any more effective. In theory, they were firmer than the promises which had gone before. Budget appropriations for agricultural support were not to rise by more than 74 per cent of the growth rate of the Community's gross national product, with the basis for the calculations being the 27.5 billion ECU (18.4 billion) budget in 1988.[2] However, there were escape clauses should the ministers wish to avail themselves of them. A so-called monetary reserve allowed for extra spending if community currencies fluctuated. There was still an allowance for real growth in the farm budget, despite its disproportionate two-thirds share in total EC spending. Moreover, the detailed measures which the farm ministers were to take to bring spending within budget might merely encourage farmers to shift from budget-constrained to less constrained crops or livestock products. The extent to which there really had been a change in the open-ended guarantees to buy up food production at particular high support prices remained an open question.

The process of reform faces the task of reversing formidable long-term trends. When EC production of a particular commodity was less than consumption, high EC support prices could be enforced by import levies designed to bring the price of imports up to the fixed price. The result was a system of agricultural support which ensured that the subsidy was paid by the consumer to the farmer, and that public exchequers actually raised money from import levies. That was the happy budgetary situation in the Community for many years: consumers paid the subsidy to farmers through higher prices. The tax cost of the policy was minimal.

The problem for the EC was simply that its high food prices encouraged rapidly growing production. As production gradually exceeded consumption for commodity after commodity, it was no longer possible to support prices merely by excluding foreign competition. There was too much home produce to go around, so that prices in EC markets could only be supported

Figure 38

The budget cost of the CAP

(Constant 1979 European Currency Units)

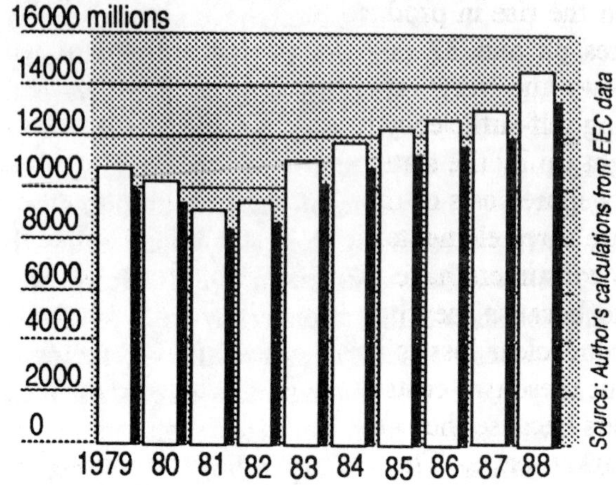

Notes: A; Australian Bureau of Agricultural Economics;
B; Buckwell Harvey, Thomson & Parton;
C; Tyers & Andersen

Figure 39

Three estimates of the cost of the CAP

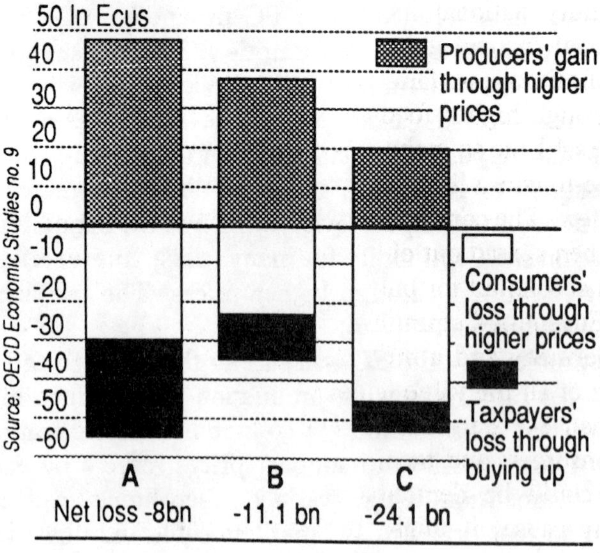

by direct official buying of goods for storage or official subsidies for export. The consumer continued to pay a higher than market price for food, but the budgetary cost also began to rise one for one with the rise in production.

Figures 38 and 39 put the problem into perspective. The first shows the very rapid increase in CAP budget costs as increasing self-sufficiency meant that all extra production had to be bought up by the state. The second shows three estimates of the net welfare costs of the CAP at particular moments in time. There are three elements: there is the loss of consumer welfare because consumers have to pay higher prices for what they do buy, and because they buy less than they would otherwise do. The second clear loss is the budget cost of buying up surplus food. But these two costs are offset to some extent by the gains to farmers because they are able to sell their produce at a higher than market price. The estimates vary in part because each group of researchers has used a slightly different methodology, but most importantly because they refer to different years. The gap between prices on world markets and on EC markets thus varied, and changed the estimates of consumer and producer costs and benefits.[3]

Put those losses into some sort of perspective: the higher prices paid by consumers are worth about 1.2 per cent of Community national income, with an additional 1 per cent of national income going in taxpayer costs. That means that a typical European family of four is paying an extra £300 a year through higher food prices, and a further £250 a year as taxpayers.[4] Like so many successful lobbies, the farm lobby has managed to take a little bit from a lot of people in order to give a lot to a few. The consumer costs may seem relatively small, especially when spread out of hundreds of individual purchases. But farmers accounted for only 7.2 per cent of civilian employment in the European Community in 1985, and only 5.5 per cent in West Germany and a mere 2.6 per cent in Britain.[5] About 40 per cent of all the value 'created' on European farms – itself no more than 3–4 per cent of total EEC output – comes straight from consumers and taxpayers.

If it could be demonstrated that this expenditure was in a worthy cause, it might be justified. But this monster of a policy is probably the single most ineffective piece of government intervention the entire length and breadth of Europe. It fails lamentably to achieve its own objectives, and its costs go far beyond even the direct and indirect consumer and budget costs detailed above – or the net loss once producers' gains are netted out. The CAP particularly benefits farmers who produce a lot, and who therefore gain most from the advantage of its high official prices. The richest quarter of farmers receive about three-quarters of the CAP's subsidy.[6] Yet it is pressure from the three-quarters of farmers with relatively small farms, and hence small incomes, which causes farm prices to be held high.

The second inequity is that the consumer loss through high prices falls disproportionately on those with low incomes, because poor families spend a higher share of their income on necessities like food. The CAP burden is equivalent to a 6 per cent additional income tax on the poorest British families, but an extra tax of only 3 per cent on the richest group.[7] The third inequity arises from the relative size of the farm sector in different member states. The more food an EC country produces, the more it benefits from the budget. In addition, the use of high support prices in international trade between the member states penalizes those countries which are net food importers and favours net exporters regardless of their overall level of income. Poor Spain loses; rich Denmark wins.

There is also a serious question about whether high price support really subsidizes farmers' incomes very much at all. After all, simple economics suggests that if you raise the price of something, you are likely to help all the factors of production – labour, capital and land – which go into making it. Labour and capital, however, are not in fixed supply. They can be sucked in from outside the farm sector, thus gently raising the price of all labour and all capital, and employing rather more in farming than might otherwise be the case. However, land is very largely in fixed supply, so that the main effect of the higher food price in the land market is to bid up rents and land values.

This is precisely what has happened in Britain. Despite very large increases in farm price support since Britain joined the Community, British farmers' incomes have not grown faster than those in the rest of the economy. However, land prices rose six-fold between 1970 and 1982, and only began to ease back as farm support was squeezed.

The extra labour which is employed on farms is, of course, one of the objectives of the policy, but it is not hard to imagine alternative ways of achieving the same objective more efficiently. If we are worried about rural depopulation, why not simply pay people a grant if they live in a rural area? Why do we have to go to the expense of getting them to produce things which no one wants to buy?

It is quite likely, indeed, that the estimates of net welfare losses – the difference between the gains to producers and the losses of consumers – seriously understate the real losses to the European economy because they are based on likely short-term responses to higher support prices. The long-term response of output to higher prices is certainly greater, which means that the degree of waste in excess production is also greater. One reason for this is simply that higher food prices attract higher investment – and higher research and development which might otherwise go into other parts of the economy or into agriculture in other parts of the world (such as the developing countries) where prices are now relatively low. Thus R&D effectively means that cereal yields are rising by about 2.5 per cent a year, merely through qualitative improvements in production rather than increased inputs.

There is also a good deal of circumstantial evidence of enormous waste of capital equipment. Britain's farmers do not have the world's lowest costs per unit of output – the economists' definition of efficiency – but they are paragons compared with their brothers-in-subsidy on the other side of the Channel. High prices encourage small farmers to buy capital equipment in order to maximize output and income from their small farm. That means, for example, that the Germans have 8.5 milking machines per 100 cows compared with only 1.9 milking machines per 100 cows in Britain. The Germans have 2.8 combine harvesters per hundred hectares of land compared with 1.4 in Britain. The Germans have 12.4 tractors per hundred hectares compared with only 2.7 in Britain. The CAP does not just subsidize farmers and landowners: it is also a massive boon to agricultural equipment and other farm input manufacturers.

If Germany could get by on the same number of tractors as Britain, it would have 1,160,000 fewer. It would have 69,500 fewer combine harvesters. And it would have 355,000 fewer sets of mechanical milking equipment.[8]

The analysis on which the calculations of welfare losses is based will also understate the full effects on the EC economy because it does not attempt to estimate the impact on all other sectors if a free market were introduced in agriculture. It is, in the economic jargon, a partial rather than a general equilibrium analysis. How would consumers spend their extra real incomes as food prices fell? And would enough extra jobs be created to absorb the unemployed farmers? These questions can only be answered by looking at a model of the whole economy, which is particularly difficult when major structural changes are supposed. One study which looked at the impact on Germany of abolishing the CAP showed that the overall gains would be enormous. Consumer prices would fall by 1.7 per cent; gross domestic product would rise by about 3.6 per cent; and total employment would rise by about 5.5 per cent.[9]

Farm reform is one area where economists are virtually unanimous: the market ought to be allowed to work, and if Governments want to subsidize rural employment or other such objectives they should do so through direct payments which do not distort the pattern of production and consumption. However, farm policy is also one area where economists' advice has been ignored in favour of pork barrel politics. No one, though, should doubt the macro-economic importance of tackling the CAP. It is beginning to be worth a real bust-up.

Notes

1 This metaphor, which is so apt, was coined by Margaret van Hattem, then of the *Financial Times*.

2 One European Currency Unit was worth about 0.67 in 1988 on average, which gives a base figure of some 18.4 billion for agricultural support spending. Preliminary draft general budget of the European Communities for the financial year 1989 COM (88)290 final, Brussels, June, 1988.

3 Australian Bureau of Agricultural Economics, *Agricultural Policies in the European Community* (Canberra: Australian Government Publishing Service, 1985); A.E. Buckwell, D.R. Harvey *et al.*, *The Cost of the Common Agricultural Policy* (London: Croom Helm, 1982); R. Tyers and K. Anderson, *Distortions*

in World Food Markets: a Quantitative Assessment, World Development Report background paper (Washington DC: World Bank, 1986).

4 'A typical family of four pays ECU 450 per annum through higher prices, and a further ECU 360 per annum as taxpayers', cited in L. Alan Winters, 'The Economic Consequences of Agricultural Support: a Survey', *OECD Economic Studies*, no. 9 (Paris: Autumn 1987).

5 Julius Rosenblatt, Thomas Mayer *et al.*, *The Common Agricultural Policy of the European Community: Principles and Consequences*, International Monetary Fund, occasional paper no. 62 (Washington DC, November 1988), table 27.

6 Author's calculations from Rosenblat, Mayer *et al.*, op cit., table 28, p. 35. Some 1,184,000 farm holdings in the EC-10 in 1985 – 23.5 per cent of all farm holdings – covered 74.9 per cent of the farmed area.

7 Andrew Dilnot and Nic Morris, Institute for Fiscal Studies, London, 1982, cited in L. Alan Winters, op cit. Moreover, all the figures cited so far are based on what economists call a 'partial equilibrium' analysis: they assume that these massive distortions have no effect on the rest of the economy outside agriculture and food, despite the evident importance of the sector.

8 Author's calculations from *Eurostat Yearbook of Agricultural Statistics, 1977–1980* (Luxembourg, 1982), p. 55, table C3. Like other interesting EC agricultural series, the figures for Germany's use of machinery appear to have dried up in the mid-seventies.

9 Rosenblatt, Mayer *et al.*, op cit., p. 64, table 51.

Europe's single market in 1992?

Why liberalization was needed

- the momentum behind change
- the Cecchini report's estimates of the effects
- private-sector scepticism unfounded
- the nature of micro-economic method
- the nature of macro-economic method
- omissions in the Cecchini analysis
- the effects on confidence
- choice through trade
- the distribution of benefits between EC and non-EC companies
- winners and losers within the EC

In one sense, the whole process of creating a single European marketplace – the project 1992 launched by the EC Commission in 1985 – is a confession of failure. After all, the twelve member states, in agreeing to the single European act which made the process of liberalization possible, were confessing that the 1958 Treaty of Rome had failed in its purpose. Almost all the objectives which needed restating in 1985 were contained in the original Treaty. The main problem is that the liberalization had run out of steam. The tariffs had gone, and trade had certainly expanded rapidly. But substantial non-tariff barriers nevertheless left the major European markets largely separate and unintegrated. The price of the same car could differ by more than 40 per cent in part because of restrictions which the manufacturers were allowed to impose, and in part because of the difficulty of trade. A lorry with a licence to transport goods from one member state to another could not pick up loads on the way. A German dentist's qualification would not be recognized in Britain. In a thousand small but cumulatively significant ways, deals which would have benefited both buyer and seller were impeded.

By 1989, though, there was little doubt among either politicians or businessmen that this time the attempt at liberalization was different. The Commission's campaign for the 300 separate EC laws which were designed to attack the paperwork, varying taxes and differing national standards which impeded trade had acquired a political momentum all of its own. Most of the Commission's draft laws were already on the table of the Council of Ministers, and the pace of legislation was far faster than it had ever been before, thanks to two important breakthroughs. The first was philosophical on the part of the Commission. It increasingly abandoned the attempt to set common standards for the whole community in favour of laws which ensured mutual recognition of standards of other community members, even if they differed. Secondly, there was the provision, within the 1985 single European act, of voting within the Council by qualified majority. This weighted majority of 75 per cent effectively abandoned the Gaullist veto which had been so corrosive of progress. No single country had enough votes to block liberalizing legislation.

The creation of a single European marketplace, unhindered by trade barriers, was an economic earthquake in the making.

Some sense of the scale of the economic effects of putting 323 million Europeans together into a genuinely common market can be gleaned from the EC Commission's Cecchini report, quite possibly the largest exercise in applied economics ever undertaken.[1] The Cecchini report has its critics. It is an heroic attempt to quantify what many regard as unquantifiable. But at least it is a stab at answering a series of key questions of fundamental importance to the European economies. The precise magnitudes themselves are less interesting than the broad conclusion that there will be substantial benefits. What Cecchini established beyond reasonable doubt is that the potential gains from creating a single market are large, and are well worth the time and talent invested in the process.

A taste of the effects is shown by the two different approaches adopted by Cecchini: the bottom-up 'micro-economic' analysis suggests welfare gains worth about 4.25–6.5 per cent of the Community's overall national income; the top-down 'macro-economic' analysis suggests significant gains to public finances and a boost to gross domestic product of up to 7 per cent, with consumer price falls of up to 6.1 per cent. The trade-off between gains in output and jobs, and falls in price, depends on the response of individual governments in setting their spending, tax and monetary policies. Cecchini suggests that if governments opt for high growth, the price fall due to increased competition between businesses would be limited to just over 4 per cent. (In an inflationary world, prices would rise by 4 per cent less than otherwise.) If governments opted to maintain tight macro-economic policies and allowed the increased competition to drive down prices fully, the gain in gross domestic product would be just over 4 per cent. The jobs gain varies from 1.8 million to 5 million. These effects would be expected roughly over a five-year period, according to the report. In other words, the whole European economy could add 1 per cent or more to its growth rate during the transition. Given its sluggish performance during the eighties, this was not a marginal gain.

Such estimates have been criticized by private-sector analysts mainly for excessive optimism. Data Resources Inc. was typical of private-sector analysts in predicting that the actual economic effects would be a boost to growth of only 0.5 per cent and a gain in jobs of some 300,000.[2] A leading City broking house said that the Commission's estimates were 'at the top end of expectations'.[3] However, much of the disagreement is about what is likely to happen, rather than the economic consequences if it did happen. Will the member states really legislate for a common market? It is easy to be cynical about Brussels, where everything takes three times as long as expected. After all, the process has to hurdle such long-standing obstacles as Britain's desire to keep customs checks against rabid dogs, and the Treasury's determination not to be inconvenienced by the approximation of differing VAT rates. There are, however, real signs of movement in the undergrowth. Who, five years ago, would have predicted the imminent introduction of free capital movements through the EEC? The effect of majority voting – and the effective abolition of an individual country's veto over 1992 legislation – has been to clear a swathe of legislation governing industrial standards. And if the 1992 liberalization looks more like Lord Cockfield's vision than that of the sceptics, its effects may be even more far-reaching than the Cecchini report's conventional analysis implies.

Cecchini's micro-economic approach starts by examining price differences between member-state markets and asks what happens if arbitrage between those markets is allowed to whittle the differences away. In the case of cars (shown in figure 40) UK consumers gain most from price falls. Producers who were benefiting from 'economic rent' – the amount paid over and above what would be necessary to keep them in the marketplace – lose out as prices fall. This will apply, for example, to Japanese car-makers in the UK market. Secondly, competitive pressure will tend to reduce business profit margins, and force more effective use of existing technology and plant. Third, there may be longer-term gains from the restructuring of industry to take advantage of economies of scale. This may in turn trigger new investment in the industry, and so forth. The total welfare gain for the economy is the benefit to consumers of the price fall, less the loss to producers of monopoly or protected profits.

This type of analysis, though, assumes that the rest of the world is unchanged by this activity: you were prepared to buy a car for £5,000, but the price is cut to £4,000. You

Figure 40

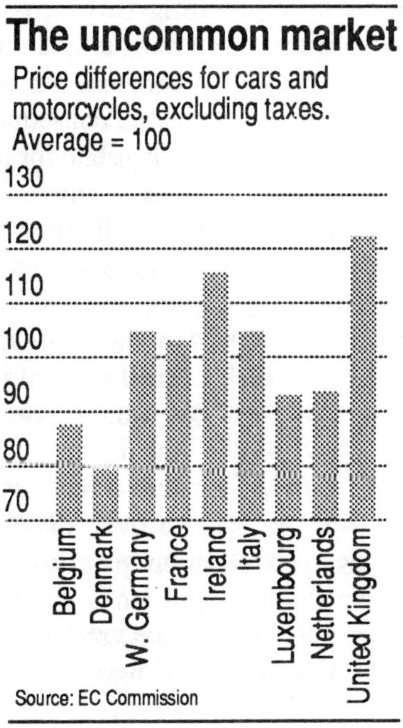

make a welfare gain of £1,000, but there is not necessarily a gain in output. Any labour or capital which is saved because of efficiency gains is assumed to be seamlessly re-employed. The analysis is essentially static: it does not tell us whether there might be any gain in economic activity, or how the balance between depressive and stimulative forces might fall out. This is where the so-called 'macro-economic' analysis is used.

The macro-analysis attempts to fill in the gaps in the micro one. It looks at changes in economy activity – not just welfare. It also asks what the knock-on effects of that initial price cut actually are. If there are enough price reductions due to increased competition, then clearly real incomes are going up. You have saved £1,000 on the car. What are you going to spend the money on? Most importantly, it relaxes the implicit assumption that all those price changes can take effect without job losses and gains: there is not necessarily full employment.

The Cecchini study is the best quantification of trade liberalization we are likely to get, but it begs some important questions. In one sense it underestimates the potential gains. First, if there is a marked quickening of the rhythm of European growth, it is likely there will also be a quickening of investment and technological change, and hence of potential output. The effect of a five-year growth spurt may be to create the conditions for a more sustained period of high growth. Indeed, it was arguable that the acceleration in European growth in 1988 and 1989 was in large part due to investment in anticipation of the creation of the single market, which had had a demonstrable impact on the revival of business confidence. One study estimated that this induced investment effect could add 2.6 to 13 per cent to Community GDP in addition to Cecchini's estimates.[4]

Nor does free trade merely lead to the more efficient production of particular goods and services, or to price cuts for consumers, the two gains singled out by Cecchini. That is a curiously simple view of what has happened to trade in the developed economies over the last three decades. The major benefit has surely been diversity of products. Trade has massively contributed to choice, which itself contributes to welfare. It is not that long ago, for example, that the choice of cheese in the average British supermarket was Cheddar, mature Cheddar or Canadian Cheddar. What is it worth to be able to buy Brie or Gorgonzola? Yet that extra choice is one of the effects of the previous wave of liberalization which came after Britain's EEC membership.[5]

Another and less happy dimension which Cecchini leaves out is the distribution of winners and losers. European industry is low-technology compared with the Americans or the Japanese, so the benefits of a large integrated market may in part flow to foreign competitors (though it is surely far fetched to argue that this will outweigh the native benefits, given transport costs). It has also been argued that American and Japanese companies are more proficient at operating on the pan-European scale which will be required after 1992, and that American- and Japanese-owned companies may therefore reap disproportionate benefits (even though the creation of output and jobs will nevertheless take place in Europe).[6]

There is a second element in assessing winners and losers. History from the Hanseatic League through to the Community itself tends to suggest the gains from liberalization are fairly evenly spread, at least between participating countries, but this cannot in theory be relied upon. There are bound to be towns and regions which lose out from the restructuring: the Consetts and the Corbys. After all, the minimum 1.8 million jobs gain which the Cecchini report projects is a net figure. There is a far larger gross number of gains but equally a large number of offsetting losses too. The Commission and national governments would be wise to put some energy into identifying the losers, and to expand training and support measures to help create alternative work where it is needed.

Notes

1 'The Economics of 1992', *European Economy*, no. 35 (Luxembourg: Office for Official Publications of the European Communities, March 1988); Paolo Cecchini, ed., *1992: The European Challenge* (London: Gower and Wildwood House, 1988).

2 DRI client analysis, 1988.

3 UBS Phillips and Drew, *Europe 1992*, June 1988.

4 Richard Baldwin, 'The Growth Effects of 1992', *Economic Policy*, no. 9 (November 1989).

5 Indeed, Professor John Kay has argued that Cecchini so misunderstands the nature of trade that its projections of gains from economies of scale are very substantially overestimated at the same time as it underestimated the likely gains from choice and diversity.

6 See Henry Neuburger, *The Economics of 1992* (1989) (mimeo), a report commissioned by the British Labour group of Euro-MPs.

Select Bibliography

Aho, C. Michael and Marc Levinson, eds., *After Reagan: Confronting the Changed World Economy*, New York: Council on Foreign Relations, 1988.

Albert, Michel and James Ball, *Towards European Recovery in the 1980s*, European Parliament working document, 31 August 1983.

Atkinson, A.B., J. Gordon and A.J. Harrison, *Trends in the Distribution of Wealth in Britain, 1923–1981*, TIDI discussion paper no. 70, London School of Economics, 1986.

Atkinson, Paul and Jean-Claude Chouraqui, 'The Origins of High Real Interest Rates', *OECD Economic Studies*, no. 5 (Autumn 1985).

Australian Bureau of Agricultural Economics, *Agricultural Policies in the European Community*, Canberra: Australian Government Publishing Service, 1985.

Baldwin, Richard, 'The Growth Effects of 1992', *Economic Policy*, no. 9 (November 1989).

Bank of England, *Bank of England Quarterly Bulletin*, London, various issues.

Barnett, Corelli, *The Collapse of British Power*, Gloucester, 1984.

Barnett, Joel, *Inside the Treasury*, London: Andre Deutsch, 1982.

Barr, Nicholas, *The Economics of the Welfare State*, London, 1987.

Barr, Nicholas, Howard Glennerster and Julian Le Grand, 'Working for Patients: the Right Approach?', *Social Policy and Administration*, vol. 23, no. 2 (August 1989), pp. 117–27.

Bauer, P.T., *Reality and Rhetoric*, London: Weidenfeld, 1984.

Bayoumi, Tamim, *Saving–Investment Correlations: Immobile Capital, Government Policy or Endogenous Behaviour?*, International Monetary Fund working paper 89/66.

Bean, Charles, 'Capital Shortages and Persistent Unemployment', *Economic Policy*, no. 8 (April 1989).

Begg, David K.H., *The Rational Expectations Revolution in Macro-economics*, Oxford: Philip Allan, 1982.

Bergsten, C. Fred, *America in the World Economy: a Strategy for the 1990s*, Washington: Institute for International Economics, 1988.

Bishop, Matthew and John Kay, *Does Privatisation Work? Lessons from the UK*, London: Centre for Business Strategy, London Business School, 1988.

Blackaby, F.T., ed., *British Economic Policy, 1960–74: Demand Management*, Cambridge, 1978.

Blake, Andrew, Nicos Christodoulakis, James E. Meade, David Vines and Martin Weale, *Macro-economic Policy: Inflation, Wealth and the Exchange Rate*, London: Unwin Hyman, 1989.

Bramley, Glen, Julian Le Grand and William Low, *How Far is the Poll Tax a 'Community Charge'? The Implications of Service Usage Evidence*, Welfare State Programme, STICERD, discussion paper WSP/42, London School of Economics.

Brittan, Samuel, *How to End the Monetarist Controversy*, Hobart Paper no. 90, London: Institute for Economic Affairs, 2nd edn, 1982.

——, 'Europe without Currency Barriers', *European Journal of International Affairs*, vol. 2, no. 4 (Spring 1989)

Brittan, Samuel and Peter Lilley, *The Delusion of Incomes Policy*, London: Temple Smith, 1977.

Brown, C.V. *et al.*, *Taxation and Family Labour Supply in Great Britain*, the final report of a project on direct taxation and short run labour supply funded by HM Treasury, Stirling University, Department of Economics, September 1986.

Brown, Lester R., *The Twenty Ninth Day*, New York: W.W. Norton, 1978.

Brown, Lester R. *et al.*, *State of the World*, Washington DC: Worldwatch Institute, various issues.

Bryant, Ralph C. *et al.*, *Empirical Macroeconomics for Interdependent Economies*, Washington DC: Brookings Institution, 1988.

Buckwell, A.E., D.R. Harvey *et al.*, *The Cost of the Common Agricultural Policy*, London: Croom Helm, 1982.

Burns, Sir Terence, 'The Interpretation and Use of Economic Predictions', *Proceedings of the Royal Society*, A 407 (1986), pp. 103–25.

Carrington, John C. and George T. Edwards, *Reversing Economic Decline*, London, 1981.

Carson, Rachel L., *Silent Spring*, Boston, 1962.

Carter, Charles, ed., *Industrial Policy and Innovation*, London: Heinemann, 1981.

Cassen, Robert and associates, *Does Aid Work? Report to an Intergovernmental Task Force*, Oxford: Clarendon Press, 1986.

Cecchini, Paolo, ed., *1992: the European Challenge*, London: Gower and Wildwood House, 1988.

Central Statistical Office, *Economic Trends*, London, various issues.

——, *Financial Statistics*, London, various issues.

——, *Regional Trends*, London, various issues.

Chiplin, Brian and Mike Wright, *The Logic of Mergers*, Hobart Paper no. 107, London: Institute of Economic Affairs, 1987.

Chisholm, Michael and Philip Kivell, *Inner City Wasteland: an Assessment of Government and Market Failure in Land Development*, Hobart Paper no. 108, London: Institute of Economic Affairs, September 1987.

Chubb, Robert N., *Urban Land Markets in the United Kingdom*, Department of Environment Land and Property Division, HMSO, September 1988.

Congdon, Tim, *Monetarism Lost and Why it Must be Regained* Centre for Policy Studies, study no. 106, London, 1989.

Cowling, K. *et al.*, *Mergers and Economic Performance*, Cambridge: Cambridge University Press, 1980.

Daoudi,M.S. and M.S. Dajani, *Economic Sanctions: Ideals and Experience*, London: Routledge, 1983.

Davies, Gavyn, *Governments can Affect Employment*, London: Employment Institute, 1985.

Davies, Gavyn, David Morrison *et al.*, *International Economics Analyst*, London: Goldman Sachs, various issues.

——, *UK Economics Analyst*, London: Goldman Sachs, various issues.

Davies, Stephen and Richard E. Caves, *Britain's Productivity Gap*, National Institute of Economic and Social Research occasional paper, Cambridge, 1987.

Department of the Environment, *Paying for local government*, Green Paper, HMSO, 1986.

Department of Employment Gazette, HMSO, various issues.

Dilnot, Andrew and Michael Kell, 'Top Rate Tax Cuts and Incentives: some Empirical Evidence', *Fiscal Studies*, vol. 9, no. 4 (November 1988).

Dilnot, A.W., J.A. Kay and C.N. Morris, *The Reform of Social Security*, Institute for Fiscal Studies and Oxford University Press, 1984.

Dow, J.C.R., *The Management of the British Economy, 1945–60*, Cambridge, 1964.

Dowd, Kevin, *Private Money*, London: Institute of Economic Affairs, 1988.

Emerson, Michael, ed., *Europe's Stagflation*, Oxford, 1984.

Englander, A. Steven and Axel Mittelstadt, 'Total Factor Productivity: Macroeconomic and Structural Aspects of the Slowdown' *OECD Economic Studies*, no. 10 (Spring 1988).

Enthoven, Alain C., *Reflections on the Management of the National Health Service*, Nuffield Provincial Hospitals Trust, 1985.

European Commission, 'Annual Economic Report', *European Economy*, Luxembourg: Office for Official Publications of the European Communities, various issues.

——, 'The Economics of 1992', *European Economy*, no. 35 (March 1988).

——, *Report of the Study Group on the Role of Public Finance in European Integration*, vol. 1, Commission of the European Communities general report (the 'MacDougall Report'), 1977.

Fallick, J.L. and R.F. Elliott, eds., *Incomes Policies, Inflation and Relative Pay*, London: George Allen & Unwin, 1981.

Financial Statement and Budget Reports ('Red Book'), HM Treasury, London, annually, various issues.

Fisher, Irving C., *The Purchasing Power of Money*, New York: Macmillan, 1911.

Fisher, P.G. *et al.*, 'Comparative Properties of Models of the UK Economy', *National Institute Economic Review*, no. 125 (August 1988).

——, *Econometric Evaluation of the Exchange Rate in Models of the UK Economy*, ESRC Macro-economic Modelling Bureau, Warwick University, June 1989 (mimeo).

Flemming, John, *Inflation*, Oxford, 1976.

Flora, Peter *et al.*, *State, Economy and Society in Western Europe, 1815–1975: a Data Handbook*, London, Frankfurt and Chicago, 1987.

Friedman, Milton, 'The Role of Monetary Policy' (Presidential Address, American Economic Association, 29 December 1967), *American Economic Review*, no. 58 (March 1968), pp. 1–17.

Friedman, Milton and Anna J. Schwartz, *Monetary Trends in the United States and the United Kingdom*, Chicago: University of Chicago Press for the National Bureau of Economic Research, 1982.

Fry, Vanessa and Panos Pashardes, 'Distributional Aspects of Inflation: Who has Suffered Most?', *Fiscal Studies*, December 1985.

Funabashi, Yoichi, *Managing the Dollar: from the Plaza to the Louvre*, Washington DC: Institute for International Economics, 1988.

Galbraith, John Kenneth, *The Great Crash*, Harmondsworth: Penguin, 1961.

George, Henry, *Progress and Poverty* (1880), London: Dent Dutton, 1976.

Giavazzi, Francesco and Alberto Giovannini, *Can the EMS be Exported? Lessons from Ten Years of Monetary Policy Co-ordination in Europe*, Centre for Economic Policy Research, discussion paper no. 285, London, 1989.

Gide, Charles and Charles Rist, *A History of Economic Doctrines*, London, 2nd edn, 1948.

Goodhart, C.A.E., *Monetary Theory and Practice: the UK Experience*, London: Macmillan, 1984.

Gray, John and David Jesson, 'Exam Results and Local Authority League Tables', *Education and Training UK, 1987*, ed. Anthony Harrison and John Grettan, Newbury, Berks.: Policy Journals.

Gray, John, David Jesson and Ben Jones, 'The Search for a Fairer Way of Comparing Schools' Examination Results', *Research Papers in Education*, Slough, 1986.

Gudgin, Graham, Barry Moore and John Rhodes, 'Employment Problems in the Cities and Regions of the UK: Prospects for the 1980s', *Cambridge Economic Policy Review*, vol. 8, no. 12 (December 1982).

Harrison, Fred, *The Power in the Land*, London: Shepheard Walwyn, 1988.

Hart, P.E., ed., *Unemployment and Labour Market Policies*, Joint Studies in Public Policy, National Institute of Economic and Social Research, Policy Studies Institute and Royal Institute of International Affairs, Gower, 1986.

Hayter, Teresa, *Aid as Imperialism*, Harmondsworth: Penguin, 1971.

Hemming, Richard and Ali M. Mansoor, *Privatization and Public Enterprises*, Washington DC: International Monetary Fund, 1988.

Hendry, David F. and Neil R. Ericsson, *Assertion without Empirical Basis: an Econometric Appraisal of 'Monetary Trends ... in the United Kingdom'*, London: Bank of England, 1983.

Hills, John, *Changing Tax: How the Tax System Works and How to Change it*, London: Child Poverty Action Group, 1988.

HMSO, *Working for Patients*, Cmnd. 555, HMSO, 1989.

Hotelling, Harold, 'The Economics of Exhaustible Resources', *Journal of Political Economy*, vol. 39 (1931).

Hufbauer, Gary Clyde and Jeffrey J Schott, *Economic Sanctions Reconsidered*, Washington DC: Institute for International Economics, 1985.

Huhne, Christopher, 'Some Lessons of the Debt Crisis: Never Again?',

International Economics and Financial Markets, ed. Richard O'Brien and Tapan Datta, Oxford, 1989.

Inland Revenue, *Comparisons of Direct Tax on Employment Income*, London: Board of Inland Revenue, December 1987.

Inland Revenue Statistics, annual, various issues.

Inner London Education Authority, *Actual and Predicted Examination Results in Schools: Research and Statistics*, Inner London Education Authority, 1987.

Institute of Employment Research, *Review of the Economy and Employment*, University of Warwick, 1987 and successive issues.

International Monetary Fund, *International Financial Statistics*, yearbook, Washington DC, various issues.

——, *World Economic Outlook*, Washington DC, various issues.

——, *Report on the World Current Account Discrepancy*, Washington DC, September 1987.

Jackman, Richard *et al.*, *A Job Guarantee for Long Term Unemployed People*, Employment Institute, 1986.

Jackman, Richard, Richard Layard, Stephen Nickell and Sushil Wadhwani, *Unemployment*, Oxford, forthcoming.

Jaidah, Ali M., *An Appraisal of OPEC Oil Policies*, London: Longman, 1983.

Johnson, Christopher, ed., *Lloyds Bank Annual Review: Privatization and Ownership*, London, 1988.

Johnson, Paul, Christoph Conrad and David Thomson, eds., *Workers versus Pensioners: Intergenerational Justice in an Ageing World*, Centre for Economic Policy Research and Manchester University Press, 1989.

Johnson, R.W., *How Long will South Africa Survive?*, London: Macmillan, 1977.

Kamarck, Andrew M., *Economics and the Real World*, Oxford: Blackwell, 1983.

Keegan, William, *Mr Lawson's Gamble*, London: John Curtis and Hodder & Stoughton, 1989.

Kenen, Peter B., *Managing Exchange Rates*, Chatham House Papers, London: Routledge, 1988.

Keynes, John Maynard, *The Economic Consequences of the Peace* (1919), *Collected Writings*, vol. 2, London: Royal Economic Society and Macmillan.

——, *The General Theory of Employment, Interest and Money*, London, 1935.

King, Mervyn, *Take-over Activity in the United Kingdom*, London School of Economics, 1987 (mimeo).

Kravis, Irving B., Alan Heston and Robert Summers, *World Product and Income: International Comparisons of Real Gross Product*, Baltimore: Johns Hopkins University Press, 1982.

Lancaster, Carol and John Williamson, eds., *African Debt and Financing*, Institute for International Economics, special report no. 5, Washington DC, May 1986.

Land Institute, *Site Value Rating: Report on Research Exercise Carried out in Whitstable*, London, 1974.

Lawson, Nigel, *Tax Reform: the Government's Record*, London: Conservative Political Centre, 1988.

Layard, Richard, *More Jobs, Less Inflation: the Case for a Counter-inflation Tax*, London: Grant McIntyre, 1982.

——, *How to Beat Unemployment*, Oxford, 1986.

Layard, Richard and Stephen Nickell, *The Thatcher Miracle?*, Centre for Labour Economics, discussion paper no. 343, London School of Economics, March 1989.

Leibenstein, Harvey, *Beyond Economic Man*, Cambridge, Mass.: Harvard University Press, 1976.

——, *Inside the Firm: the Inefficiencies of Hierarchy*, Cambridge, Mass.: Harvard University Press, 1987.

Leontief, Wassily and Faye Duchin, *The Impacts of Automation on Employment, 1963–2000*, Institute of Economic Analysis at New York University (mimeo) and Oxford, 1985.

Lever, Harold and Christopher Huhne, *Debt and Danger: the World Financial Crisis*, Harmondsworth: Penguin, 1985; 2nd edn 1987.

Likierman, Andrew, *Public Expenditure: Who Really Controls it and How*, London, 1988.

Lindbeck, Assar, 'Business Cycles, Politics, and International Economic Dependence', *Skandinaviska Enskilda Banken Quarterly*, no. 2 (1975), p. 60.

Lindsey, Lawrence B., *Taxpayer Behaviour and the Distribution of the 1982 Tax Cut*, National Bureau of Economic Research Inc., working paper no. 1760, Cambridge, Mass., October 1985.

——, *Estimating the Revenue Maximising Top Personal Tax Rate*, National Bureau of Economic Research Inc., working paper no. 1761, Cambridge, Mass., November 1985.

——, *Individual Taxpayer Response to Tax Cuts, 1982–4*, Cambridge, Mass., 15 October 1986 (mimeo).

London and Cambridge Economic Service, *The British Economy: Key Statistics, 1900–1966*, London, 1966.

London Business School, *Economic Outlook*, quarterly, various issues.

Ludlow, Peter, *The Making of the European Monetary System*, London: Butterworths, 1982.

Marshall, Alfred, *Industry and Trade*, London: Macmillan, 1919.

Mayer, Colin, *New Issues in Corporate Finance*, Centre for Economic Policy Research, paper no. 181, London, 1987.

——, assessment in *Oxford Review of Economic Policy*, vol. 3, no. 4 (Winter 1987).

Maynard, Geoffrey, *The Economy under Mrs Thatcher*, Oxford, 1988.

Meade, James E., *The Intelligent Radical's Guide to Economic Policy: the Mixed Economy*, London: George Allen & Unwin, 1975.

——, *Stagflation*, vol. 1: *Wage-fixing*, London: George Allen & Unwin, 1982.

Meadows, Donella H., Dennis L. Meadows, Jorgen Randers and William W. Behrens III, *The Limits to Growth: a Report for the Club of Rome's Project on the Predicament of Mankind*, London: Earth Island Ltd, 1972.

Meadows, Pamela, Hilary Cooper and Richard Bartholomew, *The London Labour Market*, Department of Employment, 1988.

Metcalf, David, *Water Notes Dry Up*, Centre for Labour Economics, discussion paper no. 314, London School of Economics, 1988.

Minford, Patrick, *Unemployment: Cause and Cure*, Oxford: Blackwell, 2nd edn, 1986.

Minsky, Hyman P., *Stabilising an Unstable Economy*, New Haven, 1986.

Mishan, E.J., *The Costs of Economic Growth*, Harmondsworth: Penguin, 1969.

Morganstern, Oscar, *On the Accuracy of Economic Observations*, Princeton: Princeton University Press, 1950; 2nd edn 1963.

Morris, Derek, ed., *The Economic System in the UK*, Oxford, 2nd edn, 1979.

Muellbauer, John, *The Housing Market and the UK Economy: Problems and Opportunities*, Nuffield College, Oxford, January 1987 (mimeo); revised version December 1988.

National Economic Development Council, *Pay and Productivity in the UK*, London, 1988.

National Economic Development Office, *Investment in the Public Sector Built Infrastructure*, London, 1985.

National Institute Economic Review, quarterly, various issues.

Neuburger, Henry, *The Economics of 1992*, a report commissioned by the British Labour group of Euro-MPs, London, 1989 (mimeo).

Odell, Peter R., *Oil and World Power*, Harmondsworth: Penguin, 8th edn, 1986.

Organisation for Economic Co-operation and Development, *OECD Economic Outlook*, Paris, various issues.

——, *OECD Economic Studies*, Paris, various issues.

——, *OECD Economic Surveys*: Germany, Britain, France etc., Paris, various issues.

——, *Economies in Transition: Structural Adjustment in OECD Countries*, Paris, 1989.

——, *Financing and Delivering Health Care*, Paris, 1987.

Okun, Arthur M., *Prices and Quantities: a Macroeconomic Analysis*, Oxford, 1981.

Olson, Mancur, *The Rise and Decline of Nations: Economics Growth, Stagflation, and Social Rigidities*, New Haven: University of Yale Press, 1982.

Oxford Review of Economic Policy, Templeton College, Oxford, various issues.

Page, Sheila, 'The Rise in Protection since 1974', *Oxford Review of Economic Policy*, vol. 3, no. 1 (Spring 1987).

Parker, Hermione, *Instead of the Dole*, London: Routledge, 1989.

Patel, P. and K. Pavitt, *The Technological Activities of the UK: a Fresh Look*, Science Policy Research Unit, discussion paper no. 49 (August 1987).

——, 'The Elements of British Technological Competitiveness', *National Institute Economic Review*, no. 122 (November 1987).

Pliatzky, Leo, *The Treasury under Mrs Thatcher*, Oxford, 1989.

Pollard, Sidney, *The Development of the British Economy, 1914–1967*, 2nd edn, 1981.

Powell, Stephen and Geoff Horton, *The Economic Effects of Lower Oil Prices*, HM Treasury, April 1985.

Prais, S.J., 'Vocational Qualifications of the Labour Force in Britain and Germany', *National Institute Economic Review*, no. 98 (November 1981).

——, 'Qualified Manpower in Engineering', *National Institute Economic Review*, no. 127 (February 1989).

Prais, S.J. and Hilary Steedman, 'Vocational Training in France and Britain: the Building Trades', *National Institute Economic Review*, no. 116 (May 1986).

Prebisch, Raul, 'The Spread of Technical Progress and the Terms of Trade', *United Nations Economic Survey of Latin America*, New York, 1949.

Price, Robert W.R. and Patrice Muller, 'Structural Budget Indicators and the Interpretation of Fiscal Policy Stance in OECD Economies', *OECD Economic Studies*, no. 3 (Autumn 1984).

Rajan, Amin with Julie Fryatt, *Create or Abdicate*, a report for the London Human Resources Development Group by the Institute of Manpower Studies, Sussex, John Wiley, September 1988.

Robinson, Ray and Ken Judge, *Public Expenditure and the NHS: Trends and Prospects*, King's Fund Institute for Health Policy Analysis, 1987.

Renwick, Robin, *Economic Sanctions*, Centre for International Affairs, Harvard University, 1981.

Rosenblatt, Julius, Thomas Mayer *et al.*, *The Common Agricultural Policy of the European Community: Principles and Consequences*, International Monetary Fund, occasional paper no. 62, Washington DC, November 1988.

Russell, Louise, *The Baby Boom Generation and the Economy*, Brookings Studies in Social Economics, Washington DC: Brookings Institution, 1982.

Safer, Arnold, *International Oil Policy*, Lexington Books, 1979.

Salomon Bros., *A Review of Bank Performance*, New York, 1989.

Schioppa, Tommaso Padoa, 'Policy Co-operation and the EMS Experience', *International Policy Co-ordination*, ed. Willem Buiter and Richard Marston, Cambridge, 1985.

Scott, Peter and Paul Johnson, *The Economic Consequences of Population Ageing in Advanced Societies*, Centre for Economic Policy, research paper no. 263, London, July 1988.

Schumacher, E.F., *Small is Beautiful: a Study of Economics as if People Mattered*, Blond and Briggs, 1973.

Shields, Jon, ed., *Making the Economy Work*, London: Macmillan and the Employment Institute, 1989.

——, ed., *Conquering Unemployment: the Case for Economic Growth*, London: Macmillan and the Employment Institute, 1989.

Singer, Hans, 'The Distribution of Gains between Investing and Borrowing Countries', *American Economic Review*, no. 40 (1950).

Smith, Adam, *An Inquiry into the Nature and Causes of The Wealth of Nations* (1776), Chicago: University of Chicago Press, 1976.

Smith, David, *The Rise and Fall of Monetarism*, Harmondsworth: Penguin, 1987.

——, *North and South: Britain's Growing Divide*, Harmondsworth: Penguin, 1989.

Smith, Stephen and Duncan Squire, *Local Taxes and Local Government*, Institute for Fiscal Studies, report series no. 25 (May 1987).

Stewart, Michael, *Controlling the Economic Future*, Brighton, 1983.

Taylor, Lance, 'Varieties of Stabilisation Experience: towards Sensible Macro-economics in the Third World', *WIDER Studies in Development Economics*, Oxford, 1988.

Tobin, James, *Policies for Prosperity: Essays in a Keynesian Mode*, ed. Peter M. Jackson, Brighton, 1987.

Treasury and Civil Service Select Committee of the House of Commons, *Memoranda on the European Monetary System*, 10 June 1985, session 1984–5.

Tufte, Edward R., *Political Control of the Economy*, Princeton, 1978.

Turner, David S., *Does the UK Face a Balance of Payments Constraint on Growth?*, ESRC Macro-economic Modelling Bureau, discussion paper no. 16, Warwick University, 1988.

——, *The Role of Judgement in Macro-economic Forecasting*, ESRC Macro-economic Modelling Bureau, Warwick University, April 1989 (mimeo).

Turner, D.S., K.F. Wallis and J.D. Whitley, *Explaining and Resolving Differences in the Properties of Large-scale Macro-econometric Models*, ESRC Macroeconomic Modelling Bureau, discussion paper no. 15, Warwick University, 1988.

Tyers, R. and K. Anderson, *Distortions in World Food Markets: a Quantitative Assessment*, World Development Report background paper, Washington DC: World Bank, 1986.

Tylecote, Andrew, *The Causes of the Present Inflation*, London: Macmillan, 1981.

United Nations Conference on Trade and Development, *Trade and Development Report*, Geneva, annually, various issues.

US Government Printing Office, *Economic Report of the President* (including the annual report of the Council of Economic Advisers), Washington DC, various issues.

Vickers, John and George Yarrow, *Privatization: an Economic Analysis*, Cambridge, Mass.: MIT Press, 1988.

Vines, David, Jan Maciejowski and James E. Meade, *Stagflation*, vol. 2: *Demand Management*, London: George Allen & Unwin, 1982.

Wallich, H.C. and S. Weintraub, 'A Tax-based Incomes Policy', *Journal of Economic Issues*, vol. 5, no. 2 (June 1971).

Walters, Alan, *Britain's Economic Renaissance: Margaret Thatcher's Reforms, 1979–1984*, Oxford, 1986.

Weiswiller, Rudi, ed., *Managing a Foreign Exchange Department*, London: Woodhead-Faulkner, 1985.

Wiles, Peter, 'Ideology, Methodology and Neo-classical Economics', reprinted in Alfred S. Eichner, *Why Economics is not yet a Science*, London: Macmillan, 1983.

Williamson, John, *The Exchange Rate System*, Institute for International Economics, Washington DC, revised June 1985.

Williamson, John and Marcus H. Miller, *Targets and Indicators: a Blueprint for the International Co-ordination of Economic Policy*, Washington DC: Institute for International Economics, September 1987.

Winters, L. Alan, 'The Economic Consequences of Agricultural Support: a Survey', *OECD Economic Studies*, no. 9 (Autumn 1987).

World Bank, *World Debt Tables, 1988–9*, Washington DC: International Bank for Reconstruction and Development.

——, *World Development Report*, Oxford, annually.

Yao-Su Hu, 'National Attitudes and the Financing of Industry', *Political and Economic Planning*, 1975.